DERIVATION and COUNTEREXAMPLE

An Introduction to Philosophical Logic

KAREL LAMBERT
University of California, Irvine

BAS C. van FRAASSEN
University of Toronto

DICKENSON PUBLISHING COMPANY, INC.
Encino, California, and Belmont, California

©1972 by Dickenson Publishing Company, Inc.

Library of Congress Catalog Card Number: 79-189758

Printed in the United States of America
10 9 8 7 6 5 4 3 2 1   75 74 73 72

ISBN: 0-8221-0020-7

to
Henry Siggins Leonard
(1905-1967)

that "dedicated philosopher, notable for perspicacity and patience of mind,
for absolute intellectual integrity, and for unfailing gentleness of spirit . . ."

NELSON GOODMAN

Contents

Preface

Since there are already many elementary logic texts in existence, and since logic is taught today at many levels, we shall explain, first, the specific purposes to which we think this text is suited, and second, how this text differs from other similar texts.

In many philosophy departments today a distinction is drawn between the following topics in undergraduate logic teaching:

(a) general introduction,
(b) techniques of deductive logic,
(c) metalogic,
(d) philosophical uses of logic.

In addition there are texts and courses devoted to advanced work in mathematical logic for students wishing to specialize.

We conceive the present text to be usable in the teaching of (b)–(d), to students who either have had a general introduction to logic or who are allowed (and this is frequent enough) to begin symbolic logic without such an introduction. Topics that we would normally expect to have been covered on the introductory level include the nature of arguments and validity, the use/mention distinction, the nature of definition, and perhaps the use of Venn diagrams and truth-tables. A good example of a book designed especially for this general introductory level is Wesley Salmon's *Logic* (Prentice-Hall, 1963).

After the introductory level, the instructor generally has a choice (or the student is offered a choice) whether to emphasize the philosophical side or the mathematical side of logic. Here our text is designed specifically for those whose interest is in philosophical aspects and uses of logic.

With this aim in mind, we have introduced a number of innovations into the exposition, *but at the same time have made sure that the standard body of elementary symbolic logic is covered*. In an effort to establish the (usually neglected) relation between contemporary and traditional logic, we devote the first three parts to the logic of statements, the logic of general terms (predicate logic, quantification theory), and the logic of singular terms, respectively. We have developed the standard propositional calculus and standard quantification theory both by means of natural deduction (intelim) rules and by the more mechanical method of "tableau" or counterexample rules. The latter method has been developed, in various ways, by Beth, Hintikka, Anderson and Belnap, Jeffrey, and Smullyan; by and large we have followed Beth. But we have chosen not to use Beth's diagrams; this makes it easier to show that the tableau rules do not really extend the basic logical system. In the chapters on quantificational logic, we are careful to treat the case of the empty domain of discourse. That is, unlike most logic texts, our main rules are valid for the empty domain; we add a special rule to be used when this case is not of concern. To reemphasize an earlier point, our treatment in the first five chapters covers the standard body of material through quantification theory with identity.

Our main innovations, however, are in the third part, which covers the logic of singular terms. Here we *extend the language of classical logic* by admitting singular terms, and extend our rules so as to license inferences involving such terms. The resulting extensions of classical logic are called *free logic* and *free description theory*. We take care to discuss explicitly the philosophical basis of such notions as possible worlds, domains of discourse, existence, reference and description, utilized in the first three parts, and to compare our approach with historical precedents. This is done, to some extent, as these notions are introduced, and also to some extent in Parts Four and Five.

Although there are today many good treatments of metalogic available, they are generally aimed at more advanced levels of instruction. We have aimed to make our presentation of metalogic more elementary than is usual. First of all, as soon as the student is able to use deductive techniques, he is also in a position to prove the admissibility of further deductive rules. By placing such admissibility proofs in Parts One and Two, a certain amount of proof theory is taught along with the deductive techniques. Part Four is devoted to semantics, that is, to a scrutiny of the adequacy of the logical system developed in the first three parts. Since the book is aimed specifically at the philosophy student, we treat only the finite cases; we believe that in this way the student will be able to master the main theoretical concepts and methods without the use of sophisticated mathematical techniques. It must be noted that here the previous parallel development of the tableau rules greatly simplifies the presentation.

In Part Five, we discuss the philosophical basis of the logic of existence and description theory, with special reference to the question of extensionality. In addition, we discuss the philosophical uses of free logic in connection with set theory, intentional discourse, thought and perception, modal concepts, and the concept of truth. The term "philosophical logic" is used increasingly to designate a specific discipline (indeed, the newly created *Journal of Philosophical Logic* will be entirely devoted to it), and we hope that Part Five will provide a useful introduction to some of its main areas of research.

Over the years it has become apparent to us that a text of the sort we have produced here is sorely needed in philosophy departments. Those who teach logic courses from available texts, and who hear the complaint from students, at both the graduate and undergraduate levels, completing the usual course, "Yes, but what does all this have to do with philosophy!" will appreciate, we believe, our particular approach in this book.

We would like to thank friends and colleagues who have commented on the style and content of our book while still in manuscript, but special thanks are due Professors Richmond Thomason, Ruth Barcan Marcus, and Sidney Luckenbach for their considerable help. Our major professional debts are to Henry Leonard who initiated our interest in, and persuaded us of the value of, free logic, and to some of the early writings of Jaakko Hintikka, Hugues Leblanc and Theodore Hailperin that helped to determine the very character of free logic. Finally, we wish to acknowledge the efforts of scholars who independently have developed systems of free logic, especially Rolf Schock in Sweden, Richard Routley in Australia and Nino Cocchiarella, Ronald Scales, Benson Mates, and David Kaplan in the U.S.A.

K. L.
B. v. F.

1 Introduction

In logic we study reasoning and argumentation from a special point of view. It is not the point of view of the social scientist, who charts actual practices in actual communities, nor that of the moralist, who holds forth on what practice ought to be. Still, we are concerned in some way with actual patterns of reasoning *and* with standards of right reasoning. In this introductory chapter, we explain briefly the scope and limits of our inquiry.

SECTION 1
APPRAISAL OF REASONING

To say that someone's reasoning is logical, or illogical, is to evaluate his reasoning in a certain way. In this respect it is like saying that a picture is a good picture or that it shows a keen sense of colors. Now it is often held that statements of fact are objective (objectively true or false) while evaluations are not. It would be wrong to say that the question of whether someone's reasoning is logical or illogical is a question of personal taste.

The problem is that the distinction between factual assertions and evaluations is too easily used to hide important interrelations. I can pass a negative judgment on a picture by saying that it is not a good likeness. You may counter my judgment by "But that is not what the artist was after!". Notice that if this is your response, you are not disagreeing with my judgment that the picture is not a good likeness. But you are indicating that to be explicit, I should have said that it is not a good picture because it is not a good likeness. And, explicitly, your view is that indeed it is not a good likeness, but that this is irrelevant to the value of the picture. And the reason for this may be because you think that likeness has nothing to do with aesthetic value, or because you think that likeness has something to do with aesthetic value only for a certain kind of work of art, or only if the intentions of the artist were of a certain kind, and so on.

In exactly the same way, I might pass a negative judgment on an argument by saying that it is not *valid* (a concept we shall discuss at length). And you might counter that this is irrelevant: the speaker (a demagogue or salesman) meant only to be convincing, and he was. This kind of situation does not point to a disagreement about the validity of the argument. The logical appraisal which I made was not contested; only its appropriateness or relevance. If there is anything here that is not objective, it is not the evaluation of the argument as not valid, but rather our opinions of what is important or what is appropriate.

A different kind of disagreement occasioned by logical appraisal, and which also suggests subjective value judgments, is the following. Suppose I say of an argument that it is valid, and you respond that it is worthless nevertheless. Then we have a case analogous to my saying that a picture is good because it is a good likeness and your responding that it is a bad picture not-withstanding the likeness. Notice that again there is agreement of a sort: in the one case we agree that the argument is valid, in the other case that the picture is a good likeness. And these are evaluations that we agree on. But in the one case you refuse to conclude that the argument is a good argument, in the other case that the picture is a good picture. And the reason is evidently that you are applying some further standards which in your opinion ought to be satisfied. Thus it can happen that we agree on one kind of an evaluation, and also agree on the necessity for further evaluation of a different sort. So the objectivity of the original evaluation is not drawn into question.

But now, what if I say that an argument is valid and you say it is not? If such a dispute could not be settled, then logical appraisal would indeed not be objective.

We shall not maintain that evaluation by means of the concepts developed in this book is always appropriate. Nor shall we maintain that there are no further criteria to be applied that equally deserve to be called logical criteria. But we do hope to provide a firm basis for the discussion of validity. The concept of validity developed is to be objective, and is to be widely applicable. And we will also try to indicate clearly the limits of our enterprise: many arguments formulable in natural language do not fall within our scope. But our approach is very general and while the patterns of reasoning that we study are still relatively simple, we believe that the approach we take is the correct one for further logical inquiry. In the last part of this book we shall outline a number of extensions of logical theory which are currently being developed.

SECTION 2
THE FORMAL APPROACH

If one wants to study reasoning systematically, one must deal with general patterns: application to a particular case must then begin with fitting that case in some such pattern. So the most important work first done in logic consisted in the study of a family of important argument types (called *syllogisms*). Thus the following two particular arguments

  1. All men are mortal;
     All Greeks are men;
     Hence: All Greeks are mortal.

  2. All preachers praise virtue;
     All bishops are preachers;
     Hence: All bishops praise virtue.

were said to fit the general pattern

  3. All M are P;
     All S are M;
     Hence: All S are P.

In these two particular cases, there is indeed a good and obvious fit. In many cases, however, the fitting is somewhat more Procrustean: a certain amount of adjustment, simplification, or idealization is necessary to apply the science. For example, the argument

  4. Mammals have hair;
     Whales are mammals;
     Hence: whales have hair.

is first *rewritten* as

  5. All mammals have hair;
     All whales are mammals;
     Hence: All whales have hair.

and *then* is said to fit pattern 3. Clearly the rewriting step, by which the particular case is made to fit the pattern, introduces a certain amount of "play". The discipline of logic itself should provide some guidelines for the fitting procedure, but these guidelines cannot be too strict. For example, the author of 4 might have meant only that *some* (and not all) mammals have hair.

Yet this indefiniteness at the level of application is typical. Mechanics is an exact science; but the calculation of the path of a projectile, or a comet, is fraught with approximations and idealizations. The application of mechanics can be made more and more precise by taking more and more factors into account. Similarly, the use of logic to appraise a specific argument (which must begin by fitting the various stages of the argument into the general patterns studied directly by logic) can be precise to various degrees: sometimes the consideration of alternative possible interpretations, or close interrogation of the author, or examination of other writings by the same author, or of writings by his contemporaries, is needed to reach a significant degree of precision.

In the end, of course, the science may still be found to fall short. Newton's predecessors could not construct accurate enough lunar tables for navigation: the science of mechanics had to be extended and improved. The theory of syllogisms was inadequate for the appraisal of all reasoning; and, indeed, the logic to be developed in detail in this book is not adequate to the appraisal of all reasoning, though it goes considerably further than syllogistic reasoning.

Certain patterns of reasoning are valid, others invalid. If logic is to be of some explanatory use, it cannot simply make this distinction and assert validity for some types of argument: we need an explanation of what validity is, and why certain arguments are valid. Validity cannot simply be a matter of form or pattern, though the form of an argument may be a good (or indeed sufficient) indication of validity or invalidity. The remainder of this introductory chapter is devoted to an explanation of validity and related notions. This explanation will to some extent be informal. Specifically, we shall introduce informally some concepts that are central to logical theory, and which will be made precise later in the book. We must emphasize the informal status of this first chapter: no philosophically inclined reader will be satisfied at this stage, and no one is meant to be.

The most important of these concepts is that of *possible world*. Its introduction and use in logical theory is generally credited to the seventeenth-century philosopher Leibniz. An example of such a use may help as a preliminary. Suppose one argues that whales must have hair, and gives as his reasons that whales are mammals and that all mammals that live on land have hair. For the logical appraisal of this argument it is irrelevant whether it is actually true that all mammals living on land have hair, or that whales are mammals, or that whales have hair. If the argument is to be valid, we must not be able to say: Granted that whales are mammals, and that mammals living on land have hair, the world might still have been such that mammals living in the sea (such as whales) do not have hair. Now the world as it is, is the *actual* world; the world as it might have been is a *possible* world. (For generality, we shall allow that the world might have been exactly as it is, so the actual world is one of the possible worlds.)

SECTION 3
LOGICAL TRUTH AND LOGICAL FALSEHOOD

We shall now briefly discuss the intuitive notion of possible worlds and of what is true in a given possible world, and then use this notion to characterize some central concepts of logic.

For the time being, "possible" may be taken in the sense of "conceivable" or "imaginable". In the actual world, which, of course, is also a possible world, there are no centaurs; but centaurs do occur in certain Greek myths. Using our new terminology, we can say that certain Greek myths describe possible worlds in which there are centaurs. Conversely, in the actual world there is at least one politician who has the last name "Kennedy". But we can imagine this otherwise: we can imagine a world in which no politician has the last name "Kennedy".

An easy way to "construct" new possible worlds is simply to imagine that some parts of the actual world do not exist. For example, one can imagine a world in which there are no humans. Similarly, one can speak of *the world of men* by disregarding all else in the actual world; or of *the world of numbers,* by disregarding all entities which are not numbers. Notice that these two possible worlds have different sizes: there are only finitely many men, but there are infinitely many numbers.

A possible world which is not the actual one is bound to differ from the latter in some way or other. So, some statements true in the actual world will not be true in other possible worlds. For example:

1. There exists a brick house

is true in the actual world. But it is not true in a possible world containing no houses. Nor is 1 true in the world of numbers, a world we construct by disregarding all things (including houses) that are not numbers.

But now consider the statement

2. Either there exists a brick house or there does not exist a brick house.

This statement is made up of two other statements:

3. There exists a brick house.
4. There does not exist a brick house.

In some possible worlds 3 is the case; in other possible worlds 4 is the case. But in each possible world, either 3 or 4 must be true; *therefore,* 2 is true in *all* possible worlds. Some statements are true in all possible worlds—and this fact is of special interest in logic.

Besides statements that are true in some possible world and statements that are true in all possible worlds, there are statements that are false in all possible worlds.* An example of a statement that is false in all possible worlds is

5. There exists a building which is not a building.

5 is false in all possible worlds because in any such world no object will be both a building and not a building.

The notion of a possible world is instrumental to the explanation of "logical truth" and "logical falsehood". A statement is *logically true* if and only if it is true in all possible worlds; it is *logically false* if and only if it is false in all possible worlds. 2 above is logically true, 5 is logically false, and 3 and 4 are neither logically true nor logically false.

We have indicated above that the main task of logic is to provide a systematic method for analyzing and appraising arguments. The standards which govern logical appraisal traditionally have formed the basic subject matter of logic. So the question arises: in what ways are the concepts of logical truth and logical falsehood relevant to the analysis and appraisal of arguments? It is this question to which the remainder of this chapter is directed.

---

*The statements that are false in some possible world, but not in all, are exactly the statements that are true only in some possible world. For if a statement is true only in some possible world, there is at least one possible world in which it is false.

SECTION 4
VALIDITY AND INCONSISTENCY

Validity is a characteristic of *arguments*. The sense in which we use 'argument' is of course not that in which the bank robber snaps, "Don't give me no argument" when the petrified teller stutters, "But . . . but . . . but". An argument will minimally include one statement which is specified as a *conclusion* and others which are specified to be *premises*. Typically arguments will also include other statements which are the steps of reasoning from the premises to the conclusion: the intent of most arguments is to prove the conclusion from the premises. As we are interested in appraising validity of an argument only insofar as the conclusion can be correctly inferred from the premises, the intermediate steps are irrelevant. So we will treat an argument as a finite list of statements, one of which is designated as the conclusion and the rest as premises. An argument will be said to be in *standard form* when the conclusion is the last statement in the list. The following are rather mundane examples of arguments:*

6. If Johnson is President of the U.S. in 1964, then he is a citizen;
   Now, he is the President of the U.S. in 1964;
   Therefore, he is a citizen.
7. If the priest tells the truth on the witness stand, he breaks the secrecy of the confessional;
   On the other hand, if he doesn't tell the truth, then he perjures himself;
   So, he will break the secrecy of the confessional or he will perjure himself.
8. All objects have hair;
   So if something is an object, something has hair.
9. Las Vegas is north of Arizona, if it is in Idaho;
   Las Vegas is north of Arizona;
   Hence, Las Vegas is in Idaho.

Arguments 6–8 are *valid*; argument 9 is *invalid*. But what does it mean to appraise an argument as valid (or invalid)? At the beginning of this

---

*This book is concerned only with arguments which purport to prove their conclusions *conclusively*. These are deductive arguments. Arguments which purport to establish their conclusions only with likelihood (inductive arguments) are not discussed.

section we noted that arguments are often used to prove their conclusions, and that this use consists in offering the premises as support for the conclusion. But an argument so used would fail to satisfy the purpose of its user if it were possible for it to lead from true premises to false conclusions. So the function of an argument in proof is to lead from true premises to a true conclusion.* In other words, given the truth of its premises, to prove its conclusion, an argument must be such that it *could not* lead from true premises to a false conclusion. This is what is meant when we say that the argument is valid. So the following two statements are equivalent:

> 10. The argument is valid.
> 11. If all the premises of the argument are true, then its conclusion must be true.

It is the equivalence of 10 and 11 which shows that 9 is not valid: for in our world (and indeed, in the possible world consisting just of cities and states of the U.S.), the premises of 9 are true and its conclusion is false. The equivalence between 10 and 11 does not hold merely for our world. In general, "true" means "true in our world"; but statement 11 is shorthand for

> 12. In every possible world, if all the premises of the argument are true in that world, then the conclusion is true in that world.

We shall use the word *imply* to abbreviate what 12 expresses; that is, "implies" is to be understood such that 12, and hence 10, is equivalent also to

> 13. The premises of the argument together imply its conclusion.

There is, thus, a close connection between validity and *truth in all possible worlds,* and as indicated above with respect to 9, that connection gives us the means by which to establish the invalidity of any invalid arguments.

---

*There are other features of arguments that are also important features which fall in the proper domain of the logician. In this book, however, consideration is limited to the question of whether truth of the premises *guarantees* truth of the conclusion.

A list of statements need not be an argument, since it is not always indicated (by words like "hence") that one of the statements is the conclusion and the others are premises. But an argument is a list of statements. The terms "consistent" and "inconsistent" can be found to characterize any list of statements, whether or not they make up an argument. The concept of *inconsistency* is a natural extension of that of logical falsehood: a list is inconsistent exactly if there is no possible world in which all its members are true. (To put it another way: in any given possible world, at least one of its members is false.) If a list is so short that it has only one member statement, then this list is inconsistent exactly if that statement is logically false.

For example, the following set of statements is inconsistent:

14. Nixon is a president of the U.S. only if he is a U.S. citizen.
    Nixon is president of the U.S.
    It is not the case that Nixon is a U.S. citizen.

In our world, the third of these is false, but the first and second are true. Again, we can certainly imagine a possible world in which the second is false and the first and third are true. But we cannot have a world in which all three are true.

We may note here a very important relation between validity and inconsistency. The following two assertions are equivalent:

10. The argument is valid.
15. The premises of the argument and the denial of its conclusion together form an inconsistent list.

The valid argument that corresponds to the inconsistent list in our example 14 is

14*. Nixon is a president of the U.S. only if he is a U.S. citizen.
    Nixon is a president of the U.S.
    Hence, Nixon is a U.S. citizen.

This is so because the third statement in 14 is the denial of the conclusion "Nixon is a U.S. citizen" of 14*. Of course this is only an example, but we can show the equivalence of 10 and 15 in general. If an argument is valid, then if the premises are true, the denial of the conclusion cannot be true. Conversely, suppose we have list $A_1, \ldots, A_n, A_{n+1}$ of statements, and this list is inconsistent, then if $A_1, \ldots, A_n$ are all true,

A_{n+1} cannot be true. So if A_{n+1} is the denial of B, then if $A_1, \ldots, A_n$ are all true, B must be true. Hence the argument with premises $A_1, \ldots, A_n$ and the conclusion B is valid.

The reader will notice that we have just given arguments designed to show the equivalence of 10 and 15. Since the course has not yet provided him with the tools for analyzing and appraising arguments, he may still feel somewhat at a loss when faced with an argument of this complexity. If the above paragraph is reread after studying the logic of statements, it will be possible to appraise the arguments very easily. In the meanwhile, constructing some more examples like 14 and 14* on one's own should produce a certain degree of confidence in the equivalence of 10 and 15.

SECTION 5
LOGICAL TRUTH AND LOGICAL FALSEHOOD REVISITED

Various connections among the concepts of possibility, truth, validity, and inconsistency have now been explored. But we have not yet quite fulfilled our promise of showing how the concepts of logical truth and logical falsehood are relevant to the appraisal of arguments as valid or invalid. We are now in a position to do so. Recall that statements form an inconsistent list if and only if they cannot all be true together. In 14 we gave a list of such statements; a shorter such list would be "Johnson is a U.S. citizen" and "It is not the case that Johnson is a U.S. citizen". Thus we have

> 17. "Johnson is a U.S. citizen" and "It is not the case that Johnson is a U.S. citizen" are not both true in any possible world.

Now in English we have a way of combining two statements into a new statement, their conjunction, such that this new statement is true if and only if both of the old statements are true. A conjunction is formed by writing the first statement, and then the word "and", and then the second statement. So given this convenient device of English, we can express 17 also as

> 18. "Johnson is a U.S. citizen and it is not the case that Johnson is a U.S. citizen" is not true in any possible world.

But then, in this case, the *conjunction* is what earlier we called a logically false statement. Generalizing on this, we have the principle

> 19. A list of statements is inconsistent if and only if their *conjunction* is a logically false statement.

Now we can put some pieces together. In virtue of the equivalence of 10 and 15, we find now that 19 leads to

> 20. An argument is valid if and only if the *conjunction* of its premises and the denial of its conclusion is a logically false statement.

This establishes the connection of validity and inconsistency with logical falsehood. In principal it also establishes the connection between validity and logical truth: for a logical falsehood is simply a statement of which the denial is logically true. But there is also a more straightforward connection between validity and logical truth—just as straightforward as the connection between inconsistency and logical falsehood. To this connection we now turn.

For convenience, let us consider an argument with just one premise, A, and a conclusion, B. This argument is written

> 21. $A \therefore B$

which may be read as "A; therefore, B" or "A; hence, B". Now we know that the following two statements are equivalent:

> 22. Argument 21 is valid.
> 23. In any possible world: if A is true, then B is true.

A particular instance of 21 would be:

> 24. In any world: if "John and Mary have the same parents" is true, then "John and Mary are siblings" is true.

Notice that in 24 something is said about two statements. We encountered this once before, in 17. There we had a statement to the effect that one or the other of two statements was false in every possible world. Further we were able to combine the two mentioned statements into one statement. The device of conjunction lets us go from

"- - -" is true and ". . ." is true

to

"- - - and . . ." is true

and conversely.

If we accept this device in the case of "if, then", then 24 will be the same as

> 25. In any possible world: "if John and Mary have the same parents, then John and Mary are siblings" is true,

which is in turn equivalent to

> 26. "If John and Mary have the same parents, then John and Mary are siblings" is a logically true statement.

Generalizing, we arrive at the equivalence of

> 27. (*if A then B*) is a logical truth

with

> 27*. Argument 21 is valid.

Now a statement of the form "- - - then . . ." is called a *conditional* with "- - -" the *antecedent* and ". . ." the *consequent*. Furthermore, we may think of any argument as having the form 21, because the premises of an argument may be combined by means of conjunction. So the equivalence of 21 and 27 leads us to the following important principle about the connection between validity and logical truth:

> 28. An argument is valid if and only if the *conditional* statement, whose antecedent is the conjunction of the premises of the argument and whose consequent is the conclusion of the argument, is logically true.

Certainly 28 expresses a connection between validity and logical truth which is just as straightforward as the connection between inconsistency and logical falsehood expressed in 19. This supplements the rather more awkward formulation in 20.

We have relied on certain features of language here, which made it possible to form denials, conjunctions, and conditionals. When *A* and *B* are statements, we conveniently write the denial of *A* as (*not-A*), the conjunction of *A* and *B* as (*A and B*), and the conditional which has *A* as antecedent and *B* as consequent as (*if A then B*). In English (and in natural language generally) there are of course *many* ways in which to form such combinations. For example, the conditional which has "Tom is tall" as antecedent and "Tom is heavy" as consequent is the statement "If Tom is tall, then Tom is heavy". But the very same thing can be said in different ways; for example, as "Tom is tall only if Tom is heavy". When logic is being applied, one of the first tasks is to identify various linguistic forms as conditionals, as conjunctions, and as denials. This is part of the task of fitting specific cases into general patterns, which we discussed above.

PART *I* THE LOGIC OF STATEMENTS

2 Validity and Logical Truth

In this chapter and the next, we shall take statements as our basic units. Then we shall consider how complex statements may be constructed out of simple statements, and the logical relations among simple and complex statements. The first few sections of this chapter will show how the multifarious sentence forms of English are to be related to the general patterns considered in the logic here developed. Then we shall describe basic argument patterns which we assert to be valid, and we shall give an informal justification for their assertion. The justification proper must wait until Part Four. The logic of statements thus developed is entirely standard today, though it has its origin in Aristotle and the Stoic logicians.

SECTION 1
STATEMENTS

In the *first* two chapters we will be concerned with statements whose *logical truth* or *logical falsity* is determined solely by appeal to the expressions "it is not the case that", "or" (in the sense of "and/or"), "and", and the phrases "if, then" and "if and only if". An example of this sort of logical truth is

> 1. The university will survive or it is not the case that the university will survive,

and an example of a logical falsehood of the sort in question is

2. The university will survive and it is not the case that the university will survive.

Also, in these *first* two chapters, we will be concerned with arguments whose *validity* or *invalidity* is determined solely by appeal to the words and phrases just mentioned, and with lists of statements whose *consistency* or *inconsistency* is so determined. An example of a valid argument of the sort in question is

3. If the university survives, then no one will care.
   If it is not the case that it survives, then no one will care.
   The university survives or it is not the case that it survives.
   Therefore, no one will care.

An example of an inconsistent list of statements of the sort in question is

4. If the university survives, then no one will care.
   However it is not the case that no one will care; and the university will survive.

The expressions "or", "and", "if, then", "if and only if" and "it is not the case that" are *statement connectives*. They go between statements to make up other statements. For example, "or", when placed between the pairs of statements

5. The university will survive.

and

6. No one will care,

produces another statement

7. The university will survive or no one will care.

Statement connectives differ from expressions like "is identical with", which go between words or phrases to make up other statements as in the following case:

8. Johnson is identical with the President of the U.S. in 1967.

Later we shall investigate statements like 8. In this chapter, we shall study the way in which statements and arguments can be built *from other statements*, and develop methods for determining validity and logical truth; hence, the appropriativeness of the label "the logic of statements" for this most elementary part of logic.

Grammatically, a *statement* is a declarative sentence. But declarative sentences have many other uses. For example, if a commander says "Tents will be struck at ten", he is actually giving an order (he could as well have said "Strike tents at ten!" or "See that tents be struck at ten!"). Since Aristotle, we accept a second characterization of statements: statements are expressions that are capable of being true or false. However, we do insist that statements are expressions, expressions used in a certain way; that the same expressions have other uses (are ambiguous) is one of the obstacles faced in the application of logic.

Accordingly, though

9. Nixon is the President of the U.S. in 1967

counts as a statement—it is capable of being true or false—the sentence

10. Go close the door!

does not.

Statements can be divided into two sorts: they are *simple* (or *atomic*) or they are *compound* (or *molecular*). An example of a simple statement is (9) above; an example of a compound statement is (7), that is, "The university will survive or no one will care". Simple statements do not contain any statement connectives; compound statements do. Simple statements and statements built out of them by means of the five statement connectives above make up part of what we shall call the *official idiom*. Later, in the chapter on metalogic, we shall give a precise characterization of the official idiom; until then we shall content ourselves with informal remarks on the makeup of the official idiom as the need arises.

The statement connectives will be abbreviated as follows:

  (i) "and" by "&"
  (ii) "or" by "$\lor$"
  (iii) "if, then" by "$\supset$"
  (iv) "if and only if" by "$\equiv$"
  (v) "It is not the case that" by "$\lnot$"

Statements will be abbreviated by the upper-case English letters, with or without primes or subscripts: "S", "T", "U", "S'", "T'", "U'", and so on.

The letters used to abbreviate statements differ from those used to represent the statement connectives in one key respect. What the former abbreviate ordinarily will vary from context to context, whereas the latter always and only abbreviate the same English expression no matter what the context. Finally, we use the upper-case English letters "A", "B", "C", "A_1", "B_1", "C_1", ... as metalogical symbols for talk *about* statements.

Statements and their abbreviations, as well as statement connectives and their abbreviations, are examples of *logical signs*; names of statements and the symbols "A", "B", "C", are examples of *metalogical signs*. Statement connectives and their abbreviations are often called *logical constants*.

The distinctions drawn here are a bit subtle, and some examples may help. Let us momentarily use the letter "S" as an abbreviation for "John is tall". Then "It is not the case that S" abbreviates "It is not the case that John is tall". In turn, this can be further abbreviated to "$\neg S$".

Now in addition let us use the letter "A" to denote the sentence "John is tall". Then "A is true" means the same as " 'John is tall' is true". However "S is true" makes no sense because it abbreviates "John is tall is true" which makes no sense. For "is true" is not a statement connective like "It is not the case that", but is rather a predicate that can follow the *name* of a statement.

We adopt one further convention: to use "$\neg$", "$\&$", and all other logical signs as names of themselves. So we can now say that $\neg$ is a statement connective, meaning that "$\neg$" is a statement connective. And we shall use "$\neg A$" to denote the denial of what "A" denotes, "$A \& B$" to denote the conjunction of A and B, and so on. Thus, as long as "A" denotes "John is tall", "$\neg A$" denotes "It is not the case that John is tall".

When statements become more complex, the use of *punctuation marks* becomes imperative. The only official punctuation marks we shall use are parentheses. Thus

John and Mary went up the hill, and Jack and Jill went also

is paraphrased first as

John went up the hill and Mary went up the hill, and Jack went up the hill and Jill went up the hill.

Then the punctuation is redone with parentheses:

> ((John went up the hill and Mary went up the hill) and (Jack went up the hill and Jill went up the hill))

In this new version, neither comma nor period appears, only parentheses. Then, using S, T, U, V as abbreviations we symbolize the statement as

$$((S \& T) \& (U \& V))$$

In this way we can construct statements with grammatical structures of an intricacy seldom found in natural discourse: for example,

$$(S \supset T) \supset ((S \& (S \lor \neg T) \supset \neg S))$$

which the reader may amuse himself with rendering in English (where "S" and "T" are still used to abbreviate "John went up the hill" and "Mary went up the Hill").

   In practice, it is more convenient, though less systematic, to abbreviate the punctuation somewhat. *First,* outermost parentheses (which play the role that periods do in English) may always be omitted. Second, a single pair of parentheses may be replaced by a strategically placed dot:

$$(S \supset T) \supset \cdot (S \& T) \supset \neg T$$

abbreviates

$$(S \supset T) \supset ((S \& T) \supset \neg T)$$

which abbreviates

$$((S \supset T) \supset ((S \& T) \supset \neg T))$$

The rule is: if a dot appears immediately to the *right* of a connective, you replace it by a *lefthand* parenthesis, and then you add a *righthand* parenthesis as far to the right as you can (so as to produce a correctly punctuated statement).

   We can also place a dot on the lefthand side of a connective. Then it takes the place of a *righthand* parenthesis. So the above statement can be further abbreviated to

$$S \supset T \cdot \supset \cdot (S \& T) \supset \neg T$$

Of course, then an extra lefthand parenthesis needs also to be inserted when you remove the dot • as far to the left as possible.

It is in principle possible to use double dots, triple dots, brackets, curly thingamajigs, and anything else you fancy to abbreviate statements still further. But except for very special purposes, the law of diminishing returns legislates against this. In this book, parentheses and dots are the only devices in use, and of these, only the parentheses are official.

SECTION 2
THE OFFICIAL IDIOM AND SYMBOLIC PARAPHRASE

One reason for introducing the concept of an official idiom is that it differs in some respects from ordinary English, though of course it is a close fit in many other respects. For example, the expression "if, then" in the official idiom corresponds most closely to the "if, then" in the indicative in English. Yet the official "if, then" does depart in key ways from the English "if, then" in the indicative. In this section we shall state clearly how the statements in the official idiom are to be interpreted, and point out certain disparities between the statement connectives and their English counterparts.

Consider the connective "$\neg$" prefixed to any statement A to produce the *negation* of A. For example, consider

11. $\neg S$

as an abbreviation for

12. It is not the case that John is tall.

Suppose the statement

13. John is tall

is true, then 11, and, hence, 12, will be false. Likewise, if 13 were false, then 12, and also 11, would be true. Accordingly, the *interpretation* of negation is as follows: if a given statement A is true or false, $\neg A$ will be false or true respectively.

Consider, next, the connective "&" used to combine any pair of statements A and B to produce the conjunction of A and B. For example, consider

14. $S \& T$

understood as an abbreviation for

15. John is tall and Harry is fat.

"S" and "T" each have two possible truth values. But in 14 they are combined by the *conjunction* sign, which is our name for "&", that is, "and". The interpretation of the conjunction can be expressed succinctly as follows: if both of the component statements of a conjunction— these are called its *conjuncts*—are true, the conjunction is true; otherwise, the conjunction is false.

Turn now to the connective "$\lor$". It is used to combine a pair of statements A and B to form an *alternation* or *disjunction*. For example, consider

16. $S \lor T$

understood as an abbreviation for

17. John is tall or Harry is fat.

"$\lor$" is called the *alternation* (or *disjunction*) sign. The components of a compound constructed by means of the alternation sign are called its *alternates* (or *disjuncts*).

Care must be taken when interpreting "$\lor$", that is, "or". In colloquial discourse, "or" is used in two ways. For example, consider the uses of "or" in the contexts

18. Hale wanted liberty or he wanted death

and

19. The team will lateral or it will pass.

The force of "or" in the first case is: "one or the other but not both"; the force of "or" in the second case is "one or the other and perhaps both". The latter case is sometimes expressed as "and/or". The use of "or" in 18 is called the *exclusive use* of "or"; that in 19 is called the *inclusive use* of "or". It is "or" in its inclusive sense that is symbolized by "$\lor$".

With the aid of 19 the interpretation of "∨", that is *inclusive alternation*, can be explained. 19 will be false only when "The team will lateral" and "The team will pass" are false. Otherwise, 19 will be true.

Perhaps the most important connective is that symbolized by "⊃", called the *conditional* sign, which abbreviates "if, then". It combines pairs of statements to form another statement called a conditional. For example, consider

20. $S \supset T$

understood as an abbreviation for

21. If John is tall, then Harry is fat.

The if-clause of a conditional is called its *antecedent*, for example, "S" in 20; the then-clause of a conditional is called its *consequent*, for example "T" in 20. Consider the different uses of "if, then" in the following statement.

22. If John is a man, then John is an animal,

and in 21. The use of "if, then" in 22 is stronger than its use in 21. To see this, notice that no replacement of the word "John" in 22 will ever turn 22 into a falsehood, but if we replace "John" and "Harry" in 21 by "Wilt Chamberlain" we turn an assumed truth into a falsehood. It is this weaker use of "if, then" which is the intended interpretation of "⊃".

The interpretation of the conditional may be facilitated by means of examples. Consider the following four statements:

(i) If 6 is greater than 5, then it's greater than 3.
(ii) If 4 is greater than 7, then it's greater than 2.
(iii) If 6 is greater than 5, then it's greater than 7.
(iv) If 2 is greater than 6, then it's greater than 4.

In determining the interpretation of the conditional, as in the case of "&" and "∨", combinations of truth values have to be considered. (i)–(iv) represent these four cases. (i) is the case where the statement in the antecedent is true, and the statement in the consequent is also true. It is clear that (i) is true. (ii) is the case where the antecedent is false, and the consequent is true; yet, (ii) is true as a whole. The antecedent of (iii) is true, and the consequent of (iii), as well as

(iii) as a whole, is false. Finally, (iv) is true as a whole, despite a false antecedent and a false consequent. More succinctly, a conditional is false only when its antecedent is true and its consequent is false; otherwise it is true.

The last statement connective is represented by "$\equiv$", our abbreviation for "if and only if". It joins a pair of statements to form another called a *biconditional.* Consider, for example,

23. $S \equiv T$

as an abbreviation for

24. John is tall if and only if Harry is fat.

The interpretation of the biconditional is as follows: a biconditional is true if the left and righthand components of the biconditional are both true or both false (we also say then that they "have the same truth value"); otherwise it is false. So much is fairly clear when one realizes that a biconditional is a conjunction of two conditionals; for example, in the present case it is the conjunction of "$S \supset T$" and "$T \supset S$".

This completes the *interpretations* of the connectives. It is worth emphasizing the common feature in the foregoing interpretations of the statement connectives, namely, that the "meaning" of each is specified merely in terms of the truth values of the component statements of each. The statement connectives, so interpreted, are examples of *truth-functional* connectives. A connective is truth-functional if the truth or falsity of the compound statements constructed by means of it is *solely a function of the truth or falsity* of its component statements.

There are all sorts of non-truth-functional connectives. Here are two examples:

25. If it were the case that _____ then it would be the case that . . . .

and

26. It is necessarily the case that _____ ,

where the blanks "_____" and ". . . . ." may be replaced by any statement. Suppose the blank "_____" in 25 is filled by "Mao is a Texan", and the blank ". . . . ." is filled by "Mao is

American". Both of the statements are false and 25 is true. But suppose instead that the blank "_____" in 25 is filled by the false statement "Mao is a Dubliner", and ". . . . ." filled as before. Now 25 turns out false. In other words, the truth of 25 depends upon something other than the truth or falsity of its component statements because without changing the truth value (falsity, in the present case) of the component statements of 25 we can, nevertheless, change the truth value of 25 (from true to false, in the present case). A similar situation holds for 26 if we think of the blank in 26 filled first by the true statement "Johnson is President of the U.S. in 1967" and then by the true statement "Johnson is Johnson". Given the first replacement 26 is false—Goldwater might have made it—but, given the second replacement, 26 is true. Non-truth-functional connectives like those in 25 and 26 play an important part in philosophy, especially in philosophy of science and metaphysics.

In presenting the interpretation of statements in the official idiom we exploited parallels with colloquial usage, as an aid to understanding. But it is worth emphasizing again that the official idiom departs in significent ways from colloquial discourse. To cite one example, recall the discussion of the conditional. Remember that two colloquial uses of "if, then" were distinguished, a stronger one and a weaker one, and the conditional was said to be taken in the weaker sense. More accurately, the official "if, then" most strongly resembles the weaker colloquial "if, then". But even here there are significant differences. Colloquial discourse seems to leave undecided the treatment of "if, then" in cases where the antecedent is false. Some say the conditional then may be either true or false, but do not care which; others say that it has no truth value at all. In contrast we give it the value "true". Why do we choose this unordinary interpretation of "if, then"? The answer is similar to that given for preferring simple symbolizations; for the purpose of determining validity and inconsistency, we can get by with this simple interpretation of "if, then"; a more complicated analysis of the truth conditions for the conditional is unnecessary for our purposes. Granted the differences in usage between the official "if, then" and colloquial "if, then" in the indicative, the valid arguments with which we shall be concerned in this book, and which include the latter, also turn out valid if we substitute the official "if, then" for its colloquial counterpart.

The application of logic to an argument given in English begins with two distinct stages (which after some practice the student can complete in one). First the English sentences are paraphrased in the official idiom; then the paraphrases are symbolized. The principles of paraphrase are by no means exact, but we can give some rules of thumb.

The following are all paraphrased by "John is tall and Harry is short":

> John is tall but Harry is short.
> John is tall; however, Harry is short.
> John is tall while Harry is short.
> John is tall although Harry is short.

Paraphrase is a risky business; logical relations may be destroyed by it. But we have already given the reader enough warning that the applicability of our logical systems is limited.

The rules of thumb for the conditional are more complicated; all the following are paraphrased by "If John is tall, then John is heavy":

> John is tall only if John is heavy.
> John is heavy if John is tall.
> John is heavy provided John is tall.

Statements in which "unless" occurs can also be paraphrased by conditionals. Consider "I shall go, unless it rains". This is false just if it does not rain and I do not go anyway. So we paraphrase it as "If it does not rain, then I shall go". So "unless" is taken to mean "if not". But it may be argued that the above statement is also false if it rains and I go anyway. If that is intended, then we must add "and if it rains, then I shall not go". Or we could use a biconditional "then", and give the paraphrase as "I shall go if and only if it does not rain". The second paraphrase is "stronger" than the first, and hence more audacious if the statement is being used as a premise. In general, we follow the rule that paraphrasing should proceed with as little audacity as possible.

The second stage is symbolization; and this is quite mechanical once we have our statements in official idiom. For this consists now simply in abbreviating the statement connectives by the appropriate symbols, and abbreviating the remaining simple statements by the upper-case letters.

SECTION 3
DERIVATIONS AND VALIDITY

In this section we shall carry on the discussion of arguments and logical truth begun in the introduction, give a more precise characterization of "argument" and discuss the relation of these concepts to the important concept of derivation.

An argument is a finite (but non-empty) list of statements (in the official idiom) such that the last statement in the list is designated as the conclusion and all the others, if any, as premises. This description of an argument allows both

$$(P_1) \qquad S \supset T \qquad\qquad \therefore T$$
$$(P_2) \qquad S$$

and

$$\therefore S \vee \neg S,$$

where "*S*" and "*T*" abbreviate given statements* in the official idiom, to be arguments. (That is, an argument need not have premises; if a list has only one member, then that member is its last member.)

In the Introduction we explained what it meant to call an argument valid (or invalid). Validity was associated with logical truth of the corresponding *conditional*. But the present extension of the word "argument" to cover cases where there are no premises requires a corresponding extension in the characterization of validity. We shall present the definition of validity in two steps:

(i) If an argument contains no premises, then it is *valid* if and only if the conclusion of the argument is *logically* true; otherwise it is *invalid*.

(ii) If an argument contains one or more premises, then it is *valid* if and only if the conditional statement, whose *antecedent* is the conjunction of the premises and whose consequent is the conclusion of the argument, is logically true; otherwise it is *invalid*.

Two advantages of this expanded definition of validity are as follows. First, the traditional description of deductive logic as the science of valid argument now turns out equivalent to that given in the Introduction as the science whose purpose is to discover and systematize logical truth. For, given the present characterizations of "argument" and "valid", to every valid argument there corresponds a logical truth, and vice versa. Secondly, the *methods* to be described (in the next section) for determining validity turn out to be equally appropriate to the discovery

---

*Hereafter, until further notice, "statement" means "statement in the official idiom".

of logical truths, whether the latter be in conditional form or not.

So far we have been extending our explanation of the meaning of terms like "argument" and "validity". It is now time to consider the problem of how one tells or finds out when an argument is valid; it is time to consider what many philosophers call a *criterion* for validity. What we are looking for now is not merely another way of saying what "validity" and "inconsistency" are but rather a way of identifying them. To this end we introduce the notion of a *derivation*.

As a first step in understanding a derivation one might think of it as an unpacked argument, as an argument in which the connection between the premises and the conclusion is made plain by supplying the missing steps if such are needed. The missing steps, if there are any, differ from the premises in the sense that they follow from the premises or from other steps by certain already accepted rules, called *rules of inference*. More accurately, *a derivation is a finite list of statements, each one of which is a premise or follows from other lines in the list by means of certain rules of inference*.

To illustrate, recall the argument beginning this section:

$$(P_1) \qquad S \supset T \qquad\qquad \therefore T$$
$$(P_2) \qquad S$$

To prove the validity of this argument we can construct the following derivation:

(1) $S \supset T$ Premise
(2) S Premise
(3) T From (1) and (2) by the rule of
          Conditional Elimination

The rule of *Conditional Elimination* (hereafter CE) states that from a pair of statements of the form A and $A \supset B$, the statement B may be inferred.

An inspection of the list of statements (1)–(3) will indeed show that list to be a derivation; each line is either a premise or follows from previous lines by a specified rule of inference. Hence by the definition of "derivation", the list (1)–(3) qualifies as a derivation.

Whenever a list of statements is claimed to be a derivation, that claim can be checked in a perfectly mechanical way. Simply check each line to see whether it is a premise or a consequence of other lines. Since there are only a finite number of lines, one can arrive at a definite answer with respect to the question: Is such and such a list a derivation? It is because of this feature that the definition of "derivation" is said to be *effective*. The expressions to the right of each line in the above derivation are not essential to the derivation. They are there by courtesy of the deriver and/or order of the instructor; it is easier to verify whether or not a given list is a derivation with their help. Notice that a list could be a derivation even when a line *is misidentified*. In other words, the list (1) through (3) above would be a derivation even if the deriver had mistakenly identified line (3), for example, by citing a rule of inference other than CE; one can get from (1) and (2) in a single step to (3) only by CE.

How does a derivation establish the validity of an argument? To answer this question, reflect on the notion of validity. Recall that, in a valid argument, if the premises are true, the conclusion cannot help but be true. This is part of the force of the expression "logically true" in terms of which "validity" has been defined. To say that the conditional, which has the premises of a given argument as antecedent and the conclusion of that argument as consequent, is logically true, is to say that that same conditional is true in all possible worlds, or, equivalently, that whenever its antecedent is true, its consequent is true. For example, it is because the conditional

$$((S \supset T) \& S) \supset T)$$

is logically true, that is, it is because of the fact that whenever "$((S \supset T) \& S)$" is true, "T" is true, that the argument

$$
\begin{array}{lll}
(P_1) & S \supset T & \therefore T \\
(P_2) & S &
\end{array}
$$

is valid. Now since the antecedent of the above conditional is a conjunction of the premises of the corresponding argument, it follows that *if* those premises are true, so will the conclusion of that same argument be true. In short, valid arguments are *truth preserving*, as the definition of "validity" in terms of "logical truth" makes plain. Now consider a derivation. It can be thought of as a set of statements which proves that an argument (with given premises and a certain conclusion) is truth preserving. Why? Because the rules of inference permitting the transition from line to line are truth preserving from premises to conclusion. So *if* the premises are true, and *if* the rules of inference allow one to get from those same premises to that conclusion, the conclusion cannot help but be true. The list of statements showing that this transition can be made is, of course, a derivation.

To convince yourself that the rule of CE is truth preserving, imagine that its "premises" are true but its "conclusion" false; suppose, in other words, that A and $A \supset B$ are true, no matter what statements A and B are, but that B is false. But this supposition, once made, is seen to be impossible. For remember that the truth conditions, that is, the interpretation, of $A \supset B$ tell us that $A \supset B$ is false just in case A is true and B is false. But if we suppose A to be true and B to be false, then $A \supset B$ must, by the interpretation of "$\supset$", be false. So the supposition that $A \supset B$ can be true when A is true and B is false is impossible. Therefore, if A is true and if $A \supset B$ is true, B has to be true. So CE is truth preserving. As a result any line which CE sanctions must be true if the lines from which it was derived by CE are true.

A derivation is *not* the argument despite the fact that both may be exemplified by the same set of statements, as in the present case. It is possible to have an argument with no corresponding derivation. That is, one might *offer* an argument as evidence that a certain conclusion follows from certain premises. But it does not follow that the offer is a justification. Derivations amount to a justification, and as such they are sometimes hard to come by.

Derivations are used, in part, to justify claims of validity for certain arguments. That is another reason why to the right of every line in the derivation there is an expression showing the purported "justification" for that line. If the last line of a derivation corresponds to the conclusion of an argument, then the conclusion of that argument is said to be *derived* from the premises. As we have said above, when a derivation for a given argument is supplied the argument is valid. Of course, it is not the case that because no derivation *has been found* for a given argument that therefore the argument is invalid.

Having made the distinction between a derivation and an argument, it seems unduly laborious to have to duplicate the premises of an argument every time we want to set up a derivation for proving the validity of some argument. Therefore, when producing a derivation to establish that the premises of an argument imply its conclusion it will be sufficient to list the intervening lines between premises and conclusion under the premises of the recorded argument. That is why we set the conclusion off to the right of the first premise. For example, the derivation above may be written as follows:

(P_1) $S \supset T$ $\therefore T$
(P_2) S
  (3) T From P_1 and P_2 by CE

In general a derivation to prove the validity of an argument may be recorded thusly:

$$(P_1) \qquad A_1 \qquad\qquad\qquad \therefore B$$

$$\cdot \qquad\qquad \cdot$$
$$\cdot \qquad\qquad \cdot$$
$$\cdot \qquad\qquad \cdot$$

$$(P_n) \qquad A_n$$
$$(n + 1) \qquad A_{n+1} \qquad\qquad \text{Evidence for } A_{n+1}$$

$$\cdot \qquad\qquad \cdot$$
$$\cdot \qquad\qquad \cdot$$
$$\cdot \qquad\qquad \cdot$$

$$((n + 1) + k) \qquad A_{(n+1)+k}(= B) \qquad\qquad \text{Evidence for } A_{(n+1)+k}$$

In this general scheme $A_1, \ldots, A_n$ represents the finite list of premises set off by premise designations $(P_1), \ldots, (P_n)$; $A_{n+1}, \ldots, A_{(n+1)+k}$ represent the rest of the lines in the derivation with $A_{(n+1)+k}$—the last line of the derivation—being the same as the conclusion B.

SECTION 4
SUBDERIVATIONS AND LOGICAL TRUTH

Besides derivations we shall recognize a special denizen called a *subderivation*; a subderivation is a derivation *within* a derivation. The account to be presented is essentially Fitch's technique of *subordinate proof*.* The reasons we have departed from his terminology are twofold. First, the term "derivation" has much wider current circulation, given the purposes for which we use it, than does the term "proof". Secondly, we wish to keep as clear as possible the distinction between proofs of validity and proofs of conclusions of arguments. It is better to use separate words than to run the risk of confusing what is established solely by a derivation, namely, that an argument is valid.

We start with an example of a subderivation. Consider the following abbreviated valid argument:

$$(P_1) \qquad S \qquad\qquad \therefore (S \supset T) \supset T$$

where "S" and "T" are abbreviations of certain undetermined state-

---

*Fitch, F. B., *Symbolic Logic* (New York: Ronald Press, 1952).

ments. The following will be a derivation to prove the validity of this argument:

$$(P_1) \quad | S$$

(2)	$S \supset T$	
(3)	S	From (P_1) by *Reiteration*
(4)	T	From (2) and (3) by CE
(5)	$(S \supset T) \supset T$	From (2) and (4) by *Conditional Introduction*

In this derivation lines (2)–(4) make up a subderivation; the subderivation purports to show that "T" can be derived *under* the premise "S" with the help of the *added* premise "$S \supset T$". In the course of the derivation of "T" from "S" two new rules of inference were employed. These rules, the rules of *Reiteration* (hereinafter abbreviated by "R") and *Conditional Introduction* (hereafter abbreviated by "CI") are not essential to all subderivations. There are subderivations in which neither is employed. Nevertheless, both rules are used only in derivations containing subderivations. So we might regard them as rules *of* subderivation.

These rules, as well as the rule CE, will be discussed at greater length in the next section. For now it will be sufficient to point out their purpose in the example of a subderivation above. The *rule of Reiteration*, R, is a rule which allows one to move any statement occurring in a derivation outside (to the left of) a given subderivation inside that subderivation. For example, line (3) in the subderivation above is a repetition of the statement in line (P_1)—the premise "S"—occurring outside the subderivation starting in line (2). The *rule of Conditional Introduction*, CI, allows one to move outside (to the left of) a given subderivation from inside; the idea here is that if a statement B is derivable under a premise A, then the statement $A \supset B$ is true.

What, exactly, is a subderivation? It is an ordinary derivation, except in one respect: some of its lines are brought in from outside (by the rule R). To say that lines (2)–(4) in the main derivation in our example are (taken together) a subderivation therefore means this: line (4) can be derived from line (2) with the help of line (1). In other words, line (1) plays the role of an extra premise in the derivation of (4) from (2).

The vertical lines (called *scope lines*) show pictorially exactly which lines can be used as extra premises. Consider the following more complex example:

(P₁)	S	
(P₂)	$T \supset (S \supset U)$	
(3)	$S \supset U$	
(4)	S	From (P₁) by *Reiteration*
(5)	U	From (3) and (4) by CE
(6)	$(S \supset U) \supset U$	From (3)–(5) by CI
(7)	T	
(8)	$T \supset (S \supset U)$	From (P₂) by R
(9)	$S \supset U$	From (7) and (8) by CE
(10)	$(S \supset U) \supset U$	From (6) by R
(11)	U	From (9) and (10) by CE
(12)	$T \supset U$	From (7)–(11) by CI

There are here two subderivations. In the first, lines (P₁) and (P₂) can be used as extra premises since, in effect, they may be introduced from outside by R. In the second subderivation, lines (P₁), (P₂), and (6) may similarly be used. But only those! Lines (3)–(5) may not be reiterated into the second subderivation; the scope lines show this at a glance.

A subpremise will be regarded as occurring within the scope of the subderivation which it governs. Graphically, the scope line begins at the top of the subpremise and not at the bottom. The horizontal line, of course, sets off the subpremise from the other lines of the subderivation.

The decision to regard the subpremise of a given subderivation as an occurrence inside the scope of the subderivation it introduces is not idle. For if we do not so include it, if we permit it to be outside the subderivation it introduces, then we can prove certain invalid arguments valid. For example, the invalid argument from "Johnson is tall" and "If Johnson is Premier of Russia, then Johnson is a citizen of Russia" to "Johnson is a citizen of Russia" can be proved as follows, *if* we do not include the subpremise introducing a subderivation in its own scope.

"*S*" is "Johnson is tall"
"*T*" is "Johnson is Premier of Russia"
"*U*" is "Johnson is a Russian citizen"

(P₁)	S	$\therefore U$
(P₂)	$T \supset U$	
(3)	T	
(4)	$T \supset U$	From (P₂) by R
(5)	U	From (3) and (4) by CE
(6)	$T \supset U$	From (3) and (4) by CI
(7)	U	From (3) and (6) by CE

The error in this derivation, of course, lies in the move in line (7). For unless "T" in line (3) is regarded as falling inside the scope of its own subderivation nothing prevents it from being used in an application of CE outside that subderivation. To treat a subpremise B as outside its scope is to change a derivation problem A ∴ C to that of proving the validity of $(A$ and $B)$ ∴ C, a move which is not permissible because (a) the original argument has been changed and because (b), if permitted, it allows obviously invalid arguments to be proved valid.

Subderivations can occur at any place in a derivation and, to go Shakespeare's plays within plays one better, can even occur within other subderivations. For example:

(P_1)	S		
(2)		$S \supset (S \supset T)$	∴ $(S \supset (S \supset T)) \supset (S \supset T)$
(3)		S	
(4)		$S \supset (S \supset T)$	From (2) by R
(5)		$S \supset T$	From (3) and (4) by CE
(6)		T	From (3) and (5) by CE
(7)		$(S \supset T)$	From (3) and (6) by CI
(8)	$(S \supset (S \supset T)) \supset (S \supset T)$		From (2) and (7) by CI

Perhaps the most important feature of subderivations lies in the fact that they provide a direct procedure for proving logical truths. Recall the extended definition of "validity" given in the previous section. Suppose that the argument A ∴ B has been proved valid. By the definition of "validity" it follows that $A \supset B$ is logically true. But, again, by the definition of "validity", if $A \supset B$ is logically true, then the no-premise argument ∴ $A \supset B$ is valid. Indeed, no matter what form a logical truth has (it might have the form $A \lor \neg A$, for example), our extended definition of validity tells us that a valid no-premise argument corresponds to it. The concept of subderivation makes possible the extension of the concept of validity that allows us to associate a valid argument with every logical truth, no matter what its form.

Consider the valid argument where we introduced the first example of a subderivation. It had the form A ∴ $(A \supset B) \supset B$. By our extended definition of "validity", therefore, ∴ $A \supset ((A \supset B) \supset B)$ is valid. To prove the validity of the first argument, we introduced a *single* subderivation beginning with $A \supset B$. To prove the validity of the latter it suffices to introduce *two* subderivations thusly:

(1)		A	$\therefore A \supset ((A \supset B) \supset B)$
(2)		$A \supset B$	
(3)		A	From (1) by R
(4)		B	From (2) and (3) by CE
(5)		$(A \supset B) \supset B$	From (2) and (4) by CI
(6)	$A \supset ((A \supset B) \supset B)$		From (1) and (5) by CI

The leftmost vertical line is the scope line for the main derivation. Notice that there are no lines beginning with the designation "P". The main derivation is premiseless. It has however one line, line (6), which corresponds to the conclusion represented above the justifying expressions. We have here an example of a derivation from no premises. Yet clearly any instance of the last line would be logically true.

We shall call a derivation from no premises a *categorical* derivation, and the argument it proves to be valid a valid *categorical* argument. The idea here is that the conclusion of any valid categorical argument is assertable unconditionally. All logical truths are unconditionally assertable because they comprise the class of categorical arguments. We shall call a derivation from premises a *hypothetical* argument. Every valid hypothetical argument can be turned into a valid categorical argument, but the converse is not true. This is a more precise way of saying that the logical truths outrun the valid arguments, *where "argument" is understood in the more conventional way as something having premises.* Yet the notion of a subderivation makes the distinction between arguments with premises and those with none less unconventional-looking than at first glance. For the procedure of deriving a statement from given premises and that of deriving statements from subpremises are nearly the same.

Nevertheless we are far from having an adequate set of rules for proving validity and logical truth. We have yet to consider rules for the other connectives. And until we do this it will not be possible to give support to the claim that the rules of inference we shall present are not only appropriate to showing validity but also to proving logical truths. But we have established this much at least: since all valid arguments have corresponding logically true *conditionals*, a proof of the former amounts to a proof of the latter, and vice versa. For example, we have shown in these last few pages that if an argument of the form $A \therefore ((A \supset B) \supset B)$ is valid, then the conditional statement $A \supset ((A \supset B) \supset B)$ is logically true *because* the latter is logically true just in case it is the last line of the valid categorical argument. And if $A \supset ((A \supset B) \supset B)$ is logically true then $A \therefore ((A \supset B) \supset B)$ is valid.

SECTION 5
RULES OF INFERENCE AND SOME APPLICATIONS

For each connective there is an *introduction* rule and an *elimination* rule. The set of such rules comprises the set of *intelim* rules. In addition, we shall use two other rules of inference, the rule of *Reiteration* and the rule of *Duplication*. Let us consider the latter pair of rules first.

The rule of Reiteration says: *from a statement A which is a line outside of (to the left of) and before a given subderivation infer A as a line in that subderivation.* It may be represented graphically as follows:

$$R$$

The diagram displays two scope lines, the one to the right governing a subderivation relative to the longer scope line to its left. The leftmost scope line could be the scope line of the major derivation or a certain larger subderivation. In other words, R allows one to move from the leftmost derivation (the major derivation) to the rightmost subderivation. If there are, say, ten subderivations, such that each is a member of the other, in Chinese-box fashion, R allows us to move a given line into even the innermost subderivation. The dotted lines represent the other lines, if any, in the given derivation (or subderivation).

There are two points to notice in the statement of R. The statement reiterated into a given subderivation *must* (a) already be a line in a derivation (or subderivation enclosing the given one), and (b) be outside (to the left of) the scope of a given subderivation. Let us examine (a). Assume that this condition is not met. Then indeed anything would be derivable from given premises. To see this, assume a subderivation to begin with a certain subpremise B inside a derivation with premise A. Then we show *any* conditional $B \supset C$ to be a consequence of A as follows:

(P$_1$)	A	
(2)	B	
(3)	$B \supset C$	R (Incorrect) from (5)
(4)	C	From (2) and (3) by CE
(5)	$B \supset C$	From (2) and (4) by CI

Now consider point (b) and assume that the condition is not met. Then again we run into trouble. In this case we can prove any argument of the form $A, B \supset C \therefore C$ valid. Thus consider:

(P₁)	A	
(P₂)	$B \supset C$	
(3)	B	
(4)	$B \supset C$	R (Correct) from (P₂)
(5)	C	From (3) and (4) by CE
(6)	C	R (Incorrect) from (5)

The rule of Duplication (hereafter D) says: *From any statement A which is a line in a given derivation (or subderivation) infer A as another line in that same derivation (or subderivation).* This rule may be represented graphically as follows:

The rule of Duplication differs from Reiteration in this respect: the latter rule allows one to move *between* derivations and subderivations or between subderivations; the former rule permits us to move *within* derivations or subderivations. Actually, the rule is dispensable, given R. To prove this, it will be sufficient to show that wherever A is inferred from A in a given derivation by D, we can get the same result by use of R, CE, and CI. Thus suppose a derivation (or subderivation beginning with line A:

(P₁)	A	
(2)	A	
(3)	A	From (P₁) by R
(4)	$A \supset A$	From (2) and (3) by CI
(5)	A	From (P₁) and (4) by CE

The rule D turns out to be an *admissible* rule.* We shall adopt D as a convenience; later we shall not explicitly mention it in derivations.

---

*An admissible rule is a rule which does not increase the set of sentences with categorical derivations. In other words they do not permit one to prove more things than one could without them.

Let us now turn to a discussion of the intelim rules, of which we have two for every connective. Our total bank of rules for the logic of statements will be twelve: R, D, and ten intelim rules.

The first pair of intelim rules we have already met. They are the rules of *Conditional Elimination* and *Conditional Introduction*. We shall confine ourselves to a more precise restatement of them and to the derivation strategies they suggest.

The rule of Conditional Elimination is rather easily grasped. In one way or another, the average person encounters it early in life. It also goes by other names: *Modus Ponens* and *Detachment*, for instance. The rule says: *from a statement A and a statement $A \supset B$, infer B*. It may be represented graphically as follows:

$$\text{CE} \quad \left| \begin{array}{l} A \supset B \\ \cdot \\ \cdot \\ \cdot \\ A \\ \cdot \\ \cdot \\ \cdot \\ B \end{array} \right.$$

CE is an elimination rule because the specific conditional, among the premises, containing B as its consequent, has been eliminated in the inferred line.

The rule of *Conditional Introduction* is, perhaps, the most important of all ten intelim rules because of the practical and theoretical simplifications it produces. This rule says: *from a subpremise A and any line B falling inside the scope of the subderivation governed by A, infer $A \supset B$ as a line immediately outside of (immediately to the left of) that subderivation*. This rule may be represented graphically as follows:

$$\text{CI} \quad \left| \quad \left| \begin{array}{l} A \\ \cdot \\ \cdot \\ \cdot \\ B \\ \cdot \\ \cdot \end{array} \right. \right.$$
$$A \supset B$$

In the preceding section, CI was said to allow inference of a conditional $A \supset B$, if B was derivable under the subpremise A. Now that statement was not an inaccurate statement. But it can mislead if one is not careful about the use of the word "derivable". For example, consider the derivation proving the validity of the following undetermined argument. (We shall call an argument "undetermined" for which the statement abbreviations "S", "T", "U", and so on, remain unspecified.)

(P₁)	S		$\therefore S \supset (T \supset S)$
(2)		T	
(3)		S	From (P₁) by R
(4)	$T \supset S$		From (2) and (3) by CI

In this subderivation, there is no step in which the subpremise is used. Hence if we were to understand "derivable" in the narrower sense of "being derived *from*", the application of CI in line (4) would be incorrect. But "derivable" in this book means "inferrable by any of the rules of inference". So line (3) in the above derivation *is* "derivable under the subpremise T" because it has been inferred there by means of the rule of inference R.

The next pair of intelim rules have to do with conjunction. The only complication, we shall see, a minor one, concerns the order of the conjuncts in the elimination rule for conjunction. The rule of Conjunction Elimination (hereafter, KE) says: *from a statement of the form (A & B), infer A or infer B.* KE thus has two forms which may be represented graphically as follows:

KE₁ | $A \& B$
       | .
       | .
       | .
       | A

KE₂ | $A \& B$
       | .
       | .
       | .
       | B

The need for two forms of KE can be demonstrated by examples. Consider the following valid argument:

(P₁) $S \& T$ $\therefore T$

Using only KE$_1$, the most we can obtain from (P$_1$) is:

(2) S From (P$_1$) by KE$_1$

Now it might be supposed that we could get "T" from (P$_1$) by KE$_1$, by taking A as "T" and B as "S". But this is not correct. What we would have instead is a *different* argument, namely:

(P$_1$) $T \& S$ $\therefore T$

The arguments are different because the premises are different statements.

Whereas *order* of the conjuncts does make a difference in the case of KE—it produces two forms of that rule—it does not in the case of the rule of Conjunction Introduction (hereafter, KI). KI says: *from a pair of statements A and B, infer (A & B)*. Graphically, we have

KI A

          .

          .

          .

          B

          .

          .

          .

          $(A \& B)$

The next pair of intelim rules to be presented are Alternation Elimination (AE) and Alternation Introduction (AI). Like one of the intelim rules for conjunction, one of the rules for alternation must take into account the order of components in the alternation; unlike the rules for conjunction, however, the alternation rule affected by the order of components is the introduction rule for alternation. It says: *from a statement A (or from a statement B), infer (A $\vee$ B)*. Graphically, these two forms of Alternation Introduction (AI), are as follows:

AI$_1$ A

          .

          .

          .

          $A \vee B$

$$\text{AI}_2 \quad \begin{array}{|l} B \\ \cdot \\ \cdot \\ \cdot \\ A \lor B \end{array}$$

The need for both cases of AI will be clear from the following example. Consider the valid argument

$$(\mathbf{P}_1) \qquad B \qquad\qquad \therefore A \lor B$$

and suppose only the rule AI_1 to be among the specified rules of inference. Then no derivation to prove its validity can be constructed, despite the obvious equivalence of $(A \lor B)$ and $(B \lor A)$, for the most that can be obtained using AI_1 is

$$(\mathbf{P}_1) \quad \begin{array}{|l} B \\ \hline B \lor A \end{array} \qquad \therefore A \lor B$$
$$(2)$$

Accordingly rule AI_2 is not dispensable.

The rule of Alternation Elimination (AE) says: *from $(A \lor B)$, if C is a line in a subderivation under A and C is a line in a separate subderivation under B, infer C.* Graphically, the rule looks like this:

$$\text{AE} \quad \begin{array}{|l} A \lor B \\ \quad \begin{array}{|l} A \\ \cdot \\ \cdot \\ \cdot \\ C \end{array} \\ \quad \begin{array}{|l} B \\ \cdot \\ \cdot \\ \cdot \\ C \end{array} \\ C \end{array}$$

This rule looks a bit more complicated than is the understanding required to grasp it. The best way to visualize it is with an actual example. Recall the argument symbolized in Section 2, regarding lack of concern for the survival of the university.

(P₁)	$A \supset B$	$\therefore B$
(P₂)	$(\neg A) \supset B$	
(P₃)	$A \vee \neg A$	
(4)	A	
(5)	$A \supset B$	From (P₁) by R
(6)	B	From (4) and (5) by CE
(7)	$\neg A$	
(8)	$(\neg A) \supset B$	From (P₂) by R
(9)	B	From (7) and (8) by CE
(10)	B	From (P₃); (4)–(6), (7)–(9) by AE

Now the "sense" of AI should be clear. It tells one that if one can show that C is derivable from both the alternate A and the alternate B in $(A \vee B)$ then C is derivable from $(A \vee B)$. Like CI and R, AE is a rule of subderivation.

The next pair of rules are Negation Elimination and Negation Introduction. We shall see that both reflect a technique of reasoning often used. Negation Introduction (NI) says: *from a subderivation whose subpremise is A and containing the lines B and ⌐ B, infer ⌐ A immediately outside of the subderivation.* That is:

NI

A

$\cdot$

$\cdot$

$\cdot$

B

$\cdot$

$\cdot$

$\cdot$

$\neg B$

$\neg A$

Notice, by the way, that NI differs from AE in one important way. Whereas the latter requires two subderivations, the former only requires one. The sense of NI is not hard to come by. It suggests that if from a certain assumption one gets contradictory pairs of statements, then the negate of the assumption must be true. This, of course, amounts to one form of *Reductio Ad Absurdum* because one proves a certain negated statement true by reducing the assumed unnegated statement to absurdity, that is, by showing that the assumption leads to contradiction and so must be false.

The rule of Negation Elimination (NE) says: *from a subderivation whose subpremise is* ¬ *A and containing lines B and* ¬ *B, infer A immediately outside of the subderivation.* It can be represented thusly:

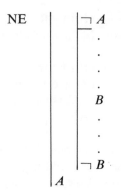

NE

NE amounts to another form of *Reductio Ad Absurdum.*

Our final intelim rule of inference concerns the biconditional. Given the fact that truth of $(A \equiv B)$ amounts to truth of the conjunction of the two conditionals $A \supset B$ and $B \supset A$, as an inspection of the truth conditions for the biconditional, conditional, and conjunction show, the sense of the rules of *Biconditional Introduction* (BI) and *Biconditional Elimination* (BE) will be easy to grasp. Thus we have, first,

BI

$$
\begin{array}{c}
A \\
\cdot \\
\cdot \\
\cdot \\
B \\
B \\
\cdot \\
\cdot \\
\cdot \\
A \\
\hline
A \equiv B
\end{array}
$$

BI says: *If B is a line in a subderivation under A, and A is a line in a separate subderivation under B, infer $A \equiv B$.* In other words, if *B* is derivable from a subpremise *A* and *A* from a subpremise *B*, infer $A \equiv B$.

The rule of Biconditional Elimination (BE) has two forms for exactly the same reasons brought forward in the explanations of KE and AI.

The rule says: *from A and (A $\equiv$ B) or (B $\equiv$ A) infer B*. Its symbolic representation is as follows:

$$
BE_1 \quad \begin{array}{|l}
A \\
\cdot \\
\cdot \\
\cdot \\
A \equiv B \\
\cdot \\
\cdot \\
\cdot \\
B
\end{array}
$$

$$
BE_2 \quad \begin{array}{|l}
A \\
\cdot \\
\cdot \\
\cdot \\
B \equiv A \\
\cdot \\
\cdot \\
\cdot \\
B
\end{array}
$$

This completes the list of rules of inference we need for the logic of statements.

We shall now give examples of derivations establishing validity and logical truth.

Argument 5a

> If Stephanie Bynge pinches the cow creamer, then Sir Watkin Bassett will put her in the nearest donjon. If Sir Watkin Bassett puts her in the nearest donjon, then Roderick Spode will beat her to jelly. Therefore, if Stephanie Bynge pinches the cow creamer, Roderick Spode will beat her to jelly.

ABBREVIATIONS

> "*S*" is "Stephanie Bynge pinches the cow creamer".
> "*T*" is "Sir Watkin Bassett will put her in the nearest donjon".
> "*U*" is "Roderick Spode will beat her to jelly".

SYMBOLIZATION OF 5ᴀ

$$(P_1)\quad S \supset T \qquad\qquad \therefore S \supset U$$
$$(P_2)\quad T \supset U$$

DERIVATION FOR 5ᴀ

(P_1)	$S \supset T$		
(P_2)	$T \supset U$		
(3)		S	
(4)		$S \supset T$	From (P_1) by R
(5)		T	From (3) and (4) by CE
(6)		$T \supset U$	From (P_2) by R
(7)		U	From (5) and (6) by CE
(8)	$S \supset U$		From (3) and (7) by CI

This is a derivation, because each line from (P_1) to (8) is either a premise or is derivable from other lines in accordance with specified rules of inference.

The following shortcuts in writing up derivations will be allowed. First, we shall drop the word "from" entirely, replace "and" with a comma, and "by" with a dash. Then, for example, the justification for line (5) may be written as follows:

  (5) T (3), (4) _____ CE

Secondly, it is a nuisance to have to rewrite a statement already appearing outside a derivation inside a subderivation whenever we wish to use it. Accordingly, we shall allow the subderivation above to be telescoped thusly:

(P_1)	$S \supset T$	$\therefore S \supset U$	
(P_2)	$T \supset U$		
(3)		S	
(4)		T	(P_1), (3) _____ CE
(5)		U	(P_2), (4) _____ CE
(6)	$S \supset U$		(3), (5) _____ CI

In other words, it will be sufficient merely to note the line being reiterated and used, because we know that it can be introduced into the subderivation only by R. Thirdly, we shall dispense with symbolizations as separate steps from here on.

Argument 5b

If either mathematicians need to take holy orders or mathematics should not be taught in a state university, then the Axiom of Choice is a theological principle. Therefore, if it is not the case that the Axiom of Choice is a theological principle then it is not the case that mathematicians need to take holy orders.

ABBREVIATIONS

"*S*" is "Mathematicians need to take holy orders".
"*T*" is "Mathematics should not be taught in a state university".
"*U*" is "The Axiom of Choice is a theological principle".

DERIVATION FOR 5B

(P_1)	$(S \lor T) \supset U$	$\therefore (\neg U) \supset \neg S$
(2)	$\neg U$	
(3)	S	
(4)	$S \lor T$	(3) _____ AI
(5)	U	(P_1), (4) _____ CE
(6)	$\neg U$	(2) _____ R
(7)	$\neg S$	(3), (5), (6) _____ NI
(8)	$(\neg U) \supset \neg S$	(2), (7) _____ CI

There is a small point about the above derivation. Putting parentheses around every compound containing negation signs gets cumbersome. So let us understand "$\neg A \supset B$" as meaning "$(\neg A) \supset B$" rather than "$\neg (A \supset B)$"; unless parentheses indicate otherwise, "$\neg$" applies to the nearest component to its right in a compound.

Argument 5c

The university will survive or it is not the case that the university will survive.

5c is a logical truth given our expanded notion of validity. Hence it must be a valid argument from no premises.

DERIVATION FOR 5c*

$$\therefore S \lor \neg S$$

(1) | $\neg (S \lor \neg S)$ | |
(2) | $\neg S$ | |
(3) | $S \lor \neg S$ | (2) _____ AI$_2$
(4) | $\neg (S \lor \neg S)$ | (1) _____ R
(5) | S | (2), (3), (4) _____ NE
(6) | $S \lor \neg S$ | (5) _____ AI$_1$
(7) | $\neg (S \lor \neg S)$ | (1) _____ D
(8) | $S \lor \neg S$ | (1), (6), (7) _____ NE

Finally, we prove the logical truth of the following undetermined argument 5d:

$$\therefore S \supset (T \supset U) \supset ((S \,\&\, T) \supset U)$$

(1) | $S \supset (T \supset U)$ | |
(2) | $S \,\&\, T$ | |
(3) | S | (2) _____ KE$_1$
(4) | $S \supset (T \supset U)$ | (1) _____ R
(5) | T | (2) _____ KE$_2$
(6) | $T \supset U$ | (3), (4) _____ CE
(7) | U | (5), (6) _____ CE
(8) | $(S \,\&\, T) \supset U$ | (2), (7) _____ CI
(9) | $S \supset (T \supset U) \supset ((S \,\&\, T) \supset U)$ | (1), (8) _____ CI

5d shows that a very simple nested conditional implies a certain un-nested conditional.

EXERCISES

1. Prove the validity of the following arguments.
   (a) Argument 7 in Chapter 1.
   (b) Philosophers are useful provided they are strange; but, in fact, they are useless. So either philosophers are wise but useless or they are neither strange nor wise.

---

*From here on we shall drop the notation (P$_i$) (i = 1,2,3, ...) in favor of (i). By now the reader should be accustomed to detecting the premises of an argument by their positions in deviations.

(c) A necessary condition for a given thing, a, being a possible object is that it could exist, that is, be concrete. The null set could never be concrete. So it is not a possible object.

(d) The king of France exists and is bald unless he wears a wig. However, the king of France does not exist. So therefore, he wears a wig.

(e) The concept of the synthetic a priori is incoherent provided that it is incoherent if unprovable. Hence that notion is either unprovable or incoherent.

2. Prove that the following sets of undetermined statements are inconsistent.

(a) $(T \supset \neg R)$, $\neg (((S \lor T) \& R) \equiv (S \& R))$

(b) $\neg (S \lor T)$, $((S \supset T) \supset T)$

(c) $(S \equiv \neg S)$

(d) $S, (S \supset \neg T), (\neg T \supset \neg S)$

(e) $\neg (\neg S \lor (S \supset T))$, $(S \supset T)$

3. Produce categorical derivations of the following.

(a) $(S \supset (T \supset R)) \supset ((S \supset T) \supset (S \supset R))$

(b) $(S \& T) \lor (\neg S \& T) \lor (S \& \neg T) \lor (\neg S \& \neg T)$

(c) $(S \supset (T \& \neg T)) \equiv \neg S$

(d) $((S \supset T) \& (R \supset U)) \supset ((S \lor R) \supset (T \lor U))$

(e) $(S \supset T) \supset ((R \& S) \supset T)$

4. Replace NI by the following rule:

NI*
$$\begin{array}{|l} A \\ \hline \neg \neg A \end{array}$$

Now show that the set of intelims rules with NI* in place of NI is equivalent to the original set of intelim rules in Chapter 2. (Here "equivalent" means "has the same set of categorical derivations").

5. Suppose the following definitions of $(A \& B)$, $(A \lor B)$ and $(A \equiv B)$ in an official idiom with $\neg$ and $\supset$ as the only primitive logical connectives.

$(A \& B) = df \ \neg (A \supset \neg B)$

$(A \lor B) = df (A \supset B) \supset B$

$(A \equiv B) = df \ \neg ((A \supset B) \supset \neg (B \supset A))$

Given these definitions—the sign "= df" means "equals by definition" —show that the intelim rules AI and AE, KI and BI and BE are derivable from the intelim rules for $\neg$ and $\supset$, and rule R.

6. The following principle is known as Peirce's Law:

$((A \supset B) \supset A) \supset A$

Is Peirce's Law derivable from CI and CE *alone*?

3 Invalidity and Consistency

In the preceding chapter we developed a method for showing that arguments are valid, or statements logically true. We should like, in addition, to be able to show that arguments are not valid (if they are not), or at least, that their validity could not be shown within the logic of statements. Similarly, we should like to be able to show that a given statement is consistent, that is, that its denial is not logically true. Henceforth we shall call the rules of the preceding chapter *intelim rules*, and we shall show how they give rise to certain other rules (*tableau rules*) which can be used to show invalidity and consistency.

SECTION 1
COUNTEREXAMPLES

Arguments can be refuted by counterexamples. What this means exactly may not be immediately obvious, but we can easily produce a case in point. Suppose I argue that if the hijacker had worn gloves he would not have left fingerprints, but he was not wearing gloves, so that he must have left fingerprints. Then you can refute me as follows: "You might as well argue that if the hijacker had been unarmed, he would not have had a gun, but he was not unarmed, so that he must have had a gun. As you well know, he was armed with a grenade instead of a gun".

This refutation proceeds by displaying a second argument, which can be symbolized in exactly the same way as the first, but which cannot be valid because its premises are true and its conclusion false. The first argument, suitably paraphrased, is

> 1. If the hijacker wore gloves, he did not leave prints;
>   The hijacker did not wear gloves;
>   Therefore: the hijacker did leave prints.

This may be symbolized as

$$1^*.\ S \supset \neg T$$
$$\neg S$$
$$\therefore T$$

where "S" abbreviates "The hijacker wore gloves" and "T" abbreviates "The hijacker did leave prints". Now the second argument is

> 2. If the hijacker was unarmed, he did not have a gun;
>   The hijacker was not unarmed;
>   Therefore: The hijacker did have a gun.

And it is pointed out, first, that 2 can be symbolized as 1* by using "S" to abbreviate "The hijacker was unarmed" and "T" to abbreviate "The hijacker did have a gun", and *second*, that 2 has true premises and a false conclusion.

There is of course a danger here that cannot be overemphasized: the symbolization in which whole statements are taken as units may obscure logical relationships. As an example, consider the argument that every raven has at least one wing because every raven has at least two wings. This seems to be a patently valid argument, but so far we can only symbolize it as, say

$$T \therefore S$$

and there are certainly invalid arguments that can be symbolized in this way too. A demonstration of invalidity is always open to the charge that it is based on too shallow an analysis of the argument.

What can we do then? Well, we can show that if an argument is correctly and adequately symbolized in a certain way, then its conclusion cannot be derived from the premises *by our rules*. For we can argue: if our rules did allow the derivation of this conclusion from those premises, then they would also allow the derivation of a false conclusion from certain true premises—and that is not possible. As an example, we thus maintain that if our rules allowed the derivation of the conclusion of 1* from its premises, then they would also allow the derivation of the false conclusion of 2 from its premises, which are true—and that is impossible.

That our rules indeed cannot lead from true premises to a false conclusion we have argued informally throughout the preceding chapter. In Part Four we shall show this rigorously.

We can also give counterexamples to claims of logical truth. Suppose, for example, that someone holds that there is a categorical derivation of a statement $(A \lor B) \supset B$. In that case, we would say we could have also a categorical derivation of

If $2 + 2$ equals either 4 or 5, then it equals 5

which is patently false. The two problems are of course closely related, since the argument from given premises $A_1, \ldots, A_n$ to conclusion B is valid exactly if the conditional $(A_1 \& \ldots \& A_n) \supset B$ is logically true.

Now there is one very practical problem in connection with the use of counterexamples. This is the problem that putative valid arguments and putative logical truths may be very complex. It is not easy to see, at a glance, whether statements symbolized as

$$((S \supset T) \supset T) \supset T$$
$$((T \supset S) \supset T) \supset T$$

are logically true, nor whether they are true or false even when we know whether the component statements are true or false. We shall therefore devote most of this chapter to showing how complex sentences may logically be transformed into equivalent sentences of a fairly simple structure, and how this procedure can be used to show either that a statement is logically true, or that it is not logically true (subject of course to cautions about adequate symbolization).

SECTION 2
A REDUCTION OF THE INTELIM RULES

Among the natural deduction rules, we have two for each connective. That makes for quite a large list. Since we have the following equivalences provable

1. $(A \supset B) \equiv (\neg A \vee B)$
2. $(A \equiv B) \equiv ((A \supset B) \& (B \supset A))$

we shall show that the C and B rules are eliminable.

From now on we shall refer to the system of rules R, D, KE$_1$, KE$_2$, KI, AI$_1$, AI$_2$, AE, NI, and NE as the system *IntElim*. And what we want to show now is that the additions of BI, BE$_1$, BE$_2$, CI, and CE are *admissible* for *IntElim*. We shall do this in detail for the C rules, and then *IntElim*, with the C rules added, can be used to do the same for the B rules.

We adopt the following abbreviatory definitions in *IntElim*:

D_1. "$(A \supset B)$" for "$(\neg A \vee B)$"
D_2. "$(A \equiv B)$" for "$((A \supset B) \& (B \supset A))$"

Now the following derivation shows that CE is admissible:

(1)	$A \supset B$				
(2)	A				
(3)	$\neg A \vee B$			(1) _____ D_1
(4)		B			
(5)		B		(4) _____ D
(6)		$\neg A$			
(7)			$\neg B$		
(8)			$\neg A$	(6) _____ R
(9)			A	(2) _____ R
(10)		B		(7), (9) _____ NE
(11)	B			(3), (4), (5), (6),
				(10) _____ AE

In this derivation we started with $A \supset B$ and A, used only definitions and rules of *IntElim* and ended with B as conclusion. The rule CE would have been a short cut, leading directly from (1) and (2) to (11); but certainly it would not have led to anything new.

Now we do the same for rule CI with the following derivation. We suppose that there really exists a derivation from A to B at a certain point in whatever derivation we are given, but before writing it out, we introduce the hypothesis $\neg (A \supset B)$. Since we obtain a contradiction, then we can use NE to conclude $A \supset B$:

(i)	$\neg (A \supset B)$	
$(i + 1)$	$\neg (\neg A \lor B)$	i _____ D_1
$(i + 2)$	$A \, \& \, \neg B$	from $i + 1$ by steps the reader can supply
$(i + 3)$	A	KE_1
	$\cdot$	
	$\cdot$	
	$\cdot$	
$(i + n)$	B	from i + 3, by the derivation whose existence we are assuming
$(i + n + 1)$	$A \supset B$	i _____ $(i + n)$, NE

Similar reasoning can be given for the admissibility of the B rules—and the use of CE and CI as shortcuts is allowed here, since the C rules have already been shown admissible. The admissibility demonstrations for the B rules are left as exercises.

SECTION 3

WORKING INSIDE CONJUNCTIONS AND ALTERNATIONS

Since A and $\neg \neg A$ are each derivable from the other, it may seem obvious to the reader that $(A \, \& \, B)$ can be derived from $(\neg \neg A \, \& \, B)$, $(B \, \& \, \neg \neg A)$ from $(B \, \& \, A)$, and so on. But the *IntElim* rules do not sanction the immediate inference of $(A \, \& \, B)$ from $(\neg \neg A \, \& \, B)$. The *IntElim* rules are applied to whole statements at a time, not to the middle of statements. For example, the following are incorrect:

(1)	$A \supset B$	
(2)	$(A \lor B) \supset B$	(1) _____ AI

(1)	$\neg (A \, \& \, B)$	
(2)	$\neg ((A \lor B) \, \& \, B)$	(1) _____ AI

although rule AI allows us to infer $A \lor B$ from A.

We are now going to see what kinds of inferential moves can be made inside multiple conjunctions and alternations. To facilitate this, we shall drop the parentheses that group conjuncts in a multiple conjunction (or alternates in a multiple alternation). So we shall write "$S \, \& \, T \, \& \, U$" to mean either "$((S \, \& \, T) \, \& \, U)$" or "$(S \, \& \, (T \, \& \, U))$". This ambiguity is useful, but we shall have to be very careful with it, and remember that a statement in which, say, "$A \, \& \, B \, \& \, C$" occurs is shorthand for two statements, one of which contains "$(A \ \& \ (B \ \& \ C))$". However, the reader can demonstrate as an exercise that each of the two indicated multiple conjunctions can be derived from the other: they are *logically equivalent*.

In addition, we shall now start using capital letters from the very end of the alphabet ("X", "Y", "Z") for a special job. These will be used exactly as "A", "B", ..., except that they may stand for nothing at all. Thus if "A" denotes "John is tall" and "X" denotes "John is heavy", then "$X \ \& \ A$" denotes "John is heavy and John is tall". But if "A" is thus while "X" and "Y" denote nothing, then "$X \ \& \ A$" and "$A \ \& \ Y$" each denote "John is tall".

When we write in this shorthand notation, the application for rules may also be conveniently telescoped. For any logical rules may be applied directly to one of the conjuncts (alternates), keeping the context the same.

I. If there is a derivation of B from hypothesis A, then there is a derivation of $X \ \& \ B \ \& \ Y$ from hypothesis $X \ \& \ A \ \& \ Y$.

To show this we need to show that the following rule (which shall remain anonymous) is admissible:

$$
\begin{array}{|l}
X \ \& \ A \ \& \ Y \\
\quad \begin{array}{|l} A \\ \cdot \\ \cdot \\ \cdot \\ B \end{array} \\
X \ \& \ B \ \& \ Y
\end{array}
$$

X and Y may themselves also be long conjunctions. Because of the systematic ambiguity of the notation (since we are not indicating how the conjuncts are grouped), this is really shorthand for four rules:

$$
\begin{array}{|l}
(X \ \& \ A) \ \& \ Y \\
\quad \begin{array}{|l} A \\ \cdot \\ \cdot \\ \cdot \\ B \end{array} \\
(X \ \& \ B) \ \& \ Y
\end{array}
\qquad
\begin{array}{|l}
(X \ \& \ A) \ \& \ Y \\
\quad \begin{array}{|l} A \\ \cdot \\ \cdot \\ \cdot \\ B \end{array} \\
X \ \& \ (B \ \& \ Y)
\end{array}
$$

$$\begin{array}{|l} X \& (A \& Y) \\ \quad\begin{array}{|l} A \\ \cdot \\ \cdot \\ \cdot \\ B \end{array} \\ (X \& B) \& Y \end{array} \qquad \begin{array}{|l} X \& (A \& Y) \\ \quad\begin{array}{|l} A \\ \cdot \\ \cdot \\ \cdot \\ B \end{array} \\ X \& (B \& Y) \end{array}$$

But since the different ways of writing the triple conjunctions are logically equivalent (as the reader may verify), it will be sufficient to show the admissibility of the first case. And this is done as follows:

$$
\begin{array}{lll}
(1) & \begin{array}{|l} (X \& A) \& Y \end{array} & \\
(2) & \begin{array}{|l} X \& A \end{array} & 1 \underline{\quad\quad} \text{KE}_1 \\
(3) & \begin{array}{|l} A \end{array} & 2 \underline{\quad\quad} \text{KE}_2 \\
(4) & \quad\begin{array}{|l} A \\ \cdot \\ \cdot \\ \cdot \end{array} & \\
(n) & \quad\begin{array}{|l} B \end{array} & \\
(n+1) & \begin{array}{|l} A \supset B \end{array} & 4(n) \underline{\quad\quad} \text{CI} \\
(n+2) & \begin{array}{|l} B \end{array} & 3\,(n+1) \underline{\quad\quad} \text{CE} \\
(n+3) & \begin{array}{|l} X \end{array} & 2 \underline{\quad\quad} \text{KE}_1 \\
(n+4) & \begin{array}{|l} X \& B \end{array} & (n+3), (n+2) \underline{\quad\quad} \text{KI} \\
(n+5) & \begin{array}{|l} Y \end{array} & 1 \underline{\quad\quad} \text{KE}_2 \\
(n+6) & \begin{array}{|l} (X \& B) \& Y \end{array} & (n+4), (n+5) \underline{\quad\quad} \text{KI}
\end{array}
$$

The use of CI and CE is allowed here, since they have been shown previously to be admissible.

II. If there is a derivation of B from hypothesis A, then there is a derivation of $X \vee B \vee Y$ from hypothesis $X \vee A \vee Y$.

Using reasoning exactly similar to that for the preceding result, it will be sufficient to show the following rule admissible:

$$\begin{array}{|l} (X \vee A) \vee Y \\ \quad\begin{array}{|l} A \\ \cdot \\ \cdot \\ \cdot \\ B \end{array} \\ (X \vee B) \vee Y \end{array}$$

This is shown admissible by noting that $X \vee B$ follows from X and also from A, and then that $(X \vee B) \vee Y$ follows from $(X \vee A)$ and also from Y. (We leave the details as an exercise.)

Derivations may now be shortened by writing down the justification for changing a single conjunct or alternate. As an example, we give the following:

(1)	$(A \vee B \vee C) \mathbin{\&} D$	
(2)	$A \vee B \vee C$	(1) KE_1
(3)	D	(1) KE_2
(4)	$(A \mathbin{\&} D) \vee B \vee C$	(2), (3) KI
(5)	$(A \mathbin{\&} D) \vee (B \mathbin{\&} D) \vee C$	(4), (3) KI
(6)	$(A \mathbin{\&} D) \vee (B \mathbin{\&} D) \vee (C \mathbin{\&} D)$	(5), (3) KI

Clearly, a certain amount of "telescoping" in the use of KI was necessary to move from (2) to (4), from (4) to (5), and from (5) to (6) with the help of (3); but we know now that such telescoping is admissible. When the reasoning is more complex, it may be convenient to insert small subderivations, to show exactly how it goes. So the above example may be given the longer form

(1)	$(A \vee B \vee C) \mathbin{\&} D$	
(2)	$A \vee B \vee C$	(1) KE_1
(3)	D	(1) KE_2
(4)	$\quad A$	
(5)	$\quad D$	(3) R
(6)	$\quad A \mathbin{\&} D$	(4), (5) KI
(7)	$(A \mathbin{\&} D) \vee B \vee C$	(2), (4–6)

and so on for the succeeding steps.

It may be helpful to say a few words about the case in which X or Y is empty, that is, "X" or "Y" denotes nothing at all. Suppose that X is empty, and B can be derived from A; can we derive $X \mathbin{\&} B$ from $X \mathbin{\&} A$? Clearly yes; for this means simply that we can derive B from A, as asserted. Similarly, can we then derive $X \vee B \vee Y$ from $X \vee A \vee Y$? This means: can we derive $B \vee Y$ from $A \vee Y$? Well, of course; for $B \vee Y$ follows from Y, but also from B, and hence also from A. The pattern of argument is exactly the same (with some clauses omitted) as for the case in which X is not empty.

SECTION 4
THE TABLEAU RULES

We shall now introduce four rules that are especially designed to be used in long alternations of conjunctions, and which have the effect of simplifying the structure of sentences to which they are applied. They are called *Tableau Rules* because they were introduced by the Dutch logician and philosopher Evert Beth* in the course of what he called his "method of semantic tableaux":

$$\text{DN} \quad \left| \begin{array}{l} X \,\&\, \neg\,\neg\, A \,\&\, Y \\ X \,\&\, A \,\&\, Y \end{array} \right.$$

$$\text{NK} \quad \left| \begin{array}{l} X \,\&\, \neg\,(A \,\&\, B) \,\&\, Y \\ (X \,\&\, \neg\, A \,\&\, Y) \vee (X \,\&\, \neg\, B \,\&\, Y) \end{array} \right.$$

$$\text{V} \quad \left| \begin{array}{l} X \,\&\, (A \vee B) \,\&\, Y \\ (X \,\&\, A \,\&\, Y) \vee (X \,\&\, B \,\&\, Y) \end{array} \right.$$

$$\text{NV} \quad \left| \begin{array}{l} X \,\&\, \neg\,(A \vee B) \,\&\, Y \\ X \,\&\, \neg\, A \,\&\, \neg\, B \,\&\, Y \end{array} \right.$$

III. The tableau rules are admissible.

Our results on inferences within conjunctions greatly facilitate the admissibility demonstration for these rules. For example, DN is proved admissible by

$$
\begin{array}{lll}
(1) & X \,\&\, \neg\,\neg\, A \,\&\, Y & \\
(2) & \quad\quad \neg\,\neg\, A & \\
(3) & \quad\quad\quad\quad \neg\, A & \\
(4) & \quad\quad\quad\quad \neg\,\neg\, A & (2)\ \text{R} \\
(5) & \quad A & (3\text{–}4)\ \text{NE} \\
(6) & X \,\&\, A \,\&\, Y & (1),\,(2\text{–}5)
\end{array}
$$

The admissibility of the other rules may be left to the reader.

Now the tableau rules may be used on alternates of a long alternation; the result is a continual simplification of the logical structure, until no further simplification is possible. In these applications, furthermore, we allow the letters X and Y in the rules to stand for *blanks*.

---

*Formal Methods, D. Reidel Publishing Co. (Dordrecht, Holland: 1962).

This means that, for example, all the following inferences are justified by DN:

(1) $\quad\vdash \neg\,\neg\,A$
(2) $\quad A$ (1) DN

(1) $\quad\vdash \neg\,\neg\,A\,\&\,B$
(2) $\quad A\,\&\,B$ (1) DN

(1) $\quad B\,\&\,\neg\,\neg\,A$
(2) $\quad B\,\&\,A$ (1) DN

As an example of how the tableau rules can be used to simplify the logical structure of a formula, we offer the following derivation:

(1) $\quad \neg\,[(S \supset T \cdot \supset S) \supset S]$
(2) $\quad \neg\,[\neg\,[\neg\,(\neg\,S \vee T)\,\vee S]\,\vee S]$ (1) D_1
(3) $\quad \neg\,\neg\,[\neg\,(\neg\,S \vee T)\vee S]\,\&\,\neg\,S$ (2) NV
(4) $\quad [\neg\,(\neg\,S \vee T)\,\vee S]\,\&\,\neg\,S$ (3) DN
(5) $\quad [\neg\,(\neg\,S \vee T)\,\&\,\neg\,S]\vee[S\,\&\,\neg\,S]$ (4) V
(6) $\quad [\neg\,\neg\,S\,\&\,\neg\,T\,\&\,\neg\,S]\vee[S\,\&\,\neg\,S]$ (5) NV
(7) $\quad [S\,\&\,\neg\,T\,\&\,\neg\,S]\vee[S\,\&\,\neg\,S]$ (6) DN

It will be obvious at a glance that (7) is a logical falsehood; and hence also that (1), from which (7) follows, must be logically false. In this way, the tableau rules serve to prove logical falsehood.

SECTION 5
CONSTRUCTION OF TABLEAU SEQUENCES

At the end of the preceding subsection we gave an example of a derivation by tableau rules, which amounted to a thorough simplification of the logical structure of the initial hypothesis. Such simplifications can be constructed mechanically by following the procedural rules:

    I. Eliminate conditionals and biconditionals by definitions D_1 and D_2.
   II. Consider the tableau rules in order, as stated. Apply the first applicable rule to the leftmost alternate (of the last line arrived at) to which any rule is applicable.

III. If any alternate is itself a conjunction, such that one conjunct is the denial of another conjunct, underline it.

Some remarks about these procedural rules are in order. In Rule II,
we call a formula *A* an alternation with *one* alternate (namely, itself)
when it does not have the form $(B \vee C)$ at all. Rule III is meant as a
convenience: in actual practice, one would stop operating on any underlined alternate, since it is a logical falsehood.

When a derivation is constructed in accordance with the above procedural rules, it is called a *tableau sequence* (*for* its initial hypothesis).
When a tableau sequence ends with a disjunction that has every one of
its disjuncts underlined, we say that the sequence *terminates*. Clearly,
if the tableau sequence for *A* terminates, then *A* is a logical falsehood,
for we can derive the denial of the last line of the tableau sequence—
and so, by NI, we can then conclude $\neg A$. (We are assuming, of
course, that our methods of derivation by intelim rules are reliable:
if we can derive $\neg A$, then *A* really is logically false. We argued this
informally in the preceding chapter, and will return to it in Part Four.)
These remarks may be summed up as follows:

IV. If the tableau sequence of *A* terminates, then $\neg A$ has a
categorical derivation in *IntElim*.

As with our other theorems, the demonstration amounts to showing the
admissibility of a rule:

$$
\begin{array}{r|l}
(1) & A \\
\cdot & \cdot \\
\cdot & \cdot \\
\cdot & \cdot \\
\cdot & \cdot \\
(n) & \cdot \\
(n+1) & \neg A
\end{array}
\qquad \text{terminating tableau sequence}
$$

Now line (n) is itself an alternation of which each alternate is underlined. An underlined alternate has either the form $(X \ \& \ P \ \& \ Y \ \& \ \neg \ P$
$\& \ Z)$ or the form $(X \ \& \ \neg \ P \ \& \ Y \ \& \ P \ \& \ Z)$, where any of X, Y, Z, may
stand for blanks. These two forms are logically equivalent; indeed,
each is logically equivalent to $(P \ \& \ \neg \ P)$. So the demonstration of
admissibility has the form

$$
\begin{array}{ll}
(1) & A \\
 & \cdot \\
 & \cdot \\
 & \cdot \\
 & \cdot \\
 & \cdot \quad\quad\text{terminating tableau sequence} \\
 & \cdot \\
 & \cdot \\
(m) & (B \,\&\, \neg\, B) \vee (C \,\&\, \neg\, C) \vee \ldots \\
(n) & \neg\,[(B \,\&\, \neg\, B) \vee (C \,\&\, \neg\, C) \vee \ldots] \\
(n+1) & \neg\, A \quad\quad\quad\quad\quad\quad (1) - (m),\, (n)\ \text{NI}
\end{array}
$$

This shows then that a terminating tableau is a good criterion of logical falsehood. (Line (n) must be derived under line (m); the reader may verify that this can be done in specific cases.)

The next question is whether we have really an "optimal" method of proving logical falsehood here. The worry is whether, in applying the structure-simplifying tableau rules, one might not oversimplify. The result of oversimplification might be that the initial formula of a tableau sequence could be logically false, while later formulas are not logically false. This worry can be laid to rest at least to the extent that we can show that if we have any chance at all of proving A to be logically false, we still have that chance after simplifying its structure with the tableau rules.

> V. If $\neg\, A$ has a categorical derivation, and B is any line in the tableau sequence for A, then $\neg\, B$ has a categorical derivation.

This we can show by proving the stronger result that if B is any line in the tableaux sequence for A, then there is a derivation of A from the hypothesis B. This means simply that the tableau rules are "reversible": if they were written backwards, they would still be admissible. So the proof of our result comes down to showing the admissibility of the rules

$$
\begin{array}{ll}
\dfrac{X \,\&\, A \,\&\, Y}{X \,\&\, \neg\,\neg\, A \,\&\, Y} &\qquad \dfrac{(X \,\&\, \neg\, A \,\&\, Y) \vee (X \,\&\, \neg\, B \,\&\, Y)}{X \,\&\, \neg\,(A \,\&\, B) \,\&\, Y} \\[2ex]
\dfrac{(X \,\&\, A \,\&\, Y) \vee (X \,\&\, B \,\&\, Y)}{X \,\&\, (A \vee B) \,\&\, Y} &\qquad \dfrac{X \,\&\, \neg\, A \,\&\, \neg\, B \,\&\, Y}{X \,\&\, \neg\,(A \vee B) \,\&\, Y}
\end{array}
$$

which will serve as further exercises.

Of course, the last line in a tableau sequence always has so simple a structure that we now expect the method of tableau rules to be a great boon.

SECTION 6
DERIVATIONS AND COUNTEREXAMPLES

We shall end with some applications of the tableau method. First, we can prove that $(A \lor \neg A)$ is logically true by constructing the tableau sequence for its denial:

$$
\begin{array}{lll}
(1) & \neg (A \lor \neg A) & \\
(2) & \neg A \,\&\, \neg\, \neg A & \text{NV} \\
(3) & \underline{\neg A \,\&\, A} & \text{DN}
\end{array}
$$

Note that X and Y are empty in this application of NV. Let us now try to show that $(A \supset B) \,\&\, (A \supset \neg B)$ is logically false.

$$
\begin{array}{lll}
(1) & (A \supset B) \,\&\, (A \supset \neg B) & \\
(2) & (\neg A \lor B) \,\&\, (\neg A \lor \neg B) & (1)\ \text{Def} \\
(3) & [\neg A \,\&\, (\neg A \lor \neg B)] \lor [\lor B \,\&\, (\neg A \lor \neg B)] & (2)\ \text{V} \\
(4) & [\neg A \,\&\, \neg A] \lor [\neg A \,\&\, \neg B] \lor [B \,\&\, (\neg A \lor \neg B)] & (3)\ \text{V} \\
(5) & [\neg A \,\&\, \neg A] \lor [\neg A \,\&\, \neg B] \lor [B \,\&\, \neg A] \lor \underline{[B \,\&\, \neg B]} & (4)\ \text{V}
\end{array}
$$

This attempt failed, since not all disjuncts in (5) are underlined, and no further rules are applicable. Does this mean that we have gained no information? Quite the contrary. In fact we can now show that $(A \supset B) \,\&\, (A \supset \neg B)$ need not stand for a logically false statement at all. For recall that the tableau rules are reversible: (1) can be derived from (5). And (5) clearly can be derived from $\neg A$ by D, KI, and AI (applied three times). So (1) can be derived from $\neg A$. But that certainty does not have the form of a logical falsehood. For example, "$\neg A$" could denote "It is not the case that there is light at the end of the tunnel", which may well be true. So the tableau technique can be used also to show that a given statement is *not* logically false.

> VI. If the tableau sequence of $\neg A$ does not terminate, then A does not have a categorical derivation.

This general principle is not proved by the preceding discussion, which only considered an example. For a completely rigorous demonstration we must refer to Part Four. But here we can justify it intuitively by linking tableau sequences with counterexamples.

Let $B_1, \ldots, B_n$ be the tableau sequence for $\neg A$, and suppose that it does not terminate. This means that B_1 is the statement $\neg A$, and that B_n is an alternation of which some parts are not underlined. Let us suppose that A does have a categorical derivation and see if this is possible. That means that we are supposing that a contradiction can be derived from $\neg A$. We already know that $\neg A$ can be derived from B_n, since the tableau rules are reversible. Therefore a contradiction can be derived from B_n. Now we are going to show that this means that our rules would allow the derivation of a false statement (namely, a contradiction) from a true statement—and this is impossible.

The final statement in the sequence, B_n, is an alternation, and some of its parts are not underlined. So let us say that B_n is the same statement as $C_1 \lor \ldots \lor C_m$, and that C_i is not underlined. It should be obvious that if C_i is a true statement, so is B_n. (Certainly B_n can be derived from C_i by repeated use of AI). The question is therefore whether C_i could be (or abbreviate) a true statement.

C_i is a conjunction, and each conjunct is either a single capital letter or a capital letter preceded by a negation sign. (For if C_i were more complex, one of the tableau rules would be applicable, and B_n would not have been the last statement in the tableau sequence.) Suppose then that the conjuncts which are single letters are "S_1", "S_2", ..., S_p" and the other conjuncts are "$\neg T_1$", ..., "$\neg T_q$". Let us agree to use each of "S_1", ..., "S_p" to abbreviate the same statement, namely "2 + 2 = 4", and each of "T_1", ..., "T_q" to abbreviate "2 + 2 = 5". Then each conjunct of C_i is true (since "2 + 2 = 4" and "It is not the case that 2 + 2 = 5" are true). Hence C_i is true.

This is rather a long argument; what it shows is that C_i can be (the symbolization of) a true statement, in which case B_n is a true statement. B_1 is just $\neg A$, and if $\neg A$ can be true, then no contradiction can be derived from it.

It is important to point out the crucial role of symbolization in this procedure. Suppose that we wish to know whether

    (a) If I am obliged to pay taxes then I should pay taxes

has a categorical derivation. We first symbolize it:

    (b) $O \supset S$

We then construct a tableau sequence:

$$
\begin{array}{lll}
(1) & \neg\,(O \supset S) & \\
(2) & \neg\,(\neg\,O \lor S) & (1)\ \ D_1 \\
(3) & \neg\,\neg\,O \lor \neg\,S & (2)\ \ NV \\
(4) & O \lor \neg\,S & (3)\ \ DN
\end{array}
$$

Next we construct the counterexample: let "O" abbreviate "$2 + 2 = 4$". Then (whatever "S" abbreviates) $\neg\,(O \supset S)$ can be derived from a true statement; hence no contradiction can be derived from it.

So we are not claiming that (a) is not logically true, nor that it could be false. We are only claiming that (b) can abbreviate a statement which is not logically true, and that *therefore* there can be no categorical derivation of (b). And because (b) is a correct symbolization of (a), the best we can produce at this point, the rules of this chapter do not allow a categorical derivation of (a).

EXERCISES

1. Provide counterexamples to show the invalidity of arguments of the following forms:
   (a) $A \supset B, B$; hence A
   (b) $A \supset B, \neg\,A$; hence $\neg\,B$
   (c) $A \lor B, C \supset A$; hence $C \lor B$
   (d) $A \,\&\, B, C \supset A$; hence $C \,\&\, B$

2. Provide examples to show that statements of the following forms are not logically true:
   (a) $A \supset (A \supset B)$
   (b) $A \supset (B \supset \neg\,A)$
   (c) $(A \supset B) \supset ((A \lor C) \supset B)$
   (d) $\neg\,((A \,\&\, B) \supset C) \lor (\neg\,A \lor C)$

3. Show that the rule $\begin{array}{|l} A \\ \hline \neg\,\neg\,A \end{array}$ is admissible.

4. Show that the rules BE and BI are admissible.

5. Derive categorically:
   (a) $(A \,\&\, B \,\&\, \neg\,(A \,\&\, C)) \supset (A \,\&\, B \,\&\, (\neg\,A \lor \neg\,C))$
   (b) $(A \,\&\, \neg\,(B \lor C) \,\&\, D) \supset (A \,\&\, \neg\,B \,\&\, \neg\,C \,\&\, D)$

6. Give derivations for
   (a) $A \,\&\, B \,\&\, D$; hence $A \,\&\, (B \lor C) \,\&\, D$
   (b) $A \,\&\, \neg\,B \,\&\, D$; hence $A \,\&\, \neg\,(B \lor \neg\,D)$
   (c) $A \,\&\, \neg\,B \,\&\, D$; hence $A \,\&\, (B \supset D) \,\&\, D$

7. Show the admissibility of rules NK, V, NV.

8. Show the logical falsehood of the following, using only the tableau rules and definitions:
   (a) $A \& B \& \neg (B \& A)$
   (b) $(A \vee B \vee C) \& \neg (A \vee C \vee B)$
   (c) $(A \vee (B \& C)) \& \neg (A \vee B)$
   (d) $\neg (A \& B) \& A$
   (e) $\neg (A \supset (B \neg A))$
   (f) $\neg (A \supset (\neg A \supset B))$
   (g) $A \supset (B \supset C) \& (A \supset B) \& \neg (A \supset C)$

9. Construct tableau sequences for the following:
   (a) $P \& Q \& \neg ((P \vee Q) \& \neg R)$
   (b) $Q \supset (P \supset \neg (P \vee Q))$
   (c) $(P \& \neg (Q \supset P)) \supset \neg P$
   (d) $(P \equiv (Q \vee \neg R)) \supset \neg (Q \& \neg R)$

10. Show the admissibility of the rules (without names) listed in the proof sketch for V.

11. Show by the tableau method that the following are logically true:
    (a) $P \& (Q \vee R) \supset ((P \& Q) \vee (R))$
    (b) $P \vee (Q \& R) \supset ((P \vee Q) \& (P \vee R))$
    (c) $((P \& Q) \vee R) \equiv ((P \vee R) \& (Q \vee R))$
    (d) $((P \supset Q) \& (R \supset Q)) \supset ((P \vee R) \supset Q)$

12. Show by the tableau method and counterexamples that the following are not logically true:
    (a) $(P \supset Q) \supset (Q \supset P)$
    (b) $(P \supset Q) \supset ((R \supset Q) \supset (P \supset R))$
    (c) $(P \supset Q) \& \neg (\neg Q \supset \neg P)$
    (d) $((P \& Q) \vee R) \supset (P \& (Q \vee R))$

PART *II* THE LOGIC OF GENERAL TERMS

PART II

THE LOGIC
OF GENERAL TERMS

4 Validity and Logical Truth

SECTION 1
GENERAL TERMS AND CATEGORICAL STATEMENTS

Many arguments that are valid in the sense explained in the Introduction can nevertheless not be proved valid by the logic of statements. Two venerable examples of such arguments are:

All Greeks are men;   Some men are Greeks;
All men are mortal;   No Greeks are barbarians;
Hence: All Greeks are mortal.   Hence: Some men are not
                                       barbarians.

None of the rules we have so far will allow us to infer the conclusions of these arguments from their premises. For none of the statements involved are constructed from smaller sentences by means of "and", "or", and so on; and our rules have all been designed so far to introduce or eliminate such connectives. Similarly, we cannot prove the logical truth of "All men are men", or the logical falsehood of "Some men are not men".

It is important to note that the statements in the above examples are of a special sort. *Categorical statements*, as they are called, are statements of one of the following forms:

(A)   All **A** is (are) **B**
(I)   Some **A** is (are) **B**
(E)   No **A** is (are) **B**
(O)   Some **A** is (are) **B**

The capital letters in parentheses are traditional labels of categorical statements of the displayed form. The boldface capitals **A**, **B** in the

69

sentences stand for (abbreviate) general terms, whether common nouns ("men", "water") or noun phrases ("salt water", "men who lie"). The statements in our examples are essentially of that form; that is, they can be rephrased without apparent distortion of meaning so as to take that form. Thus "All men are mortal" can be paraphrased as "All men are mortal beings" which has form (A), with the plural common noun "men" for the first place-holder, and the plural noun phrase "mortal beings" for the second.

Traditionally categorical statements have been analyzed (in various ways) as asserting certain relations among general terms. As an example, note that "All Greeks are men" can be analyzed as meaning that the instances of the general term "Greek" are included among the instances of the term "men". So categorical statements might be symbolized in the following way:

(A) $A \subset B$ ("A is included in B")
(I) $A \, o \, B$ ("A overlaps B")
(E) $A \perp B$ ("A is disjoint of B")
(O) $A \, os \, B$ ("A extends outside B")

These relations are easily diagrammed by drawing circles representing the classes of instances of terms (*Venn diagrams*).

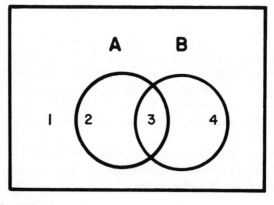

Figure 1

Thus in Figure 1, the circles divide the square into four numbered areas. Area 2, for example, represents those things to which term **A** applies and term **B** does not apply. It is customary to shade an area to represent that it is empty (there are no things belonging in that area) and to draw a bar in an area that is not empty. Thus Figure 2 represents the actual situation of there being no Greeks that are not men, and of there being some Greeks that are men.

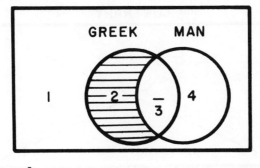

Figure 2

More generally, each of the four possible relations can be represented in Figure 1 as follows:

$A \subset B$ = area 2 is empty
$A \, o \, B$ = area 3 is not empty
$A \perp B$ = area 3 is empty
$A \, os \, B$ = area 2 is not empty

and similarly for the relations $B \subset A$, $B \, os \, A$.

It can be seen from the diagram that if the relation $A \subset B$ holds then the relation $A \, os \, B$ cannot hold, and vice versa (for in the one case area 2 is empty and in the other case area 2 is not empty). For that reason $A \subset B$ and $A \, os \, B$ were called *contradictions*. The logical relations between the four statements were said to be catalogued by the following "Square of Opposition" (Figure 3).

In Figure 3, the diagonal broken lines link contradictories (statements which cannot both be true), and an arrow indicates implication (if the first statement is true, then the second is true). *Contraries* are $A \subset B$ and $A \perp B$, because, it was said, these statements could both be false but could not both be true; *subcontraries* are $A \, o \, B$ and $A \, os \, B$ because, it was said, both may be true but both could not be false.

An inspection of the diagrams will raise problems with the square of opposition. For why is $A \subset B$ said to imply $A \, o \, B$? The former corresponds to: area 2 is empty; from this it surely does not follow that area 3 is not empty, which corresponds to the latter assertion.

The answer is that in the traditional logic of terms it was assumed that "A", "B" stood only for terms which have *some* application, but

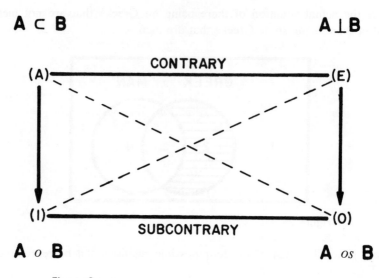

Figure 3

do not have *universal* application. This means that the following principles must be used in constructing Venn diagrams:

V_1. Either area 2 or 3 is non-empty
V_2. Either area 3 or 4 is non-empty
V_3. Either area 1 or 4 is non-empty
V_4. Either area 1 or 2 is non-empty

Later these principles were abandoned, and the traditional square of opposition pictured above was replaced by a "Square of Opposition" in which it is indicated that the old relations among statements hold only upon suitable assumptions concerning the term. This was quite an advance: it extended the logic of terms to all terms, even those which have no application in the world ("centaur", "round square"), and those whose application is universal ("entity"). The old inference of **A** *o* **B** from **A** ⊂ **B** was called the *fallacy of existential import*, and in its place the inference pattern

A ⊂ **B**
There is (are) **A**
Hence: **A** *o* **B**

was licensed.

However, the logic of terms pursued along these lines is beset with complications.* The main complications concern *relational terms* and *complex terms*. The term "father", for example, is relational: if someone is a father, then he is the father of someone (else). Now a statement may look like a categorical statement when it has a relational term in it, and yet not be categorical: "No man is his own father" cannot be symbolized as *man ⊥ father,* for this says that no man is a father. The problem of complex terms arises when we try to paraphrase all such statements, however complicated, as assertions of relations among general terms. For instance,

Some whom none dislike do not appreciate themselves,

an example due to Quine,** would become

Some non-self-appreciators are undisliked.

There must be logical relations among a simple term like "appreciator" and a complex term containing it like "non-self-appreciator". But both the grammar of these constructions and the logical rules relating them would lead us into manifold complexities.

SECTION 2
QUANTIFIERS AND VARIABLES

At the end of the nineteenth century, logicians developed a less complicated and more general approach to the logic of general terms. The basic insights leading to this fortunate development concerned the importance of *pronouns* and *quantifiers*. In the statement

All barbarians lie, and they steal if they can

the expression "All" is a quantifier, and the twice-occurring expression "they" is a pronoun. This pronoun refers back to the subject term "barbarians". Similarly, "some" is a quantifier, and "he", "she", "it", "who", and "which" may function as pronouns. All the statements

---

*The Aristotelian-Scholastic logic of syllogisms, the Boole-Schröder algebra of terms, the calculus of relations, and combinatory logic can be regarded as successive examples of this approach. The last of these is a fundamental and very important branch of contemporary logic.

**The Ways of Paradox (New York: Random House, 1966), p. 47.

which we have considered so far as examples can be rephrased more perspicuously by the use of quantifiers and pronouns:

> Everything which is a Greek, is a man.
> Everything which is a man, is mortal.
> Something which is a Greek, is a man.

In Quine's example, "themselves" also refers back to the subject, and therefore also functions as a pronoun. Hence the statement may be rephrased a bit more clearly as

> Some who are such that no one dislikes them do not appreciate themselves.

We shall now expand the official idiom to deal with statements such as those in the examples of the preceding section. We shall do this by explaining one by one the steps by which one goes from the original English statement to its paraphrase in the official idiom. We will introduce symbols for the new basic words of the official idiom as we come to them.

A. First, the words "all" and "some" must be paraphrased by means of such expressions as "everything" and "there is a thing". For example,

>   1. All Greeks are mortal

becomes

>   2. Everything which is a Greek, is mortal

and

>   3. Some Greeks are mortal

becomes

>   4. There is a thing which is a Greek, and it is mortal.

Note that "thing" is understood in the neutral sense of "entity" or "individual", so that a human is also a thing. Secondly, "there is a" is understood in the sense of "there is at least one, possibly more". But the things in question must be real, so we could also say "there exists a".

B. These paraphrases can be made even more perspicuous with the help of the *variables x, y, z, v, u, x',* . . . familiar from algebra; then 4 becomes

5. There is an x such that x is a Greek, and x is mortal

and 2 becomes

6. Every x is such that if x is a Greek then x is mortal.

The best way to understand 5 and 6 is to think of x as a *variable name*, a "name" which you can give to anything at all for the time being. Then 5 means

5a. There is a thing such that, if it is momentarily given the name "x", then the sentence "x is a Greek and x is mortal" is true.

Since we are mainly interested at this point in developing a simple and usable logical idiom, however, we shall retain the shorter 5 rather than the more perspicuous 5a.

C. Expressions of the form "there is an x such that" and "every x is such that" are called, respectively, *existential quantifiers* and *universal quantifiers*. The symbols for them are, respectively, "(Ex)" and "(x)". Thus 5 and 6 become

7. (Ex) (x is a Greek and x is mortal)
8. (x) (if x is a Greek then x is mortal)

The part of the statement that follows the quantifier and is between parentheses, is called the *scope* of the quantifier. As you see, inside the scope there are some familiar locutions, for which we already have symbols; thus we may rewrite those sentences as

9. (Ex) (x is a Greek & x is mortal)
10. (x) (x is a Greek $\supset$ x is mortal)

D. We are now almost finished; we just need to be able to symbolize such expressions as "x is a Greek".* In grammar, the expression "is a Greek" is called a *predicate*. To symbolize predicates, we use capital

_____

*We call this expression a *sentence*, because in English grammar the analogous "It is a Greek" is also called a sentence—although in either case the varying use of "it" or "x" means that the expression does not express a "complete thought", the traditional criterion for a genuine statement. Other writers sometimes call "x is a Greek" a *sentential matrix* or *quasi-statement*. We shall reserve the term "statement" for sentences that do not have variables in them without associated quantifiers; this usage will be made precise in the next section.

letters. The usual convention in logic (as opposed to English) is to place the predicate letters at the left. So "x is a Greek" becomes "Gx", and "x is mortal" can be written "Mx". (Note that we try to choose the predicate letter in such a way that it is easy to remember what it was chosen to stand for.) Thus 9 and 10 become

11. $(Ex)(Gx \,\&\, Mx)$
12. $(x)(Gx \supset Mx)$

E. In forming complex sentences, the expressions "Fx", "Gx", ... are treated just like simple sentences. Thus, "Fx" is a well-formed formula; so is "$Fx \,\&\, Gx$"; so is "$\neg Fy$", and so on. Then, given any sentence, a new sentence can be formed by prefixing a quantifier. Thus "$(y)(Fy)$" is a sentence. However, it is often useful to write this as "$(y)Fy$". Similarly, "$(Ez)(Fz \,\&\, Gy)$" and "$(Ez)(Fz) \,\&\, Gy$" are sentences; they are quite different sentences, for here the placing of the parentheses makes an obvious difference. If A is a sentence in which x does not occur, then $(x)A$ is also a sentence, and we say that the initial quantifier is *vacuous*. An example of a similar English sentence would be (the rather odd) "Everything is such that $2 + 2 = 4$".

These two ways of producing new sentences can be combined to produce for example, "$(x)(Fx \,\&\, (y)Gy)$", "$(x)(Fx) \supset (Ey)(Fy)$", "$(x)(Ey)(Fy \supset Gx)$". Colloquial counterparts can be given for all of these, though they may strain the English language somewhat. For our last two examples, the following are English counterparts (taking "F" to stand for "is colored" and "G" for "is blue"):

> $(x)(Fx) \supset (Ey)(Gy)$: If everything is colored, then there is something which is blue.
> $(x)(Ey)(Fy \supset Gx)$: Everything is such that something is such that if the latter is colored, then the former is blue.

F. There is one more topic to cover on the subject of symbolizing sentences containing general terms; namely, *relational predicates*. Some sentences assert relations among instances of general terms. Examples of these are

13. Every man likes himself
14. Every man dislikes something
15. There is a city which is between a river and a forest

It will readily be seen that we can apply steps A–D to (13) to get, successively,

13a. Everything which is a man, likes himself
13b. Everything is such that if it is a man, then it likes itself
13c. Every x is such that if x is a man, then x likes x
13d. $(x)(x$ is a man $\supset x$ likes $x)$

To the phrase "x is a man" we can apply step E (using H for "is a man (human)" to get

13e. $(x)(Hx \supset x$ likes $x)$

But this is as far as we can go, because we have as yet no way to symbolize "x likes x". We call "likes" a *two-place* or *second-degree predicate* and "is a man" a *one-place* or *first-degree predicate*. We symbolize "x likes x" as "Lxx". Therefore 13 is entirely symbolized by

16. $(x)(Hx \supset Lxx)$

Of course, we may also expect "Lxy" to occur. For example, applying our procedure to

17. Every man likes something

we get successively

17a. $(x)(Hx \supset x$ likes something$)$
17b. $(x)(Hx \supset ($there is a thing such that x likes it$))$
17c. $(x)(Hx \supset (Ey)(x$ likes $y))$
17d. $(x)(Hx \supset (Ey)(Lxy))$

Notice that "it" in 17b does not refer to x; hence we use another variable to symbolize it.
   Similarly, (14) becomes

18. $(x)(Hx \supset (Ey)(Dxy))$

if we use "D" to symbolize "dislikes". Instead one could perhaps say that "dislikes" means "does not like". Then "x dislikes y" is the same as "it is not the case that x likes y", and 14 would become:

19. $(x)(Hx \supset (Ey)(\neg Lxy))$

Besides one-place and two-place predicates there are also three-place, four-place, ..., and, in general, n-place predicates for every positive integer *n*. An *n*-place predicate, with *n* greater than 1, is called a *relational predicate*. One example of a three-place predicate is "... is between ... and ..." in example 15. Applying our paraphrase procedure to 15 we obtain

> 15a. There is an *x* such that *x* is a city and *x* is between a river and a forest.
>
> 15b. There is an *x* such that *x* is a city, and there is a *y* and also a *z* such that *y* is a river and *z* is a forest, and *x* is between *y* and *z*
>
> 15c. $(Ex)(Cx \& (Ey)(Ez)(Ry \& Fz \& Bxyz))$

Therefore we now have a unified approach to all general terms, including relational and complex terms.

SECTION 3
GRAMMAR OF QUANTIFICATIONAL LOGIC

At the end of Chapter 2, Section 1, we explained the difference between the use of "*S*" to abbreviate an English statement, and the use of "*A*" to designate an English statement (perhaps the same one). We shall continue to use these capital letters in that way. But now we have to consider the internal structure of statements. Suppose that "*A*" designates "Everything is tall"; then we can use "*S*" to symbolize (abbreviate) *A*, or, more perspicuously, we can use "$(x)Tx$" for that same purpose. For we are using capital letters to symbolize (abbreviate) predicates in just the way that we have so far used them for statements.

We interject a caution here: to avoid confusion, it is best not to use one capital letter as a symbol for both a statement and predicate *in one and the same context*. It so happens that "CIA" is an abbreviation for "Canadian Insurance Association" and for "Central Intelligence Agency", and this causes no problem with cautious use. But it would be confusing to say that the CIA is alleged to have a dossier on an employee of the CIA, in a context in which both the Central Intelligence Agency and the Canadian Insurance Association are discussed.

The capital letter "*A*" is normally used as a metalogical sign to designate a statement. In the same way we shall use the capitals "*P*", "*Q*", "*R*" normally as metalogical signs designating predicates. Logical signs, such as $\supset$, are used to designate themselves ("autonomous use"), and similarly the variables will be used to designate variables. (So it will make equal sense to say that "*x*" is a variable or that *x* is a variable.)

Thus the statement "Everything is tall" can be symbolized as "$(x)Tx$" and it can be designated by "$(x)Px$".

To confuse abbreviation symbols and metalogical signs, or to use an expression to designate itself (without having a convention to that effect) is to commit a mistake of use and mention. As mistakes go, this is a very harmless one. While the use/mention distinction is important in some cases, it is now common practice to ignore this distinction except when doing so causes confusion. So at this point we advise an exercise in tolerance of ambiguity: give no thought to the use/mention distinction except when you are feeling confused.

There is one more, minor, point about the use of our metalogical signs that we should mention. When we say simply that $A \supset A$ is logically true, this implies that $A \supset A$ is true no matter what statement A happens to be. Similarly, $A \supset (B \supset A)$ is true no matter what statements A and B are (as we can prove). Specifically, A and B may be *one and the same statement*. Now when we use "x", "y", "z" metalogically, that is, to refer to variables, we shall also allow that two of them may refer to the same variable. Thus, if we say that $(x)Px \supset (y)Py$ is logically true, we thereby imply also that $(x)Px \supset (x)Px$ is logically true. For in our assertion, we did not add the qualification that x and y were to be distinct variables. This is important to remember especially when we introduce rules for handling quantifiers.

An occurrence of a variable x is *bound* if it lies within a sentence of form $(x)B$. Hence in the sentence

$$(x)Px \ \& \ (y)(Py \supset Qx)$$
$$1 \quad 2 \quad \ \ 1 \quad \ \ 2 \quad \ \ 3$$

the first occurrence of x is bound, because it lies in the (component) sentence $(x)Px$; the second occurrence of x is bound; but the third occurrence of x is not bound. When an occurrence of a variable is not bound, we call it *free*. In addition, if an occurrence of x is within a sentence of form $(x)B$, we also say that the quantifier (x) *binds* the occurrence of x in B, or that B is the *scope* of that quantifier (x). So in

$$(x)(Px \supset (x)Qx)$$

the first quantifier (x) has scope $Px \supset (x)Qx$, the second quantifier has scope Qx. So the second occurrence of x is bound by the first quantifier, the fourth occurrence of x is bound by the second (but not by the first) quantifier.

We will now reserve the term "statement" for those sentences in which no variable occurs free. Other sentences we can refer to as "quasi-statements". It will be convenient henceforth to use our capital letters to stand for any sentences, whether statements or quasi-statements.

If we wish to draw attention to the free occurrences of a variable x, *if any*, in a sentence, we write it as Fx. When in one and the same context we use both Fx and Fy, then these sentences must differ *only* in that free occurrences of y are found in Fy wherever free occurrences of x are found in Fx, and *conversely*.

The operation of producing Fy from Fx is called *substitution* of y for x. But substitution of y for x in a sentence Fx will not always result in a sentence that can appropriately by symbolized as Fy. This may sound paradoxical, but the problem is quite simple. Suppose we have a sentence $(Py \supset Qx)$. We want to prove something, but judge that most of the structure of this sentence is irrelevant to the proof, so we just refer to it as Fx. Now substituting y for x in the original sentence produces $(Py \supset Qy)$. It is not true that this may appropriately be referred to as Fy, because it is not true that $(Py \supset Qx)$ and $(Py \supset Qy)$ differ in that the one has free occurrences of x wherever the other has free occurrences of y and conversely. The reason is of course that y already occurred free in Fx.

There is another problem which appears when we abbreviate $(y)(Py \supset Qx$ as Fx. If we substitute y for x we get $(y)(Py \supset Qy)$, and again the result cannot appropriately be abbreviated as Fy. For we do not have a *free* occurrence of y in the second sentence where we had a free occurrence of x in the first.

For these reasons we shall keep the abbreviations to Fx and Fy mainly for informal commentary and for examples, and introduce here some special notational devices to be used when we want to be precise.

First of all, we shall denote as $S_x^y(A)$ the sentence formed by replacing every free occurrence of x in A by an occurrence of y. Examples are

$$S_x^y (Px \supset (y)Ryx) = Py \supset (y)Ryy$$
$$S_x^x (Px \supset (y)Ryx) = Px \supset (y)Ryx$$
$$S_x^y (Pz \supset (y)Ryz) = Pz \supset (y)Ryz$$

Note that the substitution operation S_x^y leaves a sentence A the same in two cases: if x is not free in A or if x and y are one and the same variable.

Substitution operations only affect the free variables; hence if A is a sentence built up from simpler sentences $B_1, \ldots, B_n$ by means of statement connectives, then $S_x^y(A)$ is similarly built up from $S_x^y(B_1), \ldots, S_x^y(B_n)$. Thus we have the following *substitution equations*:

1. $S_x^y(\neg A)\quad = (\neg S_x^y(A))$
2. $S_x^y(A \& B) = (S_x^y(A) \& S_x^y(B))$
3. $S_x^y(A \vee B) = (S_x^y(A) \vee S_x^y(B))$
4. $S_x^y(A \supset B) = (S_x^y(A) \supset S_x^y(B))$

This makes it possible to carry out substitution into a complex sentence in stepwise fashion when the sentence is built up by means of connectives. When the substitution is into a quantified statement, we must observe the stipulation that substitution is only for *free* occurrences of variables. Thus, $S_x^y((x)Px)$ is not $(y)Py$, and also is not $(x)S_x^y(Px)$, that is, $(x)Py$. So we cannot say that for any three variables x, y, z, the equation $S_x^y((z)A) = (z)S_x^y(A)$; it holds only if the first and third variables are not the same. Thus the correct principle is

> if variables z and x are distinct, then
> 5a. $S_x^y((z)A) = (z)S_x^y(A)$
> 5b. $S_x^y((x)A) = (x)A$

We may note as a corollary to 5b that there is a special case in which $S_x^y((x)A) = (x)S_x^y(A)$, namely, when x is not free in A.

These equations 1–5 allow us to regard all substitutions into complex sentences as series of substitution into their simpler parts. As an example consider

$$S_x^y((z)(Pzx \supset (x)(Pxz)))$$

with the stipulation that x, y, z are distinct variables. By 5 this is the same as

$$(z)(S_x^y(Pzs \supset (x)(Pxz)))$$

which by 4 is the same as

$$(z)(S_x^y(Pxz) \supset S_x^y((x)(Pxz)))$$

which by 5 is

$$(z)((S_x^y(Pzx) \supset (x)(Pxz))$$

All that remains now is to carry out the substitution in the simple sentence Pzx to get

$$(z)(Pzy \supset (x)Pxz)$$

We turn now to a new topic closely related, however, to substitution. Suppose that the Eiffel Tower momentarily be given the name "x" and the Empire State Building the name "y". And let us abbreviate the predicate "is high" by "H". Then the sentence "Hx" says of the Eiffel Tower that it is high, and "Hy" says of the Empire State Building that it is high. Noting that "Hy" is exactly the result of substituting y for x in "Hx", we might jump to the conclusion that in general, $S_x^y(A)$ says of y exactly what A says of x. But this is not so. Consider the sentence "Nothing is taller than the Eiffel Tower" symbolized as "$(y) \neg Tyx$". The result of substituting y for x in that sentence is "$(y) \neg Tyy$". And that says that nothing is taller than itself; it does *not* say that nothing is taller than the Empire State Building.

The problem is not difficult to diagnose. In our second example, a free occurrence of x was replaced by an occurrence of y—but that occurrence of y was bound. So we must keep in mind clearly the possibility that, after substitution, the number of free occurrences of variables may be drastically diminished. This is important enough to introduce some special terminology:

> Variable y is *free for x in A* if and only if no free occurrence of x in A lies in a sentence of form $(y)B$ that is part of A.

We can now use this notion to discuss some more complex examples of substitution.

Substitution operations can be iterated: $S_x^y S_w^z(A)$ is the result of first forming $S_w^z(A)$ and then applying S_x^y to that. The following examples bring out some interesting features of this:

(i) $S_x^y S_w^z(Fw \supset (w)Rxw) = S_x^y(Fz \supset (w)Rxw) = Fz \supset (w)Ryw$

(ii) $S_x^y S_x^y(Fx \supset (y)Ryx) \;\;= S_x^y(Fy \supset (y)Ryy) \;\;= Fy \supset (y)Ryy$

(iii) $S_x^y S_y^x(Fy \supset (y)Ryx) \;\;= S_x^y(Fx \supset (y)Ryx) \;\;= Fy \supset (y)Ryy$

(iv) $S_x^y S_z^x(Fz \supset (y)Ryz) \;\;= S_x^y(Fx \supset (y)Ryx) \;\;= Fy \supset (y)Ryy$

(v) $S_z^x S_x^y(Fz \supset (y)Ryz) \;\;= S_z^x(Fz \supset (y)Ryz) \;\;= Fx \supset (y)Ryx$

From example (ii) we can draw the obvious conclusion that applying the same operation for a second time has no effect: $S_x^y S_x^y(A) = S_x^y(A)$. Example (iii) shows that substitution may not be a reversible process. In simple cases it is

$$S_x^y(Px) = Py \qquad\qquad S_y^x(Py) = Px$$

Hence: $S_x^y S_y^x(Py) = Py$

So here the complex operation $S_x^y S_y^x$ has no effect at all (just like, say, S_x^x; clearly, $S_x^x(A) = (A)$. But the complex operation $S_x^y S_y^x$ in example (iii) does have some effect; this is not a case of changing the result back into what you had. The reason is of course that, in example (iii), y was not free for x.

Finally, examples (iv) and (v) show that substitution operations in general do not *commute*: the order of their application matters a great deal. We do not generally have $S_x^y S_y^x(A) = S_y^x S_y^x(A)$—simply because x is not free in $S_x^y S_y^x(A)$ and y is not free in $S_y^x S_x^y(A)$. Thus, for example, $S_y^x S_x^y(Fx) = S_y^x(Fy) = Fx$, but $S_x^y S_y^x(Fx) = S_x^y(Fx) = Fy$.

SECTION 4
DOMAINS OF DISCOURSE

When we introduced the basic notions of this chapter, we already provided an informal interpretation: for example, $(x)Bx$ says that everything is B, or rather, that everything is such that if *it* is momentarily called x, then Bx is true. We shall now make this interpretation a little more precise.

A main figure in the development of contemporary logic was the nineteenth-century English logician Augustus De Morgan. In his *Formal Logic* of 1847 he pointed out that in normal discourse such terms as "all" or "every" are often not meant to pertain to the whole universe. He illustrates this with a science-fiction example.

Thus when we say "All animals require air", or that the name *requiring air* belongs to everything to which the name *animal* belongs, we should understand that we are speaking of things on this earth: the planets, etc., of which we know nothing, not being included.*

For this reason, De Morgan refers to the "universe" of a statement, or a "limited universe"; later writers used the terms "universe of discourse" or "domain of discourse".

De Morgan's limited universes were all parts of the whole, real universe. If a statement is logically true, then it must certainly be true in each such domain. Hence we can use these domains to show of various statements that they are not logically true. Take, for example, the statement "There are cows". In the real (whole) universe, this statement is true; to put it another way, if everything in the universe is to be considered, then there are some cows in our domain of discourse, and

---

*A. De Morgan, *Formal Logic* (London: Taylor and Walton, 1847), p. 55.

so the statement is true in our domain of discourse. But suppose that we restrict the domain to the collection of Englishmen. The statement "There are cows" is not true in *that* domain, since there are no cows in that domain. It follows then that the statement is not logically true.

In an analogous way, we can use restricted domains of discourse to show that some sentences are not logically false. For example, the statement "All fire engines are red" is not true in the domain of discourse that comprises all things in the universe. For it so happens that the fire engines in New Haven, Connecticut, are white. But if we restrict our domain of discourse to things found in Edmonton, Alberta, we find that there all fire engines are red, and so the statement is true in *that* domain. It follows then that the statement "All fire engines are red" is not logically false.

However, the method as we have presented it so far will not take us far enough. For consider the statement "No man is more than twelve feet tall" (or equivalently, "All men are twelve feet or less"). This statement is true in the domain that comprises everything; indeed, it is true in every domain. For to find a domain in which it is not true we would have to find a domain containing a man more than twelve feet tall—and there is no such man. Yet surely no one would say that this statement is logically true; giants might have existed, though in fact they do not.

Might not the method be saved by referring to "possible domains" or "domains of possibles" (as opposed to domains that are part of the real world)? Perhaps we could say: it is not logically true that no man is more than twelve feet tall, because it is not true in the land of giants. Of course, neither giants nor the land of the giants is part of the real world, but it is part of a possible world. This conception was furthered near the end of the nineteenth century by such writers as William James. In his *Principles of Psychology*, discussing what he called the problem of the perception of reality, James mentioned worlds of illusion and fantasy differentiated from the real world.

> Really there are more than two sub-universes of which we take account. . . . .For there are various categories both of illusion and of reality, and alongside the world of absolute error . . . there is the world of collective error, there are the worlds of abstract reality, of relative or practical reality, of ideal relations, and there is the supernatural world.*

There have been various philosophical reactions to this approach, from bold attempts to formulate a metaphysics doing justice to this concep-

---

*W. James, *Principles of Psychology* (New York: Henry Holt and Co., 1890), Volume II, Chapter XXI; p. 291 in the 1923 edition.

tion, to ill-concealed disgust. The proper attitude belongs to neither of these extremes. It is the task of the philosophical logician to provide reconstructions for all significant forms of discourse. In view of the philosophical puzzles and disagreements surrounding the topic of possible worlds, it would be irresponsible to use the notion of possible world without providing such a reconstruction. (Two paragraphs hence we will offer such a reconstruction, adequate for present purposes, and turn again to this topic in the part on metalogic.)

So in the present context we shall heed Russell's injunction that a philosopher should have a robust sense of reality. If someone proclaims that his domain of discourse is the collection of giants, we shall argue: there are no giants, hence that collection is empty, hence his domain of discourse is the empty domain. The statements true in the empty domain can easily be found: any statement of the form "There is (are)..." is false in the empty domain. From this fact, and the logical rules we shall develop later on, it will be possible to determine the truth values of statements of different form as well.

However this may be, we still have the problem that "No man is over twelve feet tall" is not logically true, and yet is true in all the domains we have. A somewhat more careful analysis of logical truth, however, will help to solve this problem. Logical truth can be determined by *form* alone: not the meanings of its terms, but its grammatical form, should show whether a statement is logically true. Hence the question of logical truth should not be affected if we decide to use terms in a non-standard sense. Suppose "man" were used to mean "tree"; in that case the statement "No man is over twelve feet tall" would not be true (in the domain which comprises everything, or in the domain of trees, and so on). In logical jargon this is stated as follows: we can find a domain $\mathcal{D}$ and an interpretation of the predicates, such that the statement is not true in $\mathcal{D}$ under that interpretation.

When a logician says that some statement is not true in some "possible world", he may be understood to mean exactly this: the statement is not true in some domain under some interpretation. Thus as a logical reconstruction of the notion of *possible world* we have: a possible world can be identified with a domain of discourse *plus* some interpretation of the predicates. And then we can say, keeping this reconstruction in mind, that logical truth is truth in all possible worlds.

It may at first seem strange that an argument could be refuted by giving its words a new meaning. But in logic we abstract from the meaning of most words (not all: the meanings of "and", "or", "not", "all" are not disregarded; that is why these are sometimes called *logical terms*). Sometimes this is expressed as: in logic, it is only the *form* of statements that matters, not their *content*. And a distinction may be drawn between what is true as a matter of fact ("There are bachelors"), and what is true by virtue of the meaning of the words ("Bachelors are unmarried adult male humans") and what is logically true ("Bachelors are bachelors"). The following disputation occurs in Lewis Carroll's *Alice's Adventures in Wonderland*:

> "Then you should say what you mean," the March Hare went on.
> "I do," Alice hastily replied; "at least—at least I mean what I say—that's the same thing you know."
> "Not the same thing a bit!" said the Hatter. "Why, you might just as well say that 'I see what I eat' is the same thing as 'I eat what I see'!"*

The Hatter shows that "I say what I mean if and only if I mean what I say" is not logically true. He certainly does not show that it is not factually true, nor even that it is not true by virtue of the meanings of the words. (Compare "I like what I am fond of if and only if I am fond of what I like".)

We end with two examples that may be instructive. We choose as domain of discourse (call it "$\mathcal{D}$") the collection of all natural numbers. As an interpretation we choose: "is red" means "is even", "is green" means "is an integral power of 2", "is to the left of" means "is greater than". Now in this possible world, we have

1. "All green things are red" is true because all (integral) powers of 2 are even.
2. "For every red thing x there is some green thing y such that y is to the left of x" is true because for every even number x there is some power of 2 which is greater than x.

In this example we used English predicates and gave them a new meaning. It is in general more convenient when giving an interpretation (whether of an English predicate or a predicate symbol) to stipulate simply its *extension* in the domain of discourse. What is meant by this, we shall now explain.

First, an example may be helpful. The extension of the English predicate "is red", when it has its usual meaning, is the collection of all things that are red. If we choose a limited domain of discourse, then the extension "is red" in that domain is just the collection of things that are red *and* are in that domain. More generally, if P is a one-

---

*(London: Macmillan and Co., 1879), p. 98.

place predicate, then the extension of P in a domain $\mathcal{D}$ is exactly the collection of things in $\mathcal{D}$ to which predicate P truly applies.

It is a bit more complicated to explain the extension of two-place predicates, three-place predicates, and so on. To do this we must utilize the notion of a *sequence*. This notion is of course already used in high school mathematics; for example, the sequence (1, 2, 4, 8, 16, 32) is formed by taking 1 as first member, and then each time multiplying by 2, and stopping when you have six members. A different sequence is (32, 16, 8, 4, 2, 1), which is formed by taking 32 as first member, and each time dividing by 2, until you have six members. So sequences are *ordered*: to describe a sequence you have to list its members in the right order.

Now we apply this as follows. If the Town Hall is red, then the Town Hall belongs to the extension of "is red". If the Town Hall is north of the Green, then the (two-member) sequence

(the Town Hall, the Green)

belongs to the extension of "is north of". If the Town Hall is between the Green and the Museum, then the (three-member) sequence

(the Town Hall, the Green, the Museum)

belongs to the extension of "is between . . . and - - -".

Two-member sequences are usually called *couples,* and three-member sequences, *triples.* So the extension of "is north of" is the collection of all couples of which the first member is north of the second member. To state what the extension of an n-place predicate is, in general, we must be a bit careful about the use/mention distinction, at least to begin. Let P be a predicate of degree n. Then the extension of P in a domain $\mathcal{D}$ is the collection of all sequences $(X_1, \ldots, X_n)$ such that

a) $X_1, \ldots, X_n$ all belong to $\mathcal{D}$;

b) if variables $x_1, \ldots, x_n$ are used as names for $X_1, \ldots, X_n$ respectively, then $Px_1 \ldots x_n$ is true.

Remembering that we use the lower case letters "x", "y", "z", with or without subscripts, in *two* ways (as variables and also as metalogical signs standing for variables), we can restate the above principle in a shorter way if we are prepared to ignore the use/mention distinction. Then we can say: the extension of P in $\mathcal{D}$ is the collection of all sequences $(x_1, \ldots, x_n)$ such that $Px_1 \ldots x_n$ is true.

Here then is an example using predicate symbols. As our domain $\mathcal{D}$ we choose again the class of natural numbers. The predicate letters we shall use are E, F, L, where E, F are one-place and L is two-place. The

the extension of E (in $\mathcal{D}$) is the class of even numbers;
the extension of F is the class of integral powers of 2;
the extension of L is the class of couples of numbers (m, n) such that $m > n$.

Now we have, in this possible world:

3. $(x)(Fx \supset Ex)$ is true because for all things x in $\mathcal{D}$, if x is a power of 2 then x is even.
4. $(x)(Ex \supset (Ey)(Fy \& Lyx))$ is true because for every thing x in $\mathcal{D}$, if x is even, then there is a thing y in $\mathcal{D}$ such that y is a power of 2 and $y > x$.

The two examples we have given are essentially the same: in the present case we have used predicate symbols rather than English predicates, and we have stipulated their extensions rather than their meanings.

SECTION 5
INTELIM RULES FOR QUANTIFIERS

To introduce the intelim rules for quantifiers, we shall analyze the first sample argument given at the beginning of this chapter:

All Greeks are men;
All men are mortal;
Hence: all Greeks are mortal.

This is symbolized:

$(x)(Gx \supset Hx)$
$(x)(Hx \supset Mx)$ $\therefore (x)(Gx \supset Mx)$

Notice that in the official idiom, each of these sentences is about *any individual whatsoever*. The first premise says that for any individual (in the domain), if he is Greek, then he is human. The conclusion says that for any individual (in the domain), it is the case that if he is a Greek, then he is mortal. We must therefore introduce a way of reasoning *about any individual whatsoever*. This is done by starting a subderivation preceded by the variable which is used to refer to that (arbitrarily chosen) individual. Thus the derivation will have to look like this:

$$(1) \quad (x)(Gx \supset Hx)$$
$$(2) \quad (x)(Hx \supset Mx)$$
$$(3) \quad \quad y$$

.

.

.

$$(n) \quad (x)(Gx \supset Mx)$$

Every line inside the subderivation should be true of any individual y whatsoever. We call this a *subderivation general in y*. Only subderivations, and not a derivation as a whole, can have this character.

What can be written inside a subderivation? First, any sentence which is given previously, and in which y *does not occur free*. This yields a rule of reiteration:

> R_y: any line in a derivation may be reiterated (as by rule R) into a subderivation general in y provided y does not occur free in that line

and a maxim:

> When starting a general subderivation, choose a variable which has not occurred previously in the derivation.

This maxim ensures that the restriction on R_y can not be violated. So, for example, we can reiterate the premises:*

$$(1) \quad (x)(Gx \supset Hx)$$
$$(2) \quad (x)(Hx \supset Mx)$$
$$(3) \quad \quad y \mid (x)(Gx \supset Hx) \qquad (1) \ R_y$$
$$(4) \quad \quad \quad (x)(Hx \supset Mx) \qquad (2) \ R_y$$

.

.

.

$$(n) \quad (x)(Gx \supset Mx)$$

Now, whichever individual is denoted by y, we certainly know that what is true of everything, is true of it. So if $(x)(Fx)$ is true, then so is Fy. This means that, for example, the following steps are admissible in a derivation:

---

*We drop the dash before the justifying rule in each line and also denote cases of KE_1 and KE_2 as KE. The same convention is applied to cases of AI.

(m)		y	$(x)Fx$	(m)		y		$(x)Fx$
$(m + k)$			Fy	$(m + k)$				Fy

Here Fx may be any sentence. It can be $(Gx \supset Hx)$ or $(Gx \,\&\, (y)Hy)$ or $(Ex)Gx$ or even $(Ey)Gy$. To get Fy from Fx, you must replace *all* of the free occurrences of x in Fx by occurrences of y. (If there are no free occurrences of x in Fx—as when Fx is $(Ey)Gy$—then Fy is just the same as Fx.)

We give the rule a precise but shorthand notation, covering both the above cases (the number of lines to the left is immaterial, provided at least one is flanked by the variable):

UQE y | ... | $(x)A$
.
.
.
$S^y_x(A)$ provided y is free for x in A

Now we can apply UQE to lines (3) and (4) in our sample derivation

(1)	$(x)(Gx \supset Hx)$		
(2)	$(x)(Hx \supset Mx)$		
(3)	y	$(x)(Gx \supset Hx)$	(1) Ry
(4)		$(x)(Hx \supset Mx)$	(2) Ry
(5)		$Gy \supset Hy$	(3) UQE
(6)		$Hy \supset My$	(4) UQE

and some familiar rules from Chapter 2 can be applied to lines (5) and (6):

(5)		$Gy \supset Hy$	
(6)		$Hy \supset My$	
(7)		Gy	
(8)		$Gy \supset Hy$	(5) R
(9)		Hy	(6) R
10)		$Hy \supset My$	(7) (8) CE
(11)		My	(9) (10) CE
(12)		$Gy \supset My$	(7–11) CI
	$(x)(Gx \supset Mx)$		

Looking at line (12) we see that we deduced that for an *arbitrary* individual y, it is the case that if y is a Greek, then y is mortal. All we have assumed about y is what is given by the premises as true about *any* individual. Hence our conclusion is true about *any* individual y. And that is expressed equally by "For every individual, say x, if Gx then Mx". That is, the step from (12) to the next line is valid. We embody this principle in the following rule:

UQI $\quad\Big|\quad y\ \Big|\ .$

$\qquad\qquad\qquad\quad .$

$\qquad\qquad\qquad\quad .$

$\qquad\qquad\quad\Big|\ A$

$\quad\Big|\ (x)S_y^x(A)$ $\qquad$ provided x is not free in A
$\qquad\qquad\qquad\qquad\qquad$ or x and y are the same
$\qquad\qquad\qquad\qquad\qquad$ variable; and provided x is
$\qquad\qquad\qquad\qquad\qquad$ free for y in A

If y does not occur free in A, then x is not free in $S_y^x(A)$, and we call (x) a vacuous quantifier in $(x)S_y^x(A)$.

Both our rules have sundry restrictions, and we shall now examine their necessity. Suppose we allowed the inference of $S_x^y(A)$ from $(x)A$ even if y were not free for x in A. Then we could infer $Py \supset (y)Ryy$ from $(x)(Px \supset (y)Ryx)$: for example, "Every number identical with 0 is less than every other number, therefore, if y is identical with 0, then every number is less than itself". This is surely not a valid inference.

Secondly, suppose we allowed x to be free in A in rule UQI when x is not the same variable as y. Then we could have the "derivation"

$$\Big|\ \begin{array}{l} (y)Ryx \\ \quad y\ \Big|\ \begin{array}{l}(y)Ryx \\ Ryx\end{array} \\ (x)Ryx \end{array}$$

which again allows a patently invalid inference; for example, everyone hates y; so, everyone hates himself. On the other hand, suppose we did not insist that x be free for y in A, in the rule UQI. Then we could have the "derivation"

$$\Big|\ \begin{array}{l} (z)(Ex)Rxz \\ \quad y\ \Big|\ \begin{array}{l}(z)(Ex)Rxz \qquad\quad R_y \\ (Ex)Rxy \qquad\qquad \text{UQE, } y \text{ free for } z\end{array} \\ (x)(Ex)Rxx \end{array}$$

In the conclusion, the quantifier (x) is *vacuous*; the conclusion says "Everything is such that there is something which bears R to itself".

But the premise only said "Everything is such that something bears R to it". This inference is invalid, as can be seen when we let Rxz mean that x is different from z; in that case Rxx is not true for any x.

But x does not have to be free for y in A to allow the inference of $S_x^y(A)$ from $(x)A$ by UQE. For example, the inference of $Fy \supset (x)Rxy$ from $(x)(Fx \supset (x)Rxy)$ is perfectly alright. On the other hand, we do not have to stipulate that y should be free for x in A in the rule UQI. For if x is not free in A, then y is automatically free for x in A; furthermore, y is always free for y in A. Therefore such an added stipulation in the case of UQI would be superfluous.

Finally, our logic is still essentially a logic of statements, not of quasi-statements; a *categorical derivation* is henceforth a derivation without premises, of which the last line is a statement. For example, it is wrong to say, without qualification, that the rule UQE allows us to infer Fy from $(x)Fx$. Within a derivation, $(x)Fx$ may occur flanked by a vertical line which is annotated with the variable y. In that case, Fy may be written down below that occurrence of $(x)Fx$, at a place still flanked by that same vertical line. Thus the following patterns will *not* be found:

$$(1) \quad \lfloor (x)Fx \qquad\qquad\qquad (1) \mid (x)Fx$$
$$(2) \quad \lceil Fy \qquad (1), \text{UQE} \qquad (2) \mid z \mid (x)Fx \qquad (1), R_z$$
$$\qquad\qquad\qquad\qquad\qquad\qquad (3) \mid \ \mid Fy \qquad (2), \text{UQE}$$

Similarly, when UQI is applied, then the last variable used to annotate a vertical line cannot immediately thereafter have any free occurrences. Thus the following patterns will also not be found in correctly constructed derivations:

$$(m) \quad \left|\begin{array}{c} y \\ \end{array}\right| z \qquad\qquad\qquad (m) \quad \left|\begin{array}{c} z \\ \end{array}\right|$$
$$(n) \qquad \mid \ \ Fyz \qquad\qquad\qquad (n) \qquad y\big| Fyz$$
$$(n+1) \mid (x)Fxz \quad (m)\text{–}(n), \text{UQI} \quad (n+1)\mid \ \mid (x)Fyx \quad (m)\text{–}(n)\ \text{UQI}$$

These observations are very important, because patterns such as these will allow incorrect derivations. For example, the following incorrect derivations *cannot* be turned into a correct derivation just by inserting variables annotating vertical lines:

$$(1) \mid \quad \lfloor (x)(Fx \ \& \ \neg Fx)$$
$$(2) \mid \quad \lceil Fy \ \& \ \neg Fy \qquad\qquad (1), \text{UQE}$$
$$(3) \mid \quad \mid Fy \qquad\qquad\qquad\quad (2), \text{KE}$$
$$(4) \mid \quad \mid \neg Fy \qquad\qquad\qquad (2), \text{KE}$$
$$(5) \mid \neg (x)(Fx \ \& \ \neg Fx) \qquad (1\text{–}4), \text{NI}$$

It may be thought that the last line ought to be categorically derivable (we shall discuss this below, in connection with a rule called VQE); the present point is, however, that it is not correctly derivable by the use of the rules we have so far. It must be clearly kept in mind that unlike UQI, the rules CI, NE, NI are used to terminate vertical lines *not* flanked by variables. Thus the following is incorrect also:

$$
\begin{array}{lll}
(1) & y \mid \underline{(x)(Fx \,\&\, \neg\, Fx)} & \\
(2) & \qquad\quad Fy \,\&\, \neg\, Fy & (1), \text{UQE} \\
(3) & \qquad\quad Fy & (2), \text{KE} \\
(4) & \qquad\quad \neg\, Fy & (3), \text{KE} \\
(5) & \neg\,(x)(Fx \,\&\, \neg\, Fx) & (1)\text{–}(4)\ \text{NI}
\end{array}
$$

All this may seem complicated, but it is not. Simply remember two things: annotate a new vertical line with a variable when (and only when) beginning a general subderivation, *and* terminate such a line by UQI in such a way that (a) the last such line introduced is the one being terminated, and (b) the variable that annotates it has no free occurrences immediately thereafter. (To run a quick check, look to see that each free occurrence of a variable is flanked by a vertical line annotated with that variable.)

To introduce the intelim rules for the existential quantifier we proceed somewhat differently. The sentence

There is a thing with magenta stripes

could easily be shown to be true if we could produce such an odd-looking object. But how to show it false? To show it false you would have to show for *every*thing that it does *not* have magenta stripes. So

It is not the case that there is a thing with magenta stripes

is equivalent to

For everything x, it is not the case that x has magenta stripes.

Thus $\neg(Ex)Fx$ and $(x)(\neg Fx)$ are equivalent. That means also that $\neg\,\neg(Ex)Fx$ is equivalent to $\neg(x)(\neg Fx)$. But of course we know from propositional logic that two iterated negation signs cancel each other. Therefore $(Ex)Fx$ is equivalent to $\neg(x)(\neg Fx)$. This yields the correct intelim rules at once:

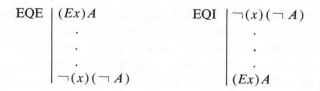

Again, A may be a sentence in which x does not occur free, in which case the exhibited quantifiers are vacuous.

The application of these rules allows us a number of shortcuts, of which we will note the first two at once. The following can be categorically derived:

$$1.\ \ \neg(Ex)Fx \equiv (x)\neg Fx$$
$$2.\ \ \neg(x)Fx \equiv (Ex)\neg Fx$$

We shall leave the derivations as exercises (with this hint: after assuming $\neg(Ex)Fx$, also assume as a subhypothesis $\neg(x)\ \neg Fx$, and then arrive at $(x)\neg Fx$ by NE). Henceforth these results may be appealed to in derivations.

As an example, consider the second argument given at the very beginning of this chapter:

Some men are Greeks;	$(Ex)(Mx\ \&\ Gx)$
No Greeks are barbarians;	$(x)(Gx \supset \neg Bx)$
Hence: Some men are not barbarians.	$(Ex)(Mx\ \&\ \neg Bx)$

The derivation should have the forms

$$
\begin{array}{ll}
(1) & \ \ (Ex)(Mx\ \&\ Gx) \\
(2) & \ \ \ \ (x)(Gx \supset \neg Bx) \\
(3) & \ \ \ \ \ \ \ \ (x)\neg(Mx\ \&\ \neg Bx) \\
(n\text{--}2) & \\
(n\text{--}1) & \ \ \neg(x)\neg(Mx\ \&\ \neg Bx) \qquad (3)\text{--}(n\text{--}2),\ \text{NI} \\
(n) & \ \ (Ex)(Mx\ \&\ \neg Bx) \qquad\quad (n\text{--}1),\ \text{EQI}
\end{array}
$$

As an exercise, the reader may fill in the lines between (3) and $(n\text{--}2)$. At some point, the first premise must be reiterated, and then be used to yield $\neg(x)\neg(Mx\ \&\ Gx)$ by EQE. As a good rule of thumb, we advise that all this be done *first*. That is, if of two premises, one begins with an existential quantifier, then *that one* should be utilized first. (And not to be coy, we may as well note that rules EQE, EQI are clumsy to work with, and that in the next section more convenient rules will be provided for practical purposes.)

Sometimes we have several quantifiers in a formula; then we may need general subderivations within general subderivations. For example:

(1)	$(x)(Fx \supset (y)(Gy))$	
(2)	$z \quad (x)(Fx \supset (y)(Gy))$	(1) R$_z$
(3)	$Fz \supset (y)(Gy)$	(2) UQE
(4)	$w \quad \quad Fz$	
(5)	$Fz \supset (y)(Gy)$	(3) R$_w$
(6)	$(y)(Gy)$	(4) (5) CE
(7)	Gw	(6) UQE
(8)	$Fz \supset Gw$	(4–7) CI
(9)	$(x)(Fz \supset Gx)$	(4–8) UQI
(10)	$(y)(x)(Fy \supset Gx)$	(2–9) UQI

In that case there are several conventions which will make the derivation more perspicuous. The first is to indicate beside the justification UQE, EQE, and so on, the variables being used. For example, in the above derivation we could write

(3)	$Fz \supset (y)(Gy)$	(2) UQE: x to z
(10)	$(y)(x)(Fy \supset Gx)$	(2–9) UQI: z to y

This is of course only a heuristic device to help keep track of what was done in the derivation. The second convention is to make the original subderivation general in both z and w, as follows:

(2)	$z, w \quad (x)(Fx \supset (y)(Gy))$	
(3)	$Fz \supset (y)(Gy)$	
(4)	Fz	
(5)	$Fz \supset (y)(Gy)$	
(6)	$(y)(Gy)$	
(7)	Gw	
(8)	$Fz \supset Gw$	
(9)	$(y)(x)(Fy \supset Gx)$	(2–8) UQI: w to x, z to y

In the Traditional Square of Opposition discussed in Section 1, we saw that "Some **A** are **B**" was said to be implied by "All **A** are **B**". We noted that this holds only when we have the extra premise "There is some **A**". Extrapolating this to the case in which everything is **A**, we must conclude that "Something is **B**" follows from "Everything is **B**" only with the additional premise "There is something". In many logical systems, the assumption that there is something is made tacitly, and the rules allow the inference of $(Ex)A$ from $(x)A$ directly. The practical reason for this is that in most interesting cases the domain of discourse is not empty.

We want to be very explicit on such questions as whether the domain is or is not empty. Our rules so far do not allow the deduction of $(Ex)B$ from $(x)B$:

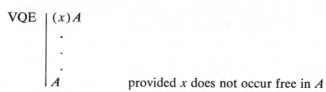

(1)	$(x)B$			
(2)		x	$(x)B$	(1) R_x
(3)			B	(2) UQE
(4)				$(x)\neg B$	(4) UQE
(5)				$\neg B$	
(6)				B	(3) R
(7)			$\neg(x)\neg B$	(4–6) NI
(8)			$(Ex)B$	(7) EQI
(9)	$(x)(Ex)B$			(2–8) UQI

The universal quantifier (x) in line (9) is vacuous; but we have no rule that eliminates vacuous quantifiers. And in general, we should not: in the empty domain, $(Ex)\neg A$ is false, and so $(x)A$ is true; but if A is $(Ey)B$, then A is not true in the empty domain.

However, for those cases in which the user is willing to assume that the domain is non-empty, we shall now provide a special rule:

VQE $\Big|\ (x)A$

$\cdot$
$\cdot$
$\cdot$

A provided x does not occur free in A

With this rule, the derivation of $(Ex)B$ on the hypothesis $(x)B$ can now be completed. With this rule it is also possible to derive $\neg(x)(Fx \,\&\, \neg Fx)$, which we noted as not derivable by the use of the rules we had given previously. We leave this as an exercise.

SECTION 6
ARGUMENTS INVOLVING QUANTIFIERS

There has so far been an asymmetry in our treatment of quantifiers, in that the intelim rules for the existential quantifier use universal quantifiers. While this has various didactic advantages, in our opinion, it does tend to make derivations involving existential quantifiers rather long. Shortcuts are available, and these we shall now provide.

Intuitively, existential statements are proved by giving examples: "There are mice in your kitchen. Why do you say that? I saw one this morning". So if somewhere in a derivation we have the line *Fx*, then we have an example of something to which *F* truly applies; hence it is reasonable to write down $(Ey)Fy$. This provides the motivation for a special rule for introducing quantifiers.

Similarly, in intuitive or informal arguments, existential quantifiers are eliminated by introducing examples: "Suppose there is a mouse in my kitchen. Let's call it Perry. Then if I put down some cheese, Perry will eat it. So, if there is a mouse in my kitchen, and I put down some cheese, that cheese will be eaten". We can do something like this in a symbolic derivation, using a new variable y as name for the (hypothetical) example. The phrase "Let's call it Perry" corresponds then to the introduction of a new vertical line, flanked by *y*, which has as its first entry to its right, the *hypothesis* that *y* is a mouse in my kitchen.

We shall now formulate precisely the special rules for the existential quantifier. (In the first, as for UQE, the number of lines to the left is immaterial, provided at least one is flanked by the variable.)

$$\text{SEQI} \quad y \left| \quad \dots \quad \right| \; S_v^y(A)$$

$$\left| \quad \right| \; (Ex)A \qquad \text{provided } y \text{ is free for } x \text{ in } A$$

The admissibility of SEQI is proved by the following derivation of $(Ex)A$ from $S_x^y(A)$ under the stated conditions.

(1)	y	$S_x^y(A)$	
(2)		$(x) \; \neg A$	
(3)		$S_x^y(\neg A)$	(2) UQE (y free for x in A)
(4)		$\neg S_x^y(A)$	(3) substitution equations
(5)		$S_x^y(A)$	(1) R
(6)		$\neg(x) \; \neg A$	(2–5) NI
(7)		$(Ex)A$	(6) EQI

To apply this rule, it is necessary to recognize when a given formula B is in fact the same as $S_x^y(A)$. In practice, the application is very easy; the rule could be written equivalently as

$$y \left| \quad \dots \quad \right| \; B$$
$$\left| \quad \right| \; (Ex)B'$$

where *B'* is formed by replacing *some* or *no* free occurrence of *y* in *B* with occurrences of *x*

So the following are correct examples:

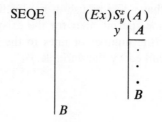

$$
\begin{array}{c|l}
y & Ryy \\
& (Ex)Rxx
\end{array}
\qquad
\begin{array}{c|l}
y & Ryy \\
& (Ex)Rxy
\end{array}
\qquad
\begin{array}{c|l}
y & Ryy \\
& (Ex)Ryy
\end{array}
$$

Because note:

$$
\begin{aligned}
Ryy &= S_x^y(Rxx) \\
Ryy &= S_x^y(Rxy) \\
Ryy &= S_x^y(Ryy)
\end{aligned}
$$

are all true!

The second special rule has more restrictions:

$$
\text{SEQE} \quad
\begin{array}{|l}
(Ex)S_y^x(A) \\
\quad
\begin{array}{c|l}
y & A \\
& \;\cdot \\
& \;\cdot \\
& \;\cdot \\
& B
\end{array} \\
B
\end{array}
$$

provided y is not free in B; and either x is not free in A or x is y; and x is free for y in A

Its admissibility is proved as follows:

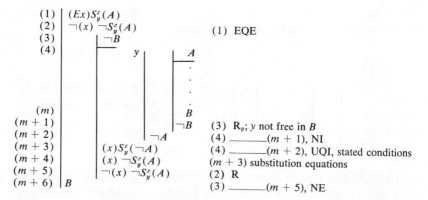

(1) | $(Ex)S_y^x(A)$
(2) | $\neg(x)\,\neg S_y^x(A)$ (1) EQE
(3) | $\neg B$
(4) | y | A

(m) B
$(m+1)$ $\neg B$ (3) R_y; y not free in B
$(m+2)$ $\neg A$ (4) _____(m + 1), NI
$(m+3)$ $(x)S_y^x(\neg A)$ (4) _____(m + 2), UQI, stated conditions
$(m+4)$ $(x)\,\neg S_y^x(A)$ (m + 3) substitution equations
$(m+5)$ $\neg(x)\,\neg S_y^x(A)$ (2) R
$(m+6)$ | B (3) _____(m + 5), NE

With these special rules, derivations can be much simplified. Recall the argument about Greeks and barbarians we examined after the introduction of the rules EQE and EQI. The derivation we can now give is very simple:

$$
\begin{array}{lll}
(1) & (Ex)(Mx \& Gx) & \\
(2) & (x)(Gx \& \neg Bx) & \\
(3) & y \;\lvert\; My \& Gy & \\
(4) & \quad (x)(Gx \& \neg Bx) & (2)\ \mathrm{R}_y \\
(5) & \quad Gy \& \neg By & (4)\ \mathrm{UQE} \\
(6) & \quad My & (3)\ \mathrm{KE} \\
(7) & \quad \neg By & (5)\ \mathrm{KE} \\
(8) & \quad My \& \neg By & (6)\text{--}(7)\ \mathrm{KI} \\
(9) & \quad (Ex)(Mx \& \neg Bx) & (8)\ \mathrm{SEQI} \\
(10) & (Ex)(Mx \& \neg Bx) & (1),\ (3)\text{--}(9)\ \mathrm{SEQE}
\end{array}
$$

Note that we are still following the rule of thumb to utilize the existentially quantified premise *first*; that is still a good maxim.

The introduction of the admissible rules SEQE and SEQI provides shortcuts and simplifies derivations; that is its *only* motivation. With exactly that same motive we shall now introduce some other new notions, which may look a bit complicated at first, but which make everything much easier in practice. To begin we introduce another admissible rule, without proving its admissibility. In rule UQI the choice of the variable x is arbitrary within very wide limits. Each of the following moves is justified by UQI:

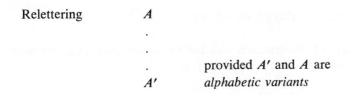

and so on. The reason is of course that if Fy and Fx are substitutionally similar sentences ($S_x^y(Fx) = Fy$ and $S_x^y(Fy) = Fx$), then $(y)Fy$ and $(x)Fx$ say exactly the same thing.

This leads us to introduce the rule of *relettering bound variables*:

Relettering A

        .

        .

        .   provided A' and A are

       A' alphabetic variants

where two sentences are said to be alphabetic variants (of *each other*) just in case *each* can be gotten from the other by the replacement of all bound occurrences of one variable by occurrences of another variable. As we mentioned before, we shall not actually prove the admissibility of this rule (which can be proved with the methods of Part Four).

For example, we can now derive $(Ex)(z)Rzx$ very quickly from $(Ey)(x)Rxy$:

$$
\begin{array}{lll}
(1) & (Ey)(x)(Rxy & \\
(2) & (Ey)(z)Rzy & (1) \ \text{Relettering } x \to z \\
(3) & (Ex)(z)Rzx & (2) \ \text{Relettering } y \to x \\
\end{array}
$$

(As an exercise, derive (3) from (1) without the use of this new rule.) The order of the relettering operations was important though; the following is *fallacious*:

$$
\begin{array}{lll}
(1) & (Ey)(x)Rxy & \\
(2) & (Ex)(x)Rxx & (1) \ \text{Relettering } y \to x \ (\text{fallacious}) \\
(3) & (Ez)(z)Rzz & (2) \ \text{Relettering } x \to z \\
\end{array}
$$

The move from (1) to (2) is fallacious because (1) cannot be gotten from (2) by the same process. Then how can we derive $(x)(y)Rxy$ from $(y)(x)Rxy$? The trick is to use an *extra* variable:

$$
\begin{array}{lll}
(1) & (x)(y)Rxy & \\
(2) & (x)(z)Rxz & (1) \ \text{Relettering } y \to z \\
(3) & (y)(z)Ryz & (2) \ \text{Relettering } x \to y \\
(4) & (y)(x)Ryx & (3) \ \text{Relettering } z \to x \\
\end{array}
$$

In this way, we achieve the effect of a "simultaneous relettering" of several variables.

The importance of relettering is that it allows us to circumvent many of the restrictions that make the quantifier intelim rules somewhat cumbersome. Consider the sentence

1. $(y)(Rxy) \ \& \ (x)(Rxy)$

The form of this sentence may not be immediately clear; by relettering twice, we find that it is equivalent to

2. $(z)(Rxz) \ \& \ (z)(Rzy)$

That is, it asserts that x bears R to everything and everything bears R to y. Now in 1, y is not free for x, and x is not free for y. But in 2,

x and y are free for each other. The result is that we can not use SEQI (x to y or y to x) on 1. But from 2 we can infer, in several steps,

$$3. \ (Ex)(Ey)\big((z)(Rxy) \ \& \ (z)(Rzy)\big)$$

Thus in those cases in which we cannot directly apply such rules as SEQI, we can still apply them after relettering.

For many purposes it is convenient to combine relettering and substitution operations. For this purpose we introduce the special notation

$$(y/x)A \text{ is } S_x^y(A')$$

where A' is formed by relettering (y to z) any part of A of the form $(y)B$ in which there are free occurrences of x, and z is an entirely new variable not occurring in A.

By this definition $(y/x)A$ is just $S_x^y(A)$ when y is free for x in A; otherwise the relettering step is necessary.

The rules UQE, UQI, SEQI, and SEQE lead then to the following much simpler rules, using this special notation:

UQE
$$y \mid (x)A$$
$$\mid \quad \cdot$$
$$\mid \quad \cdot$$
$$\mid \quad \cdot$$
$$\mid (y/x)A$$

UQI
$$y \mid \cdot$$
$$\mid \quad \cdot$$
$$\mid \quad \cdot$$
$$\mid A$$
$$(x)(x/y)A$$

provided either x is not free in A or x is y

SEQI
$$y \mid (y/x)A$$
$$\mid \quad \cdot$$
$$\mid \quad \cdot$$
$$\mid \quad \cdot$$
$$\mid (Ex)A$$

SEQE
$$(Ex)(x/y)A$$
$$y \mid A$$
$$\mid \cdot$$
$$\mid \cdot$$
$$\mid \cdot$$
$$\mid B$$
$$B$$

provided y is not free in B, and x is not free in A or x is y

By adding an automatic application of the relettering rule, we have now a fairly direct way of proceeding when the restrictions on the rules are effective. This tends to shorten the derivations. For example, see how it is possible to shorten rather longer arguments such as the following:

(1)   y | $(x)Rxy$
(2) z | $(x)Rxy$ (1) R_z
(3) | Rzy (2) UQE (x to z)
(4) $(z)Rzy$ (2–3) UQI (z to z)
(5) $(Ex)(z)Rzx$ (4) SEQI (y to x)

Even though we have not proved the admissibility of relettering, we shall henceforth allow its use in derivations. We shall also find it convenient later on to use the (y/x) substitution operation (as opposed to the S_x^y operation) in some rules introduced later in this chapter and the next.

SECTION 7
LOGICAL TRUTHS INVOLVING QUANTIFIERS

The essential job of general subderivations is to allow us to perform logical operations inside the scope of a quantifier. Thus if we have a sentence $(Ex)A$, and we can deduce B from A (using no other premises), then we may deduce $(Ex)B$ from $(Ex)A$. And, similarly, given the deducibility of B from A, we may deduce $(x)B$ from $(x)A$. But it is very important to note that the deduction of B from A, if it is to play this role, must take into consideration that the variable x in A refers to an "arbitrary" individual; that is, an individual about which we are allowed to use *only* the following information: (a) that A is true of it, and (b) that whatever is true of everything, is true of it. To guarantee that only (a) and (b) are used as evidence, we placed a restriction on reiteration into general subderivations.

The above readily suggests that the following are logical truths:

1. $(x)(Fx \supset Gx) \supset \cdot (x)(Fx) \supset (x)(Gx)$
2. $(x)(Fx \supset Gx) \supset \cdot (Ex)(Fx) \supset (Ex)(Gx)$

as, indeed, they are. (Recall the use of dots for punctuation explained in Section 1 of Chapter 2.)

Besides these the rules UQE and UQI together yield the logical truth

3. $(y)((x)(Fx) \supset Fy)$

Derivation:

$$
\begin{array}{llll}
(1) & y & \quad (x)(Fx) & \\
(2) & & \quad Fy & (1)\ \text{UQE} \\
(3) & & (x)(Fx) \supset Fy & (1)\ (2)\ \text{CI} \\
(4) & (y)((x)(Fx) \supset Fy) & & (1\text{--}3)\ \text{UQI}
\end{array}
$$

Principles (1) and (2) are called *distribution laws*; other useful distribution laws are

4. $((x)(Fx)\ \&\ (x)(Gx)) \equiv (x)(Fx\ \&\ Gx)$
5. $(Ex)(Fx) \lor (Ex)(Gx) \cdot \equiv (Ex)(Fx \lor Gx)$
6. $(x)(Fx) \lor (x)(Gx) \cdot \supset (x)(Fx \lor Gx)$—not the converse
7. $(Ex)(Fx\ \&\ Gx) \supset \cdot (Ex)(Fx)\ \&\ (Ex)(Gx)$—not the converse

Finally, a law relating the two quantifiers is

8. $(x)(Fx \supset A) \equiv ((Ex)(Fx) \supset A)$ where x is not free in A

These are important logical principles, and many derivations can be shortened by appealing to them. As exercises, the reader is asked to derive them categorically, and to give English examples of sentences of that form. An example of the converse of 6 would be

If everything is either red or not red, then either everything is red or everything is not red

which shows clearly that this converse is *not* logically true. Similarly, an example of the converse of 7 would be

If something is red all over and something is green all over, then there is something which is both red and green all over

and while the consequent is not logically contradictory, it is certainly false.

The use of the horseshoe in symbolizing "Every X is a Y" has certain important consequences. We know of course that there are no centaurs. Hence

If x is a centaur, then x is violent

is *true* in virtue of the falsity of its antecedent. And this is so for any *x* (that is, no matter what *x* is used to refer to).
Hence

$$(x)(x \text{ is a centaur} \supset x \text{ is violent})$$

must also be true. We deduced this on the assumption that there are no centaurs. Hence the following must be a logical truth:

9. $\neg(Ex)(Fx) \supset (x)(Fx \supset Gx)$

DERIVATION:

(1)	$\neg(Ex)Fx$	
(2)	$\neg(x)(\neg Fx)$	
(3)	$(Ex)Fx$	(2) EQI
(4)	$\neg(Ex)Fx$	(1) R
(5)	$(x)(\neg Fx)$	(2–4) NE
(6)	$y \quad (x)(\neg Fx)$	(5) R
(7)	$\neg Fy$	(6) UQE
(8)	$Fy \supset Gy$	[from (7) by several steps]
(9)	$(x)(Fx \supset Gx)$	(6–8) UQI
(10)	$\neg(Ex)(Fx) \supset (x)(Fx \supset Gx)$	(1–9) CI

Thus sentences like

All giants are tall
All giants are short
All giants are witches
All giants are trees

are all considered true on the basis of the assumption that there really are no giants.

The rule VQE is especially suited to proving conclusions which begin with an existential quantifier, from premises none of which begins with an existential quantifier. Thus consider

10. There is something which is either red or not red.

This is true because there really is something in the world; and of course whatever there is must be either red or not red. Thus VQE which allows us to prove 10 expresses the fact (assumption, postulate) that there really is something or other. The justification of 10 is a corollary of the following more general result (provable given VQE):

11. $(x)(Fx) \supset (Ex)(Fx)$

DERIVATION:

(1)	$(x)(Fx)$	
(2)	y $(x)Fx$	(1) R_y
(3)	Fy	(2) UQE
(4)	$(Ex)(Fx)$	(3) SEQI
(5)	$(x)((Ex)(Fx))$	(2–4) UQI
(6)	$(Ex)(Fx)$	(5) VQE
(7)	$(x)(Fx) \supset (Ex)(Fx)$	(1–6) CI

A rather curious consequence of VQE is

12. $(Ex)(Fx \supset (y)(Fy))$

sometimes known as "Henkin's formula". It says, for example, that there is someone such that, if he starves, then everyone starves. (We have proposed a research project to find that person, but so far we have not found financial backing.) The derivation of 12 shows that this logical truth is in part a consequence of the logical features of the horseshoe, and in part of VQE. The following is a sketch to be completed as an exercise:

(1)	$(y)(Fy)$	
(2)	x $(y)(Fy)$	(1) R_x
(3)	$Fx \supset (y)(Fy)$	[from (2)]
(4)	$(Ex)(Fx \supset (y)(Fy))$	(3) SEQI
(5)	$(x)((Ex)(Fx \supset (y)(Fy)))$	(2–4) UQI
(6)	$(Ex)(Fx \supset (y)(Fy))$	(5) VQE
(7)	$\neg(y)(Fy)$	
(8)	$(Ey)(\neg Fy)$	[from (7)]
(9)	x $\neg Fx$	
(10)	$Fx \supset (y)(Fy)$	[from (9)]
(11)	$(Ex)(Fx \supset (y)(Fy))$	(10) SEQI
(12)	$(Ex)(Fx \supset (y)(Fy))$	(9–11) SEQE
(13)	$(Ex)(Fx \supset (y)(Fy))$	[from (1–6), (7–12)]

SECTION 8
RELATIONS, IDENTITY, AND NUMERICAL STATEMENTS

The most familiar relations are those which are expressed by two-place predicates; these are called *binary* or *dyadic* relations. These relations can be classified through reference to some of their properties. Some common properties of dyadic relations are:

(a) R is *reflexive* if and only if $(x)(Rxx)$
(b) R is *symmetric* if and only if $(x)(y)(Rxy \supset Ryx)$
(c) R is *transitive* if and only if $(x)(y)(z)(Rxy \& Ryz \supset Rxz)$

We shall use the same adjectives to qualify relations and corresponding predicates: for example, the fatherhood relation and the predicate "is the father of" are both said not to have any of the above properties. The following table classifies some familiar relations (using $+$ for *yes* and $-$ for *no*):

	Reflexive	Symmetric	Transitive
is father of	$-$	$-$	$-$
is before	$-$	$-$	$+$
is close to	$+$	$+$	$-$
is as old as	$+$	$+$	$+$

Note that Rxy may also stand for such complex relational sentences as "x is a rich brother of y" (that is, "x is rich & x is a brother of y"), and "x is rich and y is old"—indeed, for any sentence in which zero or more occurrences of x and y are free.

An important derivation in the theory of relations is that if R is symmetric and transitive, and x bears R to anything, then x bears R to itself:

(1)		$(x)(y)(Rxy \supset Ryx)$	
(2)		$(x)(y)(z)(Rxy \& Ryz \cdot \supset Rxz)$	
(3)	v, w	$(x)(y)(Rxy \supset Ryx)$	(1) $R_{v,w}$
(4)		$(y)(Rvy \supset Ryv)$	(3) UQE (x to v)
(5)		$Rvx \supset Rwv$	(4) UQE (y to w)
(6)		$(x)(y)(z)(Rxy \& Ryz \cdot \supset Rxz)$	(2) $R_{v,w}$
(7)		$(y)(z)(Rvy \& Ryz \cdot \supset Rvz)$	(6) UQE (x to v)
(8)		$(z)(Rvw \& Rwz \cdot \supset Rvz)$	(7) UQE (y to w)
(9)		$Rvw \& Rwv \cdot \supset Rvv$	(8) UQE (z to v)
(10)		$Rvw \supset Rvv$	[from (5), (9)]
(11)		$(x)(y)(Rxy \supset Rxx)$	(3-10) UQE (v to x)
			(w to y)

We leave the further derivation of $(x)[(Ey)Rxy \cdot \supset Rxx]$ from (11) as an exercise.

Of more general interest are the laws concerning the *commutation* of quantifiers:

1. $(x)(y)(Rxy) \equiv (y)(x)(Rxy)$
2. $(Ex)(Ey)(Rxy) \equiv (Ey)(Ex)(Rxy)$
3. $(Ey)(x)(Rxy) \supset (x)(Ey)(Rxy)$—not the converse

That the converse of 3 cannot be valid follows from the consideration that even if everybody loves somebody (sometime), it does not follow that there is some person who is loved by everyone. Yet the appeal of the converse of 3 is sometimes hard to resist (especially in connection with the subject of infinity.)

In the table given above, we saw that *is as old as* is a relation which has all three properties: reflexivity, symmetry, and transitivity. Such a relation is called an *equivalence relation*. Other equivalence relations are: *has the same height as, occurs at the same time as* (simultaneously) *is equal to* (equality), *is a sibling of*.

The most important, and most restrictive, equivalence relation is *identity*: the relation which each individual bears to itself and to nothing else. We shall symbolize this by $=$, and *infix* rather than *prefix* the symbol to the variables. So "$x = y$" expresses the fact that "x" and "y" are used to refer to one and the same individual.

The rules for identity are

II $x \mid \ldots \mid x = x$ IE $y \mid \ldots \mid x = y$
$ A$
$ (y/x)A$

II means that any line of the form $x = x$ may be introduced freely anywhere in a subderivation general in x.

About IE we may note that the second and third line could be interchanged: the rule might as well have been given as

$y \mid \ldots \mid x = y$
$ \cdot$
$ \cdot$
$ \cdot$
$ (y/x)A$
$ \cdot$
$ \cdot$
$ \cdot$
$ A$

This means that from $x = y$ and Ryy, in a subderivation general in y, you can move to Rxx or Rxy or Ryx or Ryy. To show that this is really so is quite easy:

(i)	y	$\ldots$	$x = y$	
$(i + 1)$			$(y/x)A$	
$(1 + 2)$			$\neg A$	
$(1 + 3)$			$x = y$	(i) R
$(1 + 4)$			$(x/x)\neg A$	$(i + 2)$ $(i + 3)$ IE
$(1 + 5)$			$\neg(y/x)A$	same as $(i + 4)$
$(1 + 6)$			$(y/x)A$	$(i + 1)$ R
$(1 + 7)$			A	$(i + 2)$–$(i + 6)$ NE

Some logical truths concerning identity are

4. $(x)(y)(x = y \supset \cdot Fx \supset Fy)$
5. $(x)(y)(x = y \supset \cdot Fy \supset Fx)$
6. $(x)(y)(x = y \supset \cdot Rxy \supset Ryy)$
7. $(x)(y)(x = y \supset \cdot Rxx \supset Rxy)$

as well as those expressing reflexivity, symmetry, and transitivity.

The identity relation can be used to symbolize simple numerical statements.

A. *There are at least n.*

The sentence

4. There is at least one cow

is symbolized by

5. $(Ex)(Cx)$

as we know. The sentence

6. There are at least two cows

can be rephrased as

7. There is an x and a y, such that x is a cow and y is a cow, and $x \neq y$.

That is,

      8. $(Ex)(Ey)(Cx \mathbin{\&} Cy \mathbin{\&} x \neq y)$.

In general, we symbolize

      9. There are at least n cows

as

      10. $(Ex_1)(Ex_2) \ldots (Ex_n)(Cx_1 \mathbin{\&} Cx_2 \mathbin{\&} \ldots \mathbin{\&} Cx_n$
         $\mathbin{\&} x_1 \neq x_2 \mathbin{\&} \ldots \mathbin{\&} x_1 \neq x_n \mathbin{\&} x_2 \neq x_3 \mathbin{\&} \ldots$
         $\mathbin{\&} x_2 \neq x_n \mathbin{\&} \ldots \mathbin{\&} x_{n-1} \neq x_n)$

where $x_1, \ldots, x_n$ are n distinct variables.
B. *There are at most n.*
   The sentence

      11. There is at most one cow

can be paraphrased as

      12. For any x and y, if x is a cow and y is a cow, then x and y
         are one and the same.

That is,

      13. $(x)(y)(Cx \mathbin{\&} Cy \boldsymbol{\cdot} \supset x = y)$

In general we symbolize

      14. There are at most n cows

by

      15. $(x_1) \ldots (x_n)(x_{n+1})(Cx_1 \mathbin{\&} \ldots Cx_n \mathbin{\&} Cx_{n+1} \boldsymbol{\cdot} \supset \boldsymbol{\cdot}$
         $x_{n+1} = x_1 \vee \ldots \vee x_{n+1} = x_n)$

C. *There are exactly n.*
   The sentence

      16. There are exactly n cows

can be rephrased as

17. There are at least n cows and there are at most n cows

which is symbolized by the conjunction of 10 and 15. Fortunately, this can be simplified somewhat, to give the formulation

18. $(Ex_1) \ldots (Ex_n)[Cx_1 \& \ldots \& Cx_n \& (y)(Cy \supset \cdot$
$y = x_1 \lor \ldots \lor y = x_n)]$

The reader should write out both versions for the case of $n = 2$, and check their equivalence.

D. *All but n.*

The sentence

19. All but one cow is black

can be rephrased as

20. There is one cow which is not black, and every other cow is black

which can be symbolized by

21. $(Ex)(Cx \& \neg Bx \& (y)(Cy \& y \neq x \cdot \supset By)$

The generalization to "All but n cows are black" should be clear now, and is left as an exercise.

EXERCISES

1. Draw a Venn diagram in which all the following information is represented:
   (a) All men are animals.
   (b) All animals lust after blood.
   (c) Some who lust after blood are not men.
   By inspection, see whether the following information can also be read off the diagram:
   (d) Some animals are not men.
   (e) Some animals are men.
   (f) All men lust after blood.
   (g) Some men lust after blood.

2. Determine which pairs of the following statements are contradictions, contraries, or subcontraries:
   (a)–(g): as in exercise 1.
   (h) No men are animals.
   (i) Some men do not lust after blood.
   (j) Some animals do not lust after blood.

3. Symbolize (i.e., paraphrase in the official idiom) the following statements, going explicitly through steps A–F.
   (a) All men who smoke, smoke.
   (b) All men who smoke something, smoke tobacco.
   (c) Some men who smoke something, smoke everything.

4. Symbolize the following:
   (a) No one who likes wine, likes water.
   (b) No one who turns (some) water into (some) wine, likes water.
   (c) Anyone who tempts someone, tempts the fates.
   (d) The wise man thinks of nothing so little as of death.
   (e) Whoever lives authentically, thinks of death.
   (f) Living is a thing you do now or never.
   (g) Happiness is to die for one's country.*

5. Determine the bound and free occurrences of variables, indicating the binding qualifiers, in the following statements:
   (a) $((x) Px \supset Qxy) \supset (Ey) (Rxy)$
   (b) $(x) (Pxy \supset (Ez) Qzy)$
   (c) $(Ey) (Pxy \supset (x)(y) (Pxy \supset Qx))$

6. Determine the sentences denoted by
   (a) $S_y^x (Px \supset Qxy)$
   (b) $S_y^x (Py \supset (Ex)Qxy)$
   (c) $S_y^x (Py \supset (Ey)Qxy)$
   (d) $S_y^x (Px \supset (Ex)Qxy)$
   (e) $S_y^x S_z^y (Py \supset Qxy)$
   (f) $S_y^x S_z^y (Py \supset Qxy)$
   (g) $S_y^x S_z^y ((Pz \supset Qxy) \supset (Ez)Qxz)$
   (h) Examples (i)–(v) in section 3, showing each step explicitly.

7. Show that the following statements are not logically true:
   (a) Nothing is both red and green all over.
   (b) Abstract entities have no color.
   (c) No two things can occupy the same place at the same time.
   (d) Space has three dimensions.
   (e) Capitalists are benevolent.

8. Choose a domain and assign an extension to each of the predicates P and Q (one-place) and R (two-place), and then determine the truth value of:
   (a) $(x) (Px \lor Qx)$

---

*Example taken from a nineteenth-century logic text used at a military college in Pennsylvania.

    (b) $(x)(Px \supset Qx)$
    (c) $(x)(y)(Px \& Qy \cdot \supset Rxy)$

9. Do exercise 8 again, in such a way that (c) has a different truth value than the one it had the first time.

10. Provide categorical derivations, without the use of VQE, for
    (a) $(x)(y)Rxy \supset (y)(x)Rxy$
    (b) $(x)(Qx \& (Px \supset Rx)) \supset (x)(Qx \lor Rx))$
    (c) $(Ey)(x)Rxy \supset (x)(Ey)Rxy$
    (d) $(Ex)(Px) \supset ((x)(Qx) \supset (Ex)(Qx))$

11. Complete the derivations sketched after the introduction of EQE and EQI (including the lines numbered 1 and 2 and that for the example about Greeks) in section 5.

12. Provide categorical derivations (using VQE) for
    (a) $\neg (x)(Px \& \neg Px)$
    (b) $(x) \neg (Px \supset Rx) \supset (Ex)(Px \& \neg Rx)$

13. Give derivations for
    (a) $(x)(Px \supset Qx), (Ex)(Rx \& Px)$; hence $(Ex)(Rx \& Qx)$
    (b) $(Ex)(Px \& Qx)$; hence $(Ex)Px$
    (c) $(x)(Px \supset (Ex)Qx)$; hence $(Ex)(Px \supset Qx)$
    (d) $(x)(y)(Rxy \supset \neg Ryx)$; hence $\neg (Ex)Rxx$

14. Give categorical derivations for
    (a) $[(Ex)Px \supset (Ex)Qx] \supset (Ex)(Px \supset Qx)$
    (b) $(x)(Px \equiv Qx) \supset [(Ex)Px \equiv (Ex)Qx]$
    (c) $(x)(S \supset Px) \supset (S \supset (x)Px)$ where x is not free in S
    (d) $(Ex)(y)Rxy \supset (x)(Ey)Ryx$

15. Give derivations for 1–8 in section 7.

16. Give derivations for
    (a) $(Ex)(Px \lor \neg Px)$
    (b) $(Ex)((Ey)Py \supset Px)$
    (c) $(y)(Py \supset (x)(Py \lor Qx))$
    (d) $\neg (x)(y)(Ez)Rxyz \equiv (Ex)(Ey)(z) \neg Rxyz$

17. Derive $(x)[(Ey)Rxy \cdot \supset Rxx]$ from $(x)(y)[Rxy \supset Rxx]$.

18. Give derivations for 1–3 in section 8.

19. Show that identity is an equivalence relation.

20. Give derivations for 4–7 in section 8.

21. Two place predicates R are classified as follows:
    $(x)(y)(Rxy \supset Ryx)$—symmetric
    $(x)(y)(Rxy \supset \neg Ryx)$—asymmetric
    $(x)(y)(z)(Rxy \& Ryz \cdot \supset Rxz)$—transitive
    $(x)(y)(z)(Rxy \& Ryz \supset \neg Rxz)$—intransitive
    $(x)Rxx$—reflexive
    $(x)(y)(Rxy \supset \cdot Rxx \& Ryy)$—quasi-reflexive
    $(x) \neg Rxx$—irreflexive

    (a) Find examples in English of each class.
    (b) Show that R is irreflexive if it is asymmetric.
    (c) Show that R is quasi-reflexive if it is reflexive.
    (d) Show that R is irreflexive if it is intransitive.
    (e) Show that R is quasi-reflexive if it is asymmetric and transitive.
    (f) What extra assumption is needed to derive reflexivity from symmetry and transitivity?

22. Show that if there are at most two cows and at least one, then there are either exactly two cows or exactly one cow.

23. Show that if there are at least two unmitigated villains, then there is at least one villain. "Is mitigated" means, literally, "has become milder". Would the argument remain valid if "unmitigated" were replaced by "alleged"? Discuss.

5 Invalidity and Consistency

In accordance with the program of Chapter 3 we must now provide tableau rules for the quantifiers. As before, the tableau method will have two distinct uses. The first is to provide, in a rather mechanical way, categorical derivations of an especially simple structure. (Specifically, no subderivations occur, and the question which tableau rule, if any, is to be applied at a given stage always has a definite answer.) The second is to facilitate the construction of *counterexamples*, that is, examples to show that a given argument is invalid or that a given statement is contingent (not logically true) or consistent (not logically false).

As we shall see shortly, the construction of a tableau sequence will now be such that, unlike ordinary derivations, such sequences may go on forever. That means that, in principle, an attempt to prove logical falsehood may fail simply by not coming to an end. In the logic of statements this could not happen, because tableau rules always led to shorter alternates (alternates with fewer symbols). Since expressions cannot be shortened forever, the tableau sequence must end after a finite number of steps. But in the logic of quantifiers, the tableau rules sometimes add new symbols; so the process may not come to a stop.

Before turning to the tableau rules, we shall again choose some of the intelim rules as basic, and show others to be admissible.

SECTION 1
FURTHER REDUCTION OF THE INTELIM RULES

In Chapter 4 we gave two sets of intelim rules for existential quantification, showing the second set (SEQE and SEQI) to be admissible.

We shall now go one step further, and eliminate EQI and EQE. The system *IntElim* is extended by adding rules UQE and UQI, and the definition

D3. "$(Ex)A$" for "$\neg(x)\,\neg A$"

The resulting system will be referred to as *IntElim(*)*. Further systems may be constructed by adding either VQE or the rules II and IE, or both. These systems will be called, respectively, *IntElim(*v)*, *IntElim(*=)* and *IntElim(*v=)*. The following table describes the systems more exactly (where rule R henceforth includes the rules R_y).

Systems	Rules	Definitions
IntElim:	R,D,KE₁, KE₂, KI, AI₁	D1, D2
	AI₂, AE, NI, NE	
IntElim(*):	IntElim + UQI, UQE	D3
IntElim(*v):	IntElim(*) + VQE	
IntElim(*=):	IntElim(*) + II, IE	
IntElim(*v=):	IntElim(*v) + II, IE	
	or	
	IntElim(*=) + VQE	

We now turn to some admissibility considerations.

I. EQI and EQE are admissible in *IntElim(*)*.

Our considerations also show that these rules are admissible in the systems obtained by adding rules to *IntElim(*)*. The admissibility of EQE and EQI is immediate from definition D3.

Next we want to show that VQE would be admissible if we had a special rule allowing for the introduction of the line $(Ex)(Fx\lor\neg Fx)$ at any point. This shows that rule VQE does not warrant more inferences that it should.

II. If A can be deduced in *IntElim(*v)*, then $(Ex)(Fx\lor\neg Fx)$ $\supset A$ can be deduced in *IntElim(*)*. (This result carries over to the systems *IntElim(*v=)* and *IntElim(*=)* by similar reasoning.)

Let us suppose that at some point in a derivation we arrive at the line $(x)A$, with x not free in A. We can then begin a subderivation general in x, and derive A within that subderivation. Introducing $(Ex)(Fx\lor\neg Fx)$ then allows us to deduce $(Ex)(\neg A)$ from the supposition $\neg A$. But that contradicts $(x)A$. These remarks may help to understand the strategy of the following derivation:

(1)	$(x)A$		x not free in A
(2)	$(Ex)(Fx \lor \neg Fx)$		
(3)	$\neg A$		
(4)	$(Ex)(Fx \lor \neg Fx)$	(2) R	
(5)	x	$Fx \lor \neg Fx$	
(6)		$\neg A$	(3) R
(7)		$(Ex)\neg A$	(6) SEQI
(8)	$(Ex)\neg A$		(4–7) SEQE
(9)	$\neg (x)\neg \neg A$		(8)
(10)	x	$(x)A$	(1) R
(11)		A	(10) UQE
(12)		$\neg \neg A$	(11) DN reversed
(13)	$(x)\neg \neg A$		(10–12) UQI
(14)	A		(3–13) NE

The use of DN in reverse is justified because in Chapter 3 it was shown that the reverse of DN is also admissible.

It is important to note how the above derivation would have been blocked if premise (2) were omitted. In that case, line (4) would also be missing, and line (8) would not follow from the preceding: it would have to read $(x)(Ex)\neg A$ or $(x)\neg(x)\neg A$. In this way we cannot reach a formal contradiction with $(x)A$ at all.

SECTION 2
WORKING INSIDE QUANTIFIERS

The rules SEQE and SEQI allow us to work inside long formulas beginning with existential quantifiers, in roughly the way that we can work inside long alternations or conjunctions. For example, just because $(A;$ hence $A \lor B)$ is valid, the argument $((Ex)Fx;$ hence $(Ex)(Fx \lor Gx))$ is also valid, and similarly for $((Ex)(Ey)(Rxy);$ hence $(Ex)(Ey)$ $(Rxy \lor Gx))$:

(1)	$(Ex)(Ey)Rxy$		
(2)	z	$(Ey)Rzy$	
(3)		w	Rzw	
(4)			$Rzw \lor Gz$	(3) AI
(5)			$(Ey)(Rzy \lor Gz)$	(4) SEQI
(6)		$(Ey)(Rzy \lor Gz)$	(2–5) SEQE
(7)		$(Ex)(Ey)(Rxy \lor Gx)$	(6) SEQI
(8)	$(Ex)(Ey)(Rxy \lor Gx)$		(1–7) SEQE

We can "telescope" this double use of SEQE as follows, for convenience:

$$
\begin{array}{lll}
(1) & (Ex)(Ey)Rxy & \\
(2) & \quad z, w \mid Rzw & \\
(3) & \qquad Rzw \lor Gz & (2)\ \text{AI} \\
(4) & \qquad (Ey)(Rzy \lor Gz) & (3)\ \text{SEQI} \\
(5) & \qquad (Ex)(Ey)(Rxy \lor Gx) & (4)\ \text{SEQI} \\
(6) & (Ex)(Ey)(Rxy \lor Gx) & (1\text{--}5)\ \text{SEQE}
\end{array}
$$

Extrapolating to arbitrarily many variables, we see that SEQE has the immediate generalization

$$
\begin{array}{l}
(Ex_1) \ldots (Ex_n)A \\
x_1, \ldots, x_n \ \begin{array}{|l} A \\ \hline B \end{array} \\
(Ex_1) \ldots (Ex_n)B
\end{array}
$$

From now on, we shall write $E(A)$ for the formula $(Ex_1) \ldots (Ex_n)A$ where $x_1, \ldots, x_n$ are all the variables free in A (taken in some predetermined order). Note that $E(A)$ is just A when A is a statement already. With this notation the above remarks can be summed up by a principle. We call the above subderivation *entirely general* if no variable other than $x_1, \ldots x_n$ occurs free in A.

      III. If B can be derived in an entirely general subderivation from hypothesis A, then $E(B)$ can be derived from hypothesis $E(A)$, provided $E(A)$ is not A, in *IntElim*(*).

This is again an admissibility demonstration, but very short:

$$
\begin{array}{lll}
(1) & E(A) & \text{(with at most } x_1, \ldots, x_n \\
 & & \text{free in } A \text{ and } B, \text{ and some} \\
(2) & x_1, \ldots, x_n, \ \begin{array}{|l} A \\ \end{array} & \text{variable free in } A) \\
 & y_1, \ldots, y_n \quad \cdot & \\
 & \qquad\qquad\quad \cdot & \\
 & \qquad\qquad\quad \cdot & \\
(m) & \qquad\qquad\quad B & \\
(n) & \qquad\qquad\quad E(B) & (m)\ \text{SEQI repeated} \\
(n+1) & E(B) & (1\text{--}n)\ \text{SEQE}
\end{array}
$$

    The restriction that some variable occur free in A is of course exactly the condition that $E(A)$ and A are different sentences. Why is this restriction necessary? Let us suppose we did not have it. Then we could give the following derivation:

(1) | $E[(x)(Fx \lor \neg Fx)]$ (note that this is just
                                                   $(x)(Fx \lor \neg Fx)$)

(2) y | $(x)(Fx \lor \neg Fx)$
(3) | $Fy \,\&\, \neg Fy$
(4) | Fy (3) KE
(5) | $\neg Fy$ (3) KE
(6) | $\neg(Fy \,\&\, \neg Fy)$ (3–5) NI
(7) | $E[\neg(Fy \,\&\, \neg Fy)]$ (i.e.,
                                                   $(Ey)[\neg(Fy \,\&\, \neg Fy)])$

But then, by a use of CI we would get a categorical subderivation of

$$(x)(Fx \lor \neg Fx) \supset (Ey)(\neg(Fy \,\&\, \neg Fy))$$

But if the domain is empty then the antecedent is true (indeed, it also is logically true), but the consequent is false. So that restriction is important when the domain is allowed to be empty.

IV. If B can be derived in an entirely general subderivation from A, then $E(B)$ can be derived from $E(A)$, in IntElim(*v).

In this derivation we just use UQI and VQE where above we used SEQE.

Finally, we want to point out an asymmetry between existential and universal quantifiers in derivations of logical falsehood. If we can deduce $(x)(Fx \,\&\, \neg Fx)$ from A, it does not follow that we can deduce a contradiction from A in *IntElim* (*), though this would follow if we could derive $(Ex)(Fx \,\&\, \neg Fx)$ from A. In *IntElim* (*v), however, this asymmetry disappears. We can make the same point by looking at what is implied about A when a contradiction is derived in a subderivation under hypothesis A. Suppose we have the following derivation:

(1) | $E(A)$

·
· $x_1, \ldots, x_n$ | A
·
·
·
·
·
(m) | | $B \,\&\, \neg B$

Then if $E(A)$ is not just A, we can deduce $E(B \& \neg B)$; but of course it is very easy to derive $(x_1) \ldots (x_n) \neg (B \& \neg B)$ where $E(B) = (Ex_1) \ldots (Ex_n)B \ldots$; and this leads to absurdity. But if $E(A)$ is just A, then (as our preceding two results emphasize) we can conclude that an absurdity follows only if we admit VQE.

SECTION 3
FURTHER TABLEAU RULES

In view of results III and IV, it will henceforth be convenient to apply our previous tableau rules in the following generalized form.

$$\text{DN} \left| \frac{E(X \& \neg\,\neg A \& Y)}{E(X \& A \& Y)} \right.$$

$$\text{NK} \left| \frac{E(X \& \neg(A \& B) \& Y)}{E(X \& \neg A \& Y) \vee E(X \& \neg B \& Y)} \right.$$

$$\text{V} \left| \frac{E(X \& (A \vee B) \& Y)}{E(X \& A \& Y) \vee E(X \& B \& Y)} \right.$$

$$\text{NV} \left| \frac{E(X \& \neg(A \vee B) \& Y)}{E(X \& \neg A \& \neg B \& Y)} \right.$$

The admissibility of the new forms of NK and V may not be immediately obvious; we leave the demonstrations to the reader. Now we add further tableau rules for quantifiers and identity assertions.

$$\text{UI} \left| \frac{E(X \& (x)A \& Y)}{E(X \& (y_1/x)A \& \ldots \& (y_n/x)A \& Y \& (x)A)} \right.$$

where $y_1, \ldots, y_n$ are the variables free in $X \& (x)A \& Y$.

$$\text{Ur} \left| \frac{E(X \& \neg(x)A \& Y)}{E(Ey)(X \& \neg(y/x)A \& Y)} \right.$$

where y is the first variable not free in $X \& \neg(x)A \& Y$.

$$\text{VU} \left| \frac{X \& (x)A \& Y}{(Ey)(X \& (y/x)A \& Y \& (x)Fx)} \right.$$

where no variable is free in $X \& (x)A \& Y$, and y is the first variable which does not occur in $X \& (x)A \& Y$.

$$\text{I} \left| \frac{E(X \& x = y \& Y)}{E(y/x)(X \& Y)} \right.$$

We speak of the "first variable", as in "the first variable not free in X & $\neg(x)A$ & Y". This assumes that the variables have a certain order, usually called their *alphabetical* order. What this order is, is entirely immaterial; in practice, therefore, we simply pick some new variable. Secondly, VU has the same status as VQE; it is to be used only when there is something in the domain of discourse.

The rule for underlining must also be amended: any disjunct of form $E(X$ & A & Y & $\neg A$ & $Z)$ or $E(X$ & $\neg A$ & Y & $Z)$ will have to be underlined. To this topic we return in the next section.

Before turning to admissibility demonstrations, let us give an example of a derivation of logical falsehood by the new set of tableau rules.

(1)	$(Ey)[\neg(Ex)\neg Fx$ & $(Fy \supset \neg Fy)]$	
(2)	$(Ey)[(x)Fx$ & $(\neg Fy \lor \neg Fy)]$	(1) D1, D3
(3)	$(Ey)[Fy$ & $(\neg Fy \lor \neg Fy)$ & $(x)Fx]$	(2) U1
(4)	$\underline{(Ey)[Fy \ \&\ \neg Fy \ \&\ (x)Fx]} \lor \underline{(Ey)[Fy \ \&\ \neg Fy \ \&\ (x)Fx]}$	(3) V

Note that we do not use D3 to eliminate the existential quantifier on the outside, but only those inside. The outside existential quantifiers are left intact throughout in a derivation by tableau rules.

V. Ul and Ur are admissible in *IntElim*(*)

For Ul this is easily shown, utilizing UQI (and result III). To demonstrate the admissibility of Ur note that $(A$ & $(Ey)B) \supset ((Ey)A$ & $B)$ is a logical truth when y is not free in A.

VI. VU is admissible in *IntElim*(*v) and I is admissible in *IntElim*(*=).

For the demonstration of the admissibility of VU, the above logical truth must be utilized again (as well as result IV). In the case of I, we use result III and the rule IE.

SECTION 4
REVISED CONSTRUCTION OF TABLEAU SEQUENCES

Besides the preceding emendation of the set of tableau rules, there are three major revisions we must now make in the construction of tableau sequences.

First, in Chapter 3 we did not have to worry about whether an applicable rule would ever be applied: the construction has to end at some point, and ends (in principle) only when no rules are still applicable. But consider the following abortive attempt to prove something logically false:

(1) | $(x)Fx \& \neg(x) \neg \neg Fx$
(2) | $E(Fy \& \neg(x) \neg \neg Fx \& (x)Fx)$ (1) VU
(3) | $E(Fy \& \neg(x) \neg \neg Fx \& Fy \& (x)Fx)$ (2) Ul
(4) | $E(Fy \& \neg(x) \neg \neg Fx \& Fy \& Fy \& (x)Fx)$ (3) Ul

If we proceed in this way we will never finish; but the tableau would soon show a contradiction if Ur and DN were used. Now Ul comes before Ur in our list of rules, so we need a special proviso to keep it from being applied *ad nauseam*.

The necessary proviso is the following:

PROVISO: the letter X in the statement of the tableau rules must stand for a formula which does not have any conjunct of form

$$\neg \neg A$$
or $\neg(A \& B)$
or $(A \vee B)$
or $\neg(A \vee B)$
or $(x)A$
or $\neg(x)A$
or $x = y$

Now even this proviso is not enough when the tableau rules generate alternations of more than one alternate. The following is also an abortive tableau sequence, and does not run afoul of our proviso:

(1) | $\neg(\neg(x)Fx \& \neg(x)Gx)$
(2) | $\neg \neg(x)Fx \vee \neg \neg(x)Gx$ (1) NK
(3) | $(x)Fx \vee \neg \neg(x)Gx$ (2) DN
(4) | $(Fy \& (x)Fx) \vee \neg \neg(x)Gx$ (3) Ul
(5) | $(Fy \& Fy \& (x)Fx) \vee \neg \neg(x)Gx$ (4) Ul

Surely DN should be applied to the second alternate at some point; but at this rate it never will. So we add a second restriction.

PROVISO: If A' is inferred from A by tableau rule, its operation on $X \vee A \vee Y$ should "shuffle" the alternates: the next line should be $X \vee Y \vee A'$.

Of course, a little bit of non-mechanical ingenuity makes these provisos unnecessary, but we want to make the tableau sequence construction an entirely mechanical procedure. Still, in exercises, the "shuffling" proviso may be ignored.

If in spite of these provisos the construction still goes on forever without showing an explicit contradiction, then the formula cannot be shown logically false by our method. For the above provisos guarantee that any applicable rule will eventually be applied.

Finally, in the system with identity we have one further kind of explicit contradiction: formulas of form $x \neq x$ (rule CI). These must also be underlined. The following is an example of a tableau sequence:

$$(1) \; \Big|\!\!-\!\!\!- \; \underline{E(x = y \, \& \, y \neq x)}$$
$$(2) \; \Big|\!- \; \underline{E(x \neq x)} \qquad\qquad\qquad (1), \text{I}$$

Clearly, if a tableau sequence terminates, then the initial formula is such that its denial can be proven categorically.

The last question which we must consider in some detail is whether our new tableau rules are also reversible—or whether they oversimplify sometimes to the point of preventing us from proving logical falsehood. This is the final result in this chapter.

> VII. If $\neg \, E(A)$ has a categorical derivation, and $E(B)$ is any line in the tableau for A, then $\neg E(B)$ has a categorical derivation (in a system in which all the rules used up to that point are admissible).

To show this, we can adapt the demonstration of the corresponding result in Chapter 3.

We leave the demonstration for the newly generalized form of the old rules to the reader. Consider then the following rules:

$$(\text{R1}) \; \Big|\!\!-\!\!\!- \; \frac{E(X \, \& \, Fy \, \& \, Y \, \& \, (x)Fx)}{E(X \, \& \, (x)Fx \, \& \, Y)}$$

$$(\text{R2}) \; \Big|\!\!-\!\!\!- \; \frac{E(X \, \& \, \neg Fy \, \& \, Y)}{E(X \, \& \, \neg(x)Fx \, \& \, Y)}$$

$$(\text{R3}) \; \Big|\!\!-\!\!\!- \; \frac{E(x/y)(X \, \& \, Y)}{E(X \, \& \, x = y \, \& \, Y)}$$

It is easy to see that (R1) is admissible in *IntElim*(*). To show the admissibility of (R2), note that $(Ey)(A \, \& \, B) \supset A \, \& \, (Ey)B$ is a logical truth when y is not free in A. For (R3) the demonstration runs as follows:

(1)	$(Ey)(Fy \, \& \, Gy)$	
(2)	$y \; \lfloor \; Fy \, \& \, Gy$	
(3)	Fy	(2) KE_1
(4)	Gy	(2) KE_2
(5)	$y = y$	II
(6)	$Fy \, \& \, y = y$	(3–5) KI
(7)	$(Ex)Fx \, \& \, x = y \, \& \, Gy)$	(6) SEQI
(8)	$(Ey)(Ex)(Fx \, \& \, x = y \, \& \, Gy)$	(7) SEQI
(9)	$(Ey)(Ex)(Fx \, \& \, x = y \, \& \, Gy)$	(1–8) SEQE

SECTION 5
CONSTRUCTION OF COUNTEREXAMPLES

In section 4 of the preceding chapter (on domains of discourse) we discussed how a given statement can be shown *not* logically true. To do this, we specify a domain, and an interpretation (assignment of extensions to the predicates) and then show that the statement is false, given this specification. Thus "Apples are healthy" is not logically true. To show this we symbolize it as

$$(x)(Ax \supset Hx)$$

Then to construct our "counterexample" we can specify a domain, say the set of natural numbers

the domain $D = \{1, 2, 3, \ldots\}$

and assign extensions as follows:

the extension of A is the set of even numbers in D.
the extension of H is the set of odd numbers in D.

Upon this interpretation $(x)(Ax \supset Hx)$ is true exactly if all even numbers are odd numbers. But that is false.

In just the same way we can show that the statement "Apples are healthy" is "consistent", that is, not logically false. To do this we simply show that its denial is not logically true. (Or, if you wish, that it itself can be true.) This is easy: we simply modify the above interpretation by assigning H the same extension as A.

But this procedure taxes one's calculational talents exorbitantly when the logical structure of the examined sentence is more complex. So here we can look to the tableau method as in Chapter 3 to simplify the procedure. Let $B_1, \ldots, B_n$ be the tableau sequence for B_1. Then to show that B_1 can be true we need only show that B_n can be true. So we look at B_n, which is a disjunction $C_1 \vee \ldots \vee C_m$. Now if each C_k is underlined, it is impossible to show that B_n could be true. But if, say, C_k is not underlined, then all we need to do is show that *it* can be true. (For if one of the disjuncts is true, so is the disjunction.) This is exactly what we pointed out in Chapter 3 also; but here that will help *only if* the tableau sequence actually comes to a stop. Let us take an example, say, $(x)(Px \supset Qx) \,\&\, (Ex)Px \,\&\, (Ex) \neg Qx$:

(1) $(x)(Px \supset Qx) \,\&\, (Ex)Px \,\&\, (Ex) \neg Qx$

(2) $(x)(\neg Px \vee Qx) \,\&\, \neg(x) \neg \neg Qx$ (1) Def

(3) $(Ey)\{(x)(\neg Px \vee Qx) \,\&\, \neg \neg Py \,\&\, \neg(x) \neg \neg Qx\}$ (2) Ur

(4) $(Ey)\{\neg Py \vee Qy) \,\&\, \neg \neg Py \,\&\, \neg(x) \neg \neg Qx \,\&\, (x)(\neg Px \vee Qx)\}$ (3) UI

(5) $(Ey)\{\neg Py \,\&\, \neg \neg Py \,\&\, \neg(x) \neg \neg Qx \,\&\, (x)(\neg Px \vee Qx)\} \vee$
      $(Ey)\{Qy \,\&\, \neg \neg Py \,\&\, \neg(x) \neg \neg Qx \,\&\, (x)(\neg Px \vee Qx)\}$ (4) V

This calculation is going to be rather bulky, but at this point it is clear that the first disjunct is to be underlined, so we shall abbreviate it to A.

(6) $A \vee (Ey)\{Qy \,\&\, Py \,\&\, \neg(x) \neg \neg Qx \,\&\, (x)(\neg Px \vee Qx)\}$ (5) DN

(7) $A \vee (Ey)(Ez)\{Qy \,\&\, Py \,\&\, \neg \neg \neg Qz \,\&\, (x)(\neg Px \vee Qx)\}$ (6) Ur

(8) $A \vee (Ey)(Ez)\{Qy \,\&\, Py \,\&\, \neg Qz \,\&\, (x)(\neg Px \vee Qx)\}$ (7) DN'

(9) $A \vee (Ey)(Ez)\{Qy \,\&\, Py \,\&\, \neg Qz \,\&\, (\neg Pz \vee Qx \,\&\, (x)(\neg Px \vee Qx)\}$ (8) UI

(10) $A \vee (Ey)(Ez)\{Qy \,\&\, Py \,\&\, \neg Qz \,\&\, \neg Pz \,\&\, (x)(\neg Px \vee Qx)\} \vee$
     $\underline{(Ey)(Ez)\{Qy \,\&\, Py \,\&\, \neg Qz \,\&\, Qz \,\&\, (x)(\neg Px \vee Qx)\}}$ (9) V

Now the second disjunct is not underlined, and a particular example can be constructed to show that it can be true (exercises).

What have we gained here? Not nearly as much as in the case of the logic of statements. For in a tableau sequence $B_1, \ldots, B_n$, any *conjunct* of B_1 of form $(x)A$ will occur in each disjunct of B_n. In some cases the simplification is still considerable; in other cases (such as the above example) it is rather less significant. However, it can be shown (and we shall do so in Part Four) that if the tableau sequence of a statement B does not terminate, then B is *not* logically false. And although this must remain unproven at this point, we offer the tableau method here for the use of showing that a given statement is not logically false (and hence, by the considerations emphasized in Chapter 3, for the use of showing that given statements are not logically true or given arguments invalid).

EXERCISES

1. Show that if A has a categorical derivation in Intelim (*v=) then $(Ex)(x = x) \supset A$ has a categorical derivation in Intelim (*=).

2. Give a categorical derivation of the following in Intelim (*v=).
   (a) $(x)(Fx \lor \neg Fx) \supset (Ey)(\neg (Fy \& \neg Fy))$
   (b) $(x)(Ey)(Rxy) \& (x)(y)(Rxy \supset \neg Ryx) \cdot \supset$
   $(Ey)(\neg Ryy)$

3. Give the admissibility proof needed to demonstrate result IV.

4. Demonstrate the admissibility of the new forms of DN, NK, V, NV in Intelim (*).

5. Demonstrate the admissibility of Ul and Ur in Intelim (*).

6. Demonstrate the admissibility of VU in Intelim (*v).

7. Demonstrate the admissibility of I in Intelim (*=).

8. Demonstrate that the rules of the newly generalized form of DN, NK, V, NV are also admissible in Intelim (*).

9. Show the admissibility in Intelim (*) of rule (R1) and (R2) in the text (in the discussion of result VII).

10. Construct tableau sequences for
    (a) $(Ex)(Px \supset \neg (Qx \lor \neg Rx))$
    (b) $(x)(Px \supset (Ey) Rxy)$
    (c) $(x)(y)(Rxy \supset \neg Ryx) \& (Ez)(Rzz)$
    (d) $(Ez)(Fz \& (x)(Ey) Rxy)$

11. Note the peculiarity of (d)—its tableau sequence does not end—and construct another formula with the same peculiarity.

12. For the sentences in exercise 10 of which the tableau sequence ended but did not terminate, show by explicit counterexample that they are not logically false.

13. Show by explicit counterexample that sentence (d) of exercise 10 is not logically false.

14. Show that the second disjunct in line 10 in section 5 can be true.

PART *III* THE LOGIC OF SINGULAR TERMS

6 Unanalyzed Singular Terms

The system of logic developed in Parts One and Two is, except for procedural differences and attention to the empty domain, the standard logic found in most contemporary textbooks. We are now going to extend this logic in a novel way to deal with singular terms, terms such as names and titles that purport to refer to a single individual.*

SECTION 1
SINGULAR TERMS AND VARIABLES

At the beginning of Part Two we introduced the notion of a general term. In traditional grammatical terminology, general terms are common nouns, and phrases that function as common nouns (common noun phrases). These terms can be singular or plural: thus "man" is a singular common noun, "men who steal" a plural common noun phrase.

The above, grammatical, use of "singular" must be sharply distinguished from its use by logicians. For by singular terms we mean (primarily) what in traditional English grammar are proper nouns and phrases that function as proper nouns (proper noun phrases). Examples are names ("John", "Cicero"), titles ("Caesar"), combinations thereof ("General de Gaulle"), descriptive phrases ("the king of Jordan"), and a variety of other phrases that cannot be described so simply ("John's bird", "2 + 2", "that snow is white", "a certain marshall", "fatherhood", "4^2", and so on). A non-grammatical feature shared by singular

---

*Systems of logic that deal with singular terms in the way we do were named *free logics* by Karel Lambert.

terms is that they purport to refer to a single individual. We say "purport to refer", because whether the expression actually refers to something is not important. We do not intend to express an opinion on whether "God", "Heaven", or "Zeus", refer to actual entities, but these are all names, and hence singular terms. (They certainly purport to refer to actual entities; however, this does not mean that they cannot be used by someone who does not believe that they do in fact refer. For example, an atheist can use the word "God" to say "God does not exist".)

As an example of an argument in which a singular terms plays a crucial role, consider

    1. John requires surgery;
       Therefore, there is someone who is John.

Is this valid? It cannot be shown to be valid by the methods of preceding chapters. So if it is valid, we shall have to add rules that allow us to derive its conclusion from its premise.

In our symbolism we shall use lower case letters from the beginning of the alphabet ("a", "b", "c",...) to abbreviate English singular terms. Then to construct formulas we shall allow them to follow predicates in just the way that free variables do. Hence if we abbreviate "John" to "a" and "requires surgery" to "R" we can symbolize 1 as

    2. $Ra \therefore (Ex)(x = a)$

If we had a rule whereby we could derive this conclusion from that premise, what would that mean? It would mean that singular terms have *existential import*, that a simple statement containing a singular term cannot be true unless that term really refers to something. But that, in turn, would mean that a great number of common English statements could not be accommodated, or at least not accommodated in any simple or straightforward way, in our logic. For such simple-looking statements as the following could surely be true, and do not seem to entail unusual existence claims:

    Zeus is not identical with Allah.
    The ancient Greeks worshipped Zeus.
    The accident was prevented.
    The predicted storm did not occur.
    True believers fear Beelzebub.

In the past, logicians have often assumed existential import for singular terms, just as still earlier existential import was assumed for general terms. (More charitably, we should perhaps say that they limited their concern to singular terms which actually refer to something.*) However, we shall admit all singular terms into our official idiom.

As we mentioned, these will be abbreviated by lower-case letters from the beginning of the alphabet, and these letters we shall call *(individual) constants*. As a metalogical symbol referring to constants and variables alike, we shall use "t" with or without subscripts. This will be convenient since the logical rules for constants that we shall introduce will apply to variables (within general subderivations) as well. Thus "$t_1 = t_2$" can stand for "$a = b$" or "$a = a$" or "$x = b$", and so on. Further, we shall use all of these letters to refer to themselves, when that is convenient.

Finally, from the samples above it is clear that some English singular terms are more complex in structure than others, for example, "the king of Jordan". We have entitled this chapter "Unanalyzed Singular Terms" because at this stage we shall treat all singular terms as units and not attempt to analyze their internal structure.

SECTION 2
INFERENCE RULES FOR UNANALYZED
SINGULAR TERMS

We turn now to the inference rules needed to accommodate arguments whose validity, and statements whose logical truth, are determined by their constituent unanalyzed singular terms. As examples of the foregoing we offer the argument

3. No human being is God;
   Therefore, if God is a human being he doesn't exist

and the statement

4. There is at most one thing which is Hegel.

---

*In *De Interpretatione* 21a, 26–28; Aristotle asked whether "Homer is" follows from "Homer is a poet". The remarks that follow are not unambiguous, but the classic commentary by Cajetan states that the answer is negative. See R. M. Spiazzi, ed., *St. Thomae Aquinatis In Aristotelis Libros Peri Hermeneias et Posteriorum Analyticorum Expositio* (Casali: Marietti, 1955).

In those systems in which 4 is a logical truth, peculiarity, in one sense of the word, becomes a point of logic.

Because variables are a kind of singular term, the problem of which rules, if any, in addition to the rules we have already, are needed to deal with cases like 3 and 4, may be construed as a substitution problem. Specifically, the problem is one of determining which of the rules in Chapter 3 operating within a subderivation general in some variable can be extended to singular terms. Accordingly, our problem is reduced to the consideration of four rules UQI, UQE, II, and IE; the other rules, that is, VQE, R, EQI, and EQE carry over unchanged.

Beginning with UQE, let us suppose that we allow the inference of Ft, rather than just Fx, from $(x)Fx$. Then we are committed to the validity of the argument

> Everything exists;
> Therefore, Pegasus exists.

But this argument is invalid, as we can see by recalling that our quantificational variables range only over the things which exist. Thus "Everything exists" is symbolized as "$(x)(x \text{ exists})$" and is true; but "Pegasus exists" is false.

Before going on, we wish to discuss the predicate "exists" that occurs in some examples above. At the beginning of Part Two we already emphasized that the quantifiers concern real things, things that actually exist. Thus the following two sentences we consider synonymous:

> There is at least one cow.
> There exists at least one cow.

And therefore, we consider the following redundant:

> There exists at least one cow which exists.

Now, it does not seem very audacious to claim that

> Ichabod exists if and only if Ichabod is identical with some thing which exists

is logically true. However, in the second part of this statement, we regard the phrase "which exists" as redundant for the same reason as before. Therefore we may claim equivalently that

Ichabod exists if and only if Ichabod is identical with some thing

is logically true. Since "Ichabod is identical with something" is para-phrased in our official idiom as "There is some x such that Ichabod is identical with x", we now regard

$$(Ex)(x = \text{Ichabod})$$

as a correct and adequate symbolization of "Ichabod exists".

In general "a exists" is symbolized as "$(Ex)(x = a)$", "y exists" as "$(Ex)(x = y)$", and "x exists" as "$(Ez)(z = x)$"; note the need for a new variable in the last case. It is important to see that our variables are always used to refer to real things, members of the domain of dis-course. When a variable occurs free (inside a general subderivation) it functions as a *referring singular term*, a term which does in fact have a referent. This is clearly shown in the following derivation:

(1) | x | $x = x$ | II
(2) | | $(Ey)(y = x)$ | (1) SEQI
(3) | $(x)((Ey)(y = x))$ | | (1–2) UQI

This also shows at once that if we extended UQE as supposed above to apply to any singular term, we could derive further

(4) $(Ey)(y = \text{Ichabod Crane})$ (3) UQE

which is a patently false conclusion.

The situation for UQI is somewhat different. Suppose that we can prove categorically

(1)

   .
   .
   .
   .
   .
(n) | Fa

Can we now conclude not only that Fa but also that $(x)Fx$ is a logical truth? It is easy to see that the above derivation can be extended as follows:

$$
\begin{array}{ll}
(1) \\
\quad \cdot \\
\quad \cdot \\
\quad \cdot \\
(n) & Fa \\
(n+1) & a \text{ exists} \\
(n+2) & Fa & (n),\ \mathrm{R} \\
(n+3) & (a \text{ exists}) \supset Fa & (n+1,\, n+2),\ \mathrm{CI}
\end{array}
$$

In other words, it is a logical truth that if a exists, then a is F—with no assumptions being made about which existent "a" denotes. So then it is a logical truth for *any* existent that it is F—that is, we may infer that $(x)Fx$ is a logical truth. The change of UQI to

$$
\begin{array}{l}
\quad\quad a \\
\quad\quad\ \ \Big| Fa \\
(x)Fx
\end{array}
$$

would not lead us into error. On the other hand, it must be emphasized that *nothing would be gained* from this change. There is no reason for not leaving UQI as it is, for as the above shows, when we can prove Fa categorically, we can also prove Fx categorically, since in the rules a free variable functions like a name assumed to refer to an existent. So we shall not extend UQI either.

It is worthwhile noting that an argument exactly parallel to that brought against the Traditional Square of Opposition can be brought against the substitution of names for variables in the rules UQE and SEQI; for they would then support what we shall call the Modern Square of Opposition. The square in question looks like this:

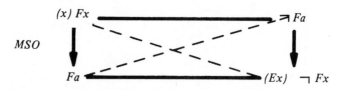

Here "a" is an (undetermined) name. In many texts the statements in MSO, in virtue of extended UQE and extended SEQI, bear exactly the same semantical relations to each other that the Tradition acknowledged to hold between the statements in the Traditional Square of Opposition. For example, "$(x)Fx$" and "$(Ex)\neg Fx$" are contradictories. "$(Ex)\neg Fx$"

is related by subalternation to "$\neg Fa$"; "Fa" and "$(Ex)\neg Fx$" are sub-contraries, and so on. Consider again the case where "a" abbreviates "Ichabod Crane" and "F" abbreviates "exists" (that is, "there exists something which is"). Then the relations alleged to hold *around* MSO fail; in contrast, those on the diagonals still hold. Recall also that the difficulties in the Traditional Square of Opposition arose in relation to general terms true of nothing and that the least restrictive way out of the inferential problems caused by introduction of such general terms into the Traditional Square was to insert a specific existence premise in those arguments originally licensed by the relations around the Traditional Square. Similarly, in the present case, the problems with MSO arise only when "a" is taken as an abbreviation for a non-referential singular term; matters can be set aright simply by adding an existence premise to those arguments originally licensed by the relations *around* MSO.*

Accordingly, one would expect an adequate logic of unanalyzed singular terms to be able to establish the validity of at least the following (undetermined) arguments:

5. $(x)Fx$ $\therefore Fa$
  $(Ex)(x = a)$
6. $\neg Fa$ $\therefore \neg(x)Fx$
  $(Ex)(x = a)$
7. $\neg Fa$ $\therefore (Ex)\neg Fx$
  $(Ex)(x = a)$
8. $\neg(Ex)\neg Fx$ $\therefore Fa$
  $(Ex)(x = a)$

That 5–8 are demonstrably valid in free logic will be shown shortly. The preceding remarks on MSO support the claim in the previous section that free logic can be viewed as an extension (to singular terms) of the philosophical attitude of standard logic toward general terms.

Finally we come to the rules II and IE. Can either of these rules be extended to the entire class of singular terms? The situation here is quite unlike that for the other rules in that we can extend them in this way without precipitating any logical difficulties, but we are not forced to do so. If we do so extend the rules, we must restate them as follows:

---

*See further, K. Lambert, "Existential Import Revisited", *Notre Dame Journal of Formal Logic* 4 (1963), pp. 288–292.

$$
\text{II} \quad
\begin{array}{|l}
\cdot \\
\cdot \\
\cdot \\
t = t \\
\cdot \\
\cdot \\
\cdot \\
\end{array}
\qquad
\text{IE} \quad
\begin{array}{|l}
t_1 = t_2 \\
\cdot \\
\cdot \\
\cdot \\
A \\
\cdot \\
\cdot \\
\cdot \\
(t_2/t_1)A \\
\end{array}
$$

By (t_2/t_1) we mean $(y/x)A$ if t_2 and t_1 happen to be variables y and x; by $(b/x)A$ we mean the replacement of each free occurrence of x in A by an occurrence of b, and by $(b/c)A$ we mean the replacement of each occurrence of c in A by an occurrence of b. This is a very natural extension of our notation. Of course, if "t_1" or "t_2" is a variable, the earlier restriction on II and IE, that this variable must flank some scope line to the left, must continue to be observed.

If these extended rules are accepted, such sentences as "Pegasus = Pegasus", and "the golden mountain = the golden mountain", as well as "Cicero = Cicero" are categorically provable. That "Cicero = Cicero" is true, is no doubt indisputable since the person referred to by "Cicero" must be exactly the person referred to by "Cicero", namely, Cicero, whom everyone knows to exist. But this only establishes that "Cicero = Cicero" is true, not that it is logically true. And while it sounds odd to our ears to say that Pegasus is not Pegasus—we would not expect any-one but a philosopher to say so—it is *prima facie* not inconsistent.

Let us consider these extended rules in more detail. Cicero exists, hence "Cicero" refers to a real person who must be exactly the person referred to by "Cicero"; hence "Cicero = Cicero" is true. In general, if t is a referring term, then $t = t$ is true. Thus II must be strengthened at least to allow the derivation of

9. $(Ex)(x = t) \supset t = t$

Similarly, the Dauphin existed, so if the man in the iron mask was the Dauphin, then the man in the iron mask must have existed. Generalizing on this example we must allow the derivation of

10. $[(Ex)(x = t) \,\&\, t = t'] \supset (Ex)(x = t')$

Still more generally, if t refers to something, and $t = t'$ is true, then t' may replace t everywhere:

11. $((Ex)(x = t) \,\&\, t = t' \,\&\, A) \supset (t'/t)A$

(Note that 10 follows from 11.) So IE must at least be strengthened in such a way that 11 can be proved.

What we have seen now is that the ordinary rules governing identity must at least apply to referring terms. Should non-referring terms function in logical inference in just the same way? We choose the alternative of extending II and IE to *all* singular terms, whether they refer or not. In the case of non-referring terms, correct usage of identity ascriptions cannot be decided by appealing to sameness of reference. So we choose to accept the principles of self-identity and substitutivity of identity to govern correct usage there. If anyone feels that this is wrong, that our extension of II and IE does not fit his intuitions about identity ascriptions at all, agreement, where agreement is possible, can be secured by the following paraphrase: When he says that a and b are identical we shall symbolize his statement as "$a = b$ & $(Ex)(x = a)$ & $(Ex)(x = b)$", and when he says that a and b are not identical, we shall symbolize his statement as "$\neg(a = b) \vee \neg(Ex)(x = a) \vee \neg (Ex)(x = a)$".

To sum up, only the rules II and IE are extended to the entire class of singular terms.

SECTION 3
ARGUMENTS AND LOGICAL TRUTHS INVOLVING UNANALYZED SINGULAR TERMS

Examples 5–8 in the preceding section were left unproved for the time being. We are now in a position to prove their validity, and the reader may do so as exercise. But these derivations are enormously facilitated by the following admissible rules:

$$
\text{RUQE:} \quad \begin{array}{|l} (x)A \\ (Ex)(x = t) \\ \hline (t/x)A \end{array} \qquad \text{where } t \text{ is not } x
$$

$$
\text{RSEQI} \quad \begin{array}{|l} A \\ (Ex)(x = t) \\ \hline (Ex)(x/t)A \end{array} \qquad \text{where } t \text{ is not } x
$$

The derivations are very straightforward. To simplify them somewhat in appearance, we shall use the convention of writing "Fx", "Fy", "Fz", "Fa" for sentences which are exactly alike except for a uniform replacement of (free) occurrences of a term (for example, "Fa" and "Fx" are exactly alike except that the one contains occurrences of a where the other contains free occurrences of x, and vice versa):

RUQE   (1) | $(x)Fx$
          (2) | $(Ex)(x = t)$
          (3) | x | $x = t$
          (4) | | $(x)Fx$ (1) R
          (5) | | Fx (4) UQE
          (6) | | Ft (3) (5) IE
          (7) | Ft (2) (3) (6) SEQE

RSEQI   (1) | Ft
          (2) | $(Ex)(x = t)$
          (3) | x | $x = t$
          (4) | | Ft (1) R
          (5) | | Fx (3) (4) IE
          (6) | | $(Ex)Fx$ (5) SEQI
          (7) | $(Ex)Fx$ (2) (3) (6) SEQE

We shall now prove the validity of example 3, letting "F" stand for "is a human being" and "a" for "God":

(P_1) | $(x)(Fx \supset x \neq a)$ $\therefore Fa \supset \neg(Ex)(x = a)$
(2) | | Fa
(3) | | | $(Ex)(x = a)$
(4) | | | | $(x)(Fx \supset x \neq a)$ (P_1) R
(5) | | | | $Fa \supset a \neq a$ (3) (4) RUQE
(6) | | | | Fa (2) R
(7) | | | | $a \neq a$ (5) (6) CE
(8) | | | | $a = a$ II
(9) | | | $\neg(Ex)(x = a)$ (3) (7) (8) NI
(10) | $Fa \supset \neg(Ex)(x = a)$ (2) (9) CI

We shall present two more examples of arguments whose validity turns on their constituent singular terms before training our methods on logical truths:

12. Pegasus has wings, but Nixon doesn't;
    The Flying Horse is Pegasus;
    Therefore, Nixon is not the Flying Horse.
13. The Absolute exists;
    At most the Absolute exists;
    So, all and only those things which exist are identical with the Absolute.

The validity of 12 is shown by the derivation below, letting "a" stand for "Pegasus", "b" for "Nixon", "c" for "the Flying Horse" and

"*F*" for "has wings":

(1)	Fa		$\therefore \neg (b = c)$
(2)	$\neg Fb$		
(3)	$c = a$		
(4)	$c = c$	II	
(5)	$a = c$	(3) (4) IE	
(6)	Fc	(1) (5) IE	
(7)		$b = c$	
(8)		$b = b$	II
(9)		$c = b$	(7) (8) IE
(10)		Fc	(6) R
(11)		Fb	(9) (10) IE
(12)		$\neg Fb$	(2) R
(13)	$\neg (b = c)$		(7) (11) (12) NI

To prove the validity of 13 let "*a*" stand for the "Absolute" and "*F*" for "exists". Then we have

(1)	Fa		$\therefore (x)(Fx \equiv x = a)$
(2)	$(x)(Fx \supset x = a)$		
(3)	y	$(x)(Fx \supset x = a)$	(2) R
(4)		$Fy \supset y = a$	(3) UQE
(5)		$y = a$	
(6)		$y = y$	II
(7)		$a = y$	(5) (6) IE
(8)		Fa	(1) R
(9)		Fy	(7) (8) IE
(10)		$y = a \supset Fy$	(5) (9) CI
(11)		$Fy \equiv y = a$	(4) (10) BI
(12)	$(x)(Fx \equiv x = a)$		(11) UQI

It must be pointed out here that the preceding valid argument cannot be inverted. That is, we cannot argue validly

$(x)(Fx \equiv x = z)$; hence Fa.

A counterexample to this inference is the following:

$(x)(x$ is both round and not round if and only if x is Pegasus); Hence, Pegasus is both round and not round.

The premise is true just because no existent is Pegasus, and no existent is both round and not round. If we were to make the assumption (rejected in our logic) that every name has a referent, then no such counterexample could be given. That is, the following slightly different inference is valid.

$$(x)(Fx \equiv x = a) \ \& \ (Ey)(y = a); \text{hence } Fa.$$

When there are no quantifiers in the premises (as in the second to last derivation), there is of course no need to add premises corresponding to the assumption that certain names refer to existents.

Some special terminology may help to bring out some features of derivations in which the difference between variables and other singular terms is crucial. Let us say that if t is any term, then $(t/x)B$ is a *specification* of $(x)B$. Note that even if $(x)B$ is a statement, some of its specifications may be quasi-statements. Thus 14–16 are specifications of 17:

14. $(x)Fx \supset Fy$
15. $(x)Fx \supset Fx$
16. $(x)Fx \supset Fb$
17. $(y)((x)Fx \supset Fy)$

But the following statement has only one specification:

18. $(y)((y)Py)$

namely, $(y)Py$. (For $(t/y)((y)Py)$ is just $(y)Py$.)

Now the first thing we must notice is that a statement may be true while some of its specifications are not true. For example, "Everything exists" is true, but its specification "Pegasus exists" is not true. The reason for this disparity is of course that we reserve variables for reference to things, but a name need not refer to anything. Thus 19 is derivable:

19. $(x)((Ey)(y = x))$

but its specification "$(Ey)(y = b)$" is not. Another such pair is

20. $(y)((x)(Ez)(z = x) \supset (Ez)(z = y))$
21. $(x)(Ez)(z = x) \supset (Ez)(z = a))$

So we cannot derive all statements that have the form of

22. $(x)A \supset (t/x)A$

but we can derive what all those statements are specifications of, namely,

23. $(y)((x)A \supset (y/x)A)$

For exactly similar reasons, we cannot accept that

24. $A \supset (Ex)(x/t)A$

is logically true, but we can derive

25. $(y)(A \supset (Ex)(x/y)A)$

For in a subderivation general in y we can infer $(y/x)A$ from $(x)A$, and $(Ex)(x/y)A$ from A. But nowhere can we infer $(a/x)A$ from $(x)A$ or $(Ex)(x/y)A$ from A.

It is only through the rules for identity that some logically true statements are such that all their specifications are true. Examples of these are

26. $(z)(x)(y)((x = z \& y = z) \supset x = y)$
27. $(x)(x = x)$

Why this is so we leave as an exercise.

However, from the logically true 23 and 25 we can infer what must be added in 22 and 24 to produce derivable statements. In place of 22 and 24 we have derivable

28. $(x)A \supset ((Ex)(x = t) \supset (t/x)A)$
29. $A(t/x) \supset ((Ex)(x = t) \supset (Ex)A)$

The reader should note the connections between 28 and RUQE and 29 and RSEQI.

Consider the following list of undetermined statements:

30. $(Ex)(x = a)$
31. $(x)(x = a \supset Fx) \supset Fa$
32. $(x)(x = a \supset Fx) \supset (Ex)(x = a \& Fx)$
33. $(Fa \lor \neg Fa) \supset ((Ex)(x = a \& Fx) \lor (Ex)(x = a \& \neg Fx))$
34. $(x)(Fx \equiv x = a) \supset (Fa \& (x)(Fx \supset x = a))$

These statements are not provable by our rules; logical truths can be gotten from them by taking them as consequents of conditionals whose antecedent is, in each case, "$(Ex)(x = a)$". The resulting conditionals *are* logically true. In short, 30–31 hold only on the condition that "*a*" is a referential name. Another interesting feature of 30–34 is this: if "*a*" is replaced by a variable, and the whole sentence is universally quantified with respect to that variable, then the result is logically true. This emphasizes that our treatment and more standard treatments of logic do *not* differ in their accounts of logical truth with respect to statements not containing singular terms other than variables.

Russell* once argued against the termlike character of expressions like "the present king of France" on the ground that the pair of sentences "the present king of France is wise" and "the present King of France is not wise" would violate the Law of Excluded Middle.. His argument apparently assumed the logical truth of 33 with "*a*" replaced by an expression like "the present king of France". For since there is no present king of France, the consequent of 33 is false and hence the antecedent is false also. In free logic Russell's argument does not go through because 33 is not logically true; it holds only on the condition that "*a*" actually refers. Consequently, Russell's argument only establishes that "the present king of France" does not refer and not that either the Law of Excluded Middle fails or that the expression in question is not a *singular term*. We shall derive the logical truth of restricted 33 and 34, and shall complete this section by showing the logical truth of 4 at the beginning of Section 2 and the logical truth of the following important statement:

$$35. \quad (x)((Ey)(y = x) \supset Fx) \supset (x)Fx$$

Proof of restricted 33:

(1)	$(Ex)(x = a)$	
(2)	$Fa \lor \neg Fa$	
(3)	Fa	
(4)	$(Ex)(x = a)$	(1) R
(5)	$a = a$	II
(6)	$a = a \,\&\, Fa$	(3) (5) KI
(7)	$(Ex)(x = a \,\&\, Fx)$	(4) (6) RSEQI
(8)	$(Ex)(x = a \,\&\, Fx) \lor (Ex)(x = a \,\&\, \neg Fx)$	(7) AI
(9)	$\neg Fa$	
(10)	$(Ex)(x = a)$	(1) R
(11)	$a = a$	II
(12)	$a = a \,\&\, \neg Fa$	(9) (11) KI
(13)	$(Ex)(x = a \,\&\, \neg Fx)$	(10) (12) RSEQI
(14)	$(Ex)(x = a \,\&\, Fx) \lor (Ex)(x = a \,\&\, \neg Fx)$	(13) AI
(15)	$(Ex)(x = a \,\&\, Fx) \lor (Ex)(x = a \,\&\, \neg Fx)$	(2) (3) (8) (9) (14) AE

---

*B. Russell, "On Denoting", in *Logic and Knowledge*, R. C. Marsh, ed. (London: George Allen & Unwin, 1956), p. 48.

Restricted 33, of course, follows now by two applications of CI.
   Proof of restricted 34:

$$
\begin{array}{lll}
(1) & (Ex)(x = a) & \\
(2) & \quad (x)(Fx \equiv x = a) & \\
(3) & \qquad y \mid Fy & \\
(4) & \qquad\quad (x)(Fx \equiv x = a) & (2)\ \text{R} \\
(5) & \qquad\quad Fy \equiv y = a & (4)\ \text{UQE} \\
(6) & \qquad\quad y = a & (3)\ (5)\ \text{BE} \\
(7) & \qquad Fy \supset y = a & (3)\ (6)\ \text{CI} \\
(8) & \qquad (x)(Fx \supset x = a) & (1)\ \text{R} \\
(9) & \qquad Fa \equiv a = a & (1)\ (8)\ \text{RUQE} \\
(10) & \qquad a = a & \text{II} \\
(11) & \qquad Fa & (9)\ (10)\ \text{BE} \\
(12) & \qquad Fa\ \&(x)(Fx \supset x = a) & (8)\ (11)\ \text{KI} \\
\end{array}
$$

Restricted 34 follows now by two uses of CI. This conditional says
that if a exists, then if all and only F are the same as a, then a, and a
only, is F. For example, that the Absolute (and the Absolute only)
exists if all and only existents are identical with the Absolute is the case
provided the Absolute exists. Free logic, it appears, offers little comfort
to the Friends of the Concrete Universal; for the argument is question-
begging with respect to the existence of the Absolute.
   The logical truth 4, which might be called the "Principle of Peculiarity", is derived by a *Reductio Ad Absurdum* kind of argument. The
assumption with which we begin, then, is the contradictory of 4, that
is, "$(x)(Ey)(y = a\ \&\ y \neq x)$ where "a" is "Hegel":

$$
\begin{array}{lll}
(1) & (x)(Ey)(y = a\ \&\ y \neq x) & \\
(2) & \quad z \mid (x)(Ey)(y = a\ \&\ y \neq x) & (1)\ \text{R} \\
(3) & \qquad (Ey)(y = z\ \&\ y \neq z) & (2)\ \text{UQI} \\
(4) & \qquad x \mid x = a\ \&\ y \neq z & \\
(5) & \qquad\quad x = a & (4)\ \text{KE} \\
(6) & \qquad\quad (Ey)(y = a) & (5)\ \text{SEQI} \\
(7) & \qquad (Ey)(y = a) & (3)\ (4)(6)\ \text{SEQE} \\
(8) & \qquad z_1 \mid z_1 = a & \\
(9) & \qquad\quad (Ex)(x = a) & (8)\ \text{SEQI} \\
(10) & \qquad (Ex)(x = a) & (7)\ (8)\ (9)\ \text{SEQE} \\
(11) & \qquad (Ey)(y = z\ \&\ y \neq a) & (1)(10)\ \text{RUQE} \\
(12) & \quad (x)(Ey)(y = a\ \&\ y \neq a) & (11)\ \text{UQI} \\
(13) & (Ey)(y = a\ \&\ y \neq a) & (12)\ \text{VQE} \\
\end{array}
$$

Since (13) leads immediately to contradiction, we obtain by NI the negation of (1), which is equivalent to 4.

The derivation of the logical truth of 35 is equally straightforward:

(1)	$(x)((Ey)(y = x) \supset Fx)$	
(2)	$z \mid (x)((Ey)(y = x) \supset Fx)$	(1) R
(3)	$(Ey)(y = z) \supset Fz$	(2) UQE
(4)	$z = z$	II
(5)	$(Ey)(y = z)$	(4) SEQI
(6)	Fz	(3)(5) CE
(7)	$(x)Fx$	(6) UQI

35, of course, follows now by a single application of CI.

Recall that "a exists" is symbolized by "$(Ey)(y = a)$". With the help of 35, letting F be "$(Ey)(y = \ldots)$", we obtain "$(x)((Ey)(y = x) \supset (Ey)(y = x))$", that is, that every existent exists. 35 thus can be viewed as making explicit the range of the quantifier context "$(x)(\ldots x \ldots)$"; hence of the quantifier context "$(Ex)(\ldots x \ldots)$". The latter is equivalent to "$(Ex)((Ey)(y = x) \& \ldots x \ldots)$". In other words, the quantifiers range over the existents. On the other hand, failure of "$(Ey)(y = a)$" to be logically true makes explicit in the object language that singular terms do *not* invariably refer.

SECTION 4
TABLEAU RULES FOR UNANALYZED SINGULAR TERMS

Virtually no changes in the rules for constructing counterexamples other than those discussed in Section 2 on inference rules for simple singular terms are needed. It suffices, therefore, to rewrite I and CI with $t, t_1 \ldots$ and so on, in the place of the variable designators. Thus we have

$$\text{I} \quad \frac{X \& t = t_1 \& Y}{(t_1/t) \ (X \& Y)}$$

CI   If a conjunct contains $t \neq t$, underline it.

Essentially the justification for the above extensions of I and CI is present already in the discussion of extended II and IE in Section 2. Thus, for example, since $t = t$ is true for all t, it is clear that $t \neq t$ is false for all t. Hence $t \neq t$ is inconsistent. So much is reflected, of course, in the convention that when $t \neq t$ occurs in a conjunct, underline it. The reader may interpolate the justification for I from the discussion of extended IE.

Again, as in the case of the inference rules RUQE and RSEQI, one would expect the tableau rule Ul to hold for unanalyzed singular terms only under the restriction that these singular terms actually refer. Thus suppose that the variables $u_1 \ldots u_n$ in Ul are replaced by $t_1 \ldots t_n$. Then one can prove the inconsistency of, for example "$(x)(x$ exists$)$ & Ichabod Crane does not exist". But, as suggested in the previous section, free logic can be construed as counting the (undetermined) statement "$(x)Fx$ & $\neg Fa$" consistent if "a" does not refer; indeed it must, given the relationship between logical truth and inconsistency recounted in the previous chapters. For if "$(x)Fx$ & $\neg Fa$" where "a" is non-referential were inconsistent, its denial "$\neg((x)Fx$ & $\neg Fa)$" would be logically true; and this would contradict the established claims of Sections 2 and 3 in this chapter. Hence we shall *not* amend Ul so as to allow substitution of names for variables in its application. However, we may use a derived inconsistency rule RUl analogous to the derived rule RUQE:

$$\text{RUl} \qquad \frac{X \,\&\, (x)\, A \,\&\, Y}{X \,\&\, (t_1/x)A \,\&\, \ldots \,\&\, (t_n/x)\, A \,\&\, Y \,\&\, (x)\, A}$$

where $i = 1, \ldots, n$, t_i is a free variable in X & (x) A & Y, or t_i is a name and $(Ey)(y = t_i)$ is a conjunct in X or Y, for some variable y. The derivation of this rule is of course easy by a use of the rule RUQE.

Notice that Ur is not a tableau or counterexample rule applying to singular terms, referential or non-referential. It is analogous to SEQE in this respect and not analogous to RUQE.

Finally, we note that the relationship (outlined in Chapter 4) between our natural deduction technique and our counterexample procedure carries over to our extended procedures in this chapter. The only difference is that now there may occur logical truths and inconsistent statements containing no free variables but whose logical truth or inconsistency cannot be determined merely by the inference and counterexample rules for the logic of statements and/or general terms. Nevertheless it still is true that if A is a formula which contains no free variables and is inconsistent by our counterexample rules, then $\neg A$ is logically true by our inference rules. We end this chapter with two illustrations of this point. We shall show that "$a = b \supset b = a$" and "$(Ey)(y = a) \supset (Fa \supset (Ey)(Fy))$" are valid. This is the case if, respectively, "$a = b$ & $\neg(b = a)$" and "$(Ey)(y = a)$ & $\neg(Fa \supset (Ey)(Fy))$" are inconsistent.

The inconsistency (logical falsehood) of "$a = b \mathbin{\&} \neg(b = a)$" is evident in the failure of the following counterexample:

$$
\begin{array}{ll}
(1) & \lfloor\ a = b \mathbin{\&} \neg(b = a) \\
(2) & \lceil\ \underline{a = a \mathbin{\&} \neg(a = a)} \qquad (1)\ \mathrm{I} \\
\end{array}
$$

The logical truth of the formula in question is shown by the following categorical derivation:

$$
\begin{array}{lll}
(1) & \quad\ \lfloor\ a = b & \\
(2) & \quad\ \lceil\ a = a & \mathrm{II} \\
(3) & \quad\ \lfloor\ b = a & (1)\ (2)\ \mathrm{IE} \\
(4) & \lfloor\ a = b \supset b = a & (1)\ (3)\ \mathrm{CI} \\
\end{array}
$$

That "$(Ey)(y = a) \mathbin{\&} (Fa \supset (Ey)Fy)$" is logically false is clear from the following:

$$
\begin{array}{lll}
(1) & \lfloor\ (Ey)(y = a) \mathbin{\&} \neg(Fa \supset (Ey)Fy) & \\
(2) & \lceil\ (Ey)(y = a) \mathbin{\&} Fa \mathbin{\&} \neg(Ey)Fy & (1)\ \mathrm{NC} \\
(3) & \mid\ \neg(y)\ \neg(y = a) \mathbin{\&} Fa \mathbin{\&} \neg(Ey)Fy & (2)\ \mathrm{EI} \\
(4) & \mid\ \neg\neg(z = a) \mathbin{\&} Fa \mathbin{\&} \neg(Ey)Fy & (3)\ \mathrm{Ur} \\
(5) & \mid\ z = a \mathbin{\&} Fa \mathbin{\&} \neg(Ey)Fy & (4)\ \mathrm{DN} \\
(6) & \mid\ z = a \mathbin{\&} Fa \mathbin{\&} \neg Fz & (5)\ \mathrm{Er} \\
(7) & \mid\ z = a \mathbin{\&} Fa \mathbin{\&} \neg Fz & (6)\ \mathrm{Ul} \\
(8) & \lfloor\ \underline{Fa \mathbin{\&} \neg Fa} & (7)\ \mathrm{I} \\
\end{array}
$$

The following categorical derivation establishes the logical truth of "$(Ey)(y = a) \supset (Fa \supset (Ey)Fy)$".

$$
\begin{array}{lll}
(1) & \quad\ \lfloor\ (Ey)(y = a) & \\
(2) & \quad\quad\ \lfloor\ Fa & \\
(3) & \quad\quad\ \lceil\ (Ey)(y = a) & (1)\ \mathrm{R} \\
(4) & \quad\quad\ \mid\ (Ey)Fy & (2)\ (3)\ \mathrm{RSEQI} \\
(5) & \quad\ \lfloor\ Fa \supset (Ey)Fy & (2)\ (4)\ \mathrm{CI} \\
(6) & \lfloor\ (Ey)(y = a) \supset (Fa \supset (Ey)Fy) & (1)\ (5)\ \mathrm{CI} \\
\end{array}
$$

EXERCISES

1. Establish the validity of the following arguments:
    (a) There are no nonentities. So, at most one theory is a nonentity.
    (b) No one who is not an absolute Idealist is identical with Hegel. Hegel, who actually exists, is not an absolute Idealist. So, all philosophers are Logical Positivists.

(c) No number is greater than itself. For any three numbers, if the first is greater than the second and the second is greater than the third, then the first is greater than the third. Hence, for any pair of numbers, if the first is greater than the second, the second is not greater than the first.

(d) A given thing is a member of itself if and only if it is the same as the set that does not contain itself as a member and is not a member of itself. Therefore, the set that does not contain itself as a member does not exist.

(e) Something is a god, and at most one thing is a god. So there is exactly one god.

2. Produce categorical derivations for the following undetermined statements:

(a) $(x)(Mx \supset Nx) \supset \cdot (Ex)Mx \supset (Ex)Nx$

(b) $(Ex)(Mx \supset (y)My)$

(c) $(x)[(y)(y = x \supset My) \equiv (Ey)(y = x \& My)]$

(d) $(Ex)(x = a) \equiv [(Ex)(x = a \& \neg Mx) \lor (Ex)(x = a \& Mx)]$

(e) $(x)(Mx \supset Nx) \supset (x)[(Ey)(Oxy \& Mx) \supset (Ey)(Nx \& Oxy)]$

3. Establish the consistency or inconsistency of the following sets of undetermined statements:

(a) $(Ex)(Mx \supset \neg S), (x)Mx, Ma$

(b) $(Ey)(x)(Rxy), (Ex)(y)(\neg Rxy)$

(c) $(Ex)(x = a), b = a, (y)(\neg (y = a \equiv y = b))$

(d) $(a = b \& b = c) \supset a = c, a = a, (Ex)(\neg x = b \lor b = x)$

(e) $(x)((Ey)(Ny \& \neg Oxy) \supset \neg Mx), (x)(Px \supset Nx),$
$\neg (y)[Py \supset \neg (z)(Qz \supset Oyz)], (x)(y)(z)[(Oxy \& Oyz) \supset Oxy],$
$(Ex)[Mx \& (Ez(Qz \& \neg Qxz)]$

4. Suppose the set of intelim rules in Chapter 6 are supplemented by the following rules:

$$y \left| \begin{array}{l} \dots \\ \end{array} \right. \begin{array}{|l} (x)A \\ \underline{E!t} \\ \overline{(t/x)A} \end{array} \qquad y \left| \begin{array}{l} \dots \\ \end{array} \right. \begin{array}{|l} (x)(E!x \supset A) \\ \overline{(x)A} \end{array}$$

Now show that $E!t \equiv (Ex)(x = t)$ is a categorically derivable. (This result is due originally to Jaakko Hintikka. See his paper "Studies in the Logic of Existence and Necessity. I. Existence", *The Monist*, 50, (1966), 54–76.)

5. Show that $E!t \equiv (Ex)(x = t \& E!x)$ is categorically derivable, given the rules for the predicate $E!$ in Exercise 4.

6. Is $(x)(x = t \equiv x = t') \equiv t = t'$ categorically derivable?

7. Is $(x)(Fx \equiv Gx) \& Ft \& \neg Gt$ consistent or inconsistent? How about $(x)(Fx \equiv Gx) \& \neg Ft \& Gt$?

7 Analyzed Singular Terms

We have so far treated all singular terms as unanalyzed units. In this chapter, we shall analyze the internal structure of such terms, and discuss logical truths and arguments to which this structure is crucial.

ARGUMENTS AND DEFINITE DESCRIPTIONS

In Part One we treated statements as units when they were not constructed by the use of certain connectives. By the rules of that part, we could demonstrate the validity of

> 1. Roderick Spode is a cad;
>   Therefore, Roderick Spode is a cad or a bounder

but we could not demonstrate the validity of

> 2. Everything perishes,
>   Therefore, everything perishes or remains.

Yet 2 has as much claim to validity as 1, and that is why, in Part Two, we began to analyze the internal structure of statements that are not built up out of other statements by connectives.

We now face a similar situation. In the preceding chapter, all singular terms were treated as units. By those rules, we cannot demonstrate the validity of

148

3. Quine is the author of *Word and Object*;
Quine is the existent Edgar Peirce Professor of Philosophy;
Therefore, the Edgar Peirce Professor of Philosophy wrote
Word and Object.

Yet this is a valid argument, and is valid, in part, because of relations
between the complex singular terms "the author of *Word and Object*"
and "the Edgar Peirce Professor of Philosophy".

There are unfortunately a large variety of singular terms. Consider
the following examples:

(a)   John
(b)   you
(c)   your father
(d)   the father of John
(e)   fatherhood
(f)   3 + 2
(g) $\sqrt{2}$
(h)   a certain father
(i)   that snow is white
(j)   running

Without much effort, we can satisfy ourselves that each of these terms
can be the subject of a verb in third person singular, *and* each of them
at least purports to refer to a single thing. And without much further
effort we could find still more grammatical variety among singular terms.

While we cannot hope to do justice to all these kinds of terms, we
do wish to point out that many can be paraphrased adequately by what
are called *definite descriptions*. The English form of a definite description is "the (one and only) thing which is ...". Some of the above
examples can be paraphrased as follows:

(c′)   the thing which is a father of you
(d′)   the thing which is a father of John
(f′)   the thing which is a sum of 3 and 2
(g′)   the thing which is a square root of 2

It is important to note that the word "the" is meant to convey that the
description in question is supposed to be unique. In the case of "your
father" that condition cannot help but be satisfied. But if I say "your
brother", and you have two brothers, then I am being ambiguous; I

should say, for example, "your elder brother", or "your younger brother".

The other examples cannot be so paraphrased in a way that is at once significant and straightforward, so we shall continue to treat them as units. In general, there is no harm in phrasing the definite descriptions in a more idiomatic way. The idiomatic forms of the above paraphrases are, of course,

> (c″) the father of you
> (d″) the father of John
> (f″) the sum of 3 and 2
> (g″) the square root of 2

But the single primed forms are the official ones; they are the ones (as we shall see) which can be symbolized directly. In the next subsection we shall treat the paraphrase and symbolization of argument 3 in detail.

In the ensuing discussion we will confine ourselves mainly to the topics of the validity (logical truth) of arguments (statements) containing definite descriptions. In Part Four we shall take up briefly the topic of counterexample rules for proving the inconsistency (logical falsehood) of sets of statements containing definite descriptions.

Because there has been considerable philosophical controversy over the topic of definite descriptions for more than fifty years, our procedure in this chapter will differ a bit from that in the preceding chapters. First we shall, as before, make some informal remarks about the changes required in the official idiom to accommodate definite descriptions. Secondly, we shall introduce and explain the inference rules for the logic of definite descriptions in the context of a critical account of the Meinong-Russell debate.

SECTION 2
DEFINITE DESCRIPTIONS AND THE OFFICIAL IDIOM

Our official idiom already comprises all (English) singular terms, including those which are definite descriptions. So any definite description may be abbreviated to a lower-case letter from the beginning of the alphabet (just as any statement may be abbreviated to a capital letter). But, in addition, we may abbreviate a definite description in another way, which will bring out its internal structure.

As an example, consider the term "my mother's father". We can treat this as a unit, and abbreviate it to "a". On the other hand, we can paraphrase it into "the father of my mother" (in which "my mother" is an unanalyzed subunit), and then further into "the thing which is a father of my mother". As with quantifiers, "thing which" becomes "x such that x"; so we arrive at

    the x such that x is a father of my mother

Noting that "is a father of" is a two-place predicate, we can abbreviate this to

    the x such that Rxa

where "a" abbreviates "my mother" and "R" abbreviates "is a father of". Finally, we shall abbreviate "the x such that" to "Ix". The symbol "I" (an upper case English "I") is a new logical symbol, and will be used to denote itself just as the other logical symbols do.

It is clear that by the use of variables we have concocted expressions that are not English expressions, so we are adding to our official idiom. The addition is exactly this: if A is any statement or quasi-statement, and x is a variable, then $(Ix)A$ is a singular term in our official idiom. The English terms to which it corresponds can be found by reflecting on the paraphrasing procedure outlined above. We shall call all the new terms that we have added *(definite) descriptions* of our official idiom. The letter "t" with or without subscripts will now be a metavariable for both variables and singular terms including all descriptions.

In a definite description $(Ix)A$, we say that the description operator (Ix) binds all the free occurrences of x in A. Thus in the sentence "$(Px \supset Qx)$", x has two free occurrences; in the sentence "$P(Ix)(Px \supset Qx)$", x has no free occurrences. In this way description operators are like quantifiers. Now, there can still be free occurrences of variables inside a definite description. Thus, in "$(Ix)(Px \supset Qy)$", y has a free occurrence. We call a description *proper* if no variables occur free in it, and *improper* otherwise. In a sentence containing an improper description, a quantifier may bind the free occurrences of a variable inside that description. As an example, consider "John is someone's father". We can paraphrase this into "There is someone such that John is his (or her) father", and more explicitly into "There is some y such that John is the father of y". Using obvious abbreviations, this is symbolized as

    $(Ey)(j = (Ix)(Rxy))$

We may read the improper description "$(Ix)Rxy$" informally as "the father of y"; in our paraphrases this will correspond to English descriptive phrases containing pronouns.

Descriptions, like names, can be either referential or non-referential. "The author of *Word and Object*" is referential; "the queen of the U.S." is non-referential.

Finally, we want to add a cautionary note. The remarks in Chapter 5 may suggest support for the philosophic view that there is some absolute distinction between grammatically proper names and definite descriptions. No such thing is intended, however. True, we did take names as our prime examples of unanalyzed singular terms; but that was a heuristic device on a par with illustrating and explaining the logic of statements only with singular statements. We do not intend to argue for some philosophical or linguistic reason which discriminates between names as unanalyzable singular terms and descriptions as analyzable singular terms; but equally we do not wish to legislate against those philosophers who think there is no absolute distinction between names and descriptions. Our attitude rather is that expressed at the beginning of the last section; the question of whether an expression like "the author of *Word and Object*" is to be treated as an unanalyzed singular term or as an analyzed singular term is dependent on the inferential purpose at hand. In this respect, to reemphasize the analogy, the logic of descriptions is like that of statements. For some inferential purposes, "All men are mortal" is most simply treated as an unanalyzed unit; for other purposes, as described in Chapters 4 and 5, the statement in question must be analyzed further. In short, our logic is compatible either with the thesis that names are eliminable in favor of descriptions or with its denial. Nevertheless, as we shall see in the next section, our logic of descriptions does have a philosophical basis, and one which does run contrary to that tradition proceeding from Russell's treatment of descriptional inference in *Principia Mathematica*.

SECTION 3
THE RUSSELL-MEINONG DEBATE

We have characterized definite descriptions as *singular terms*, and in our official idiom both "the father of Mary" and "$(Ix)(x$ is a father of Mary$)$" appear. The former may be paraphrased into the latter when an argument is being analyzed, but it need not be so paraphrased. For we can give a shallow analysis, treating "the father of Mary" as a unit by itself, or a less shallow analysis in which we regard "the father of

Mary" as being somehow constructed out of the singular term "Mary" and the two-place predicate "is a father of".

This point of view concerning descriptions was contested by Bertrand Russell, who argued that definite descriptions cannot be treated as singular terms. According to Russell, if an English sentence contains a definite description, then we must first paraphrase it into a sentence not containing a definite description prior to symbolization. And he provided a procedure for such paraphrases.

Russell's theory of descriptions seems to have originated in an exchange with the German philosopher A. Meinong at the turn of the century. According to Meinong, there is a widespread "prejudice in favor of the actual" among philosophers causing them to overlook the fact that "the totality of what exists . . . is infinitely small in comparison with the Objects of knowledge".* Meinong's point can be put quite simply; a singular term, for example, "the gold mountain", need not refer (that is, refer to an existing thing) to occur in a *true* statement.

Meinong made virtually the same point in another way; being-thus-and-so (Sosein), he said, is independent of being (Sein).** The gold mountain, for example, may be thus-and-so even though it does not exist. For Meinong, then, the principle

1. if t is F then t exists

is unacceptable. This principle concerns any singular term t and, of course, is familiar from earlier chapters.

What evidence did Meinong have for rejecting 1? Meinong held that "the gold mountain is made of gold, and the round square is surely round". In general, he seems to have believed that any statement of the form

2. The thing which is F, is F

is logically true. But since some instances of 2 are about nonexistent objects, indeed even about objects that could not possibly exist, he therefore rejected 1.

Russell vigorously challenged Meinong's analysis. 2, he held, has two immediate, catastrophic consequences which demolish its claim to being a logical truth; 2 yields

---

Realism and the Background of Phenomenology, R. Chisholm (ed.), (Glencoe, Illinois: The Free Press, 1960), p. 79. This volume contains a translation of some relevant work of Meinong. Russell's articles in the exchange with Meinong are in *Mind*, 1904–1905.

**Ibid.*, p. 82.

3. The thing which is round and not round is round, and also is not round

and

4. The existent gold mountain is an existent gold mountain.

4, however, is false and 3 is *logically* false. In symbols, 2–4 are

2′. $F(Ix)Fx$
3′. $F(Ix)(Fx \& \neg Fx) \& \neg F(Ix)(Fx \& \neg Fx)$
4′. $E!(Ix)(E!x \& Fx) \& F(Ix)(E!x \& Fx)$

where "F", in 3′ abbreviates "is round", in 4′ abbreviates "golden mountain" and is undetermined in 2′, and where "E!" abbreviates "exists".

To example 4 Meinong answered that the existent gold mountain is an existent but doesn't exist. This purely verbal maneuver would not have worked had Russell used "The gold mountain which exists is a gold mountain which exists" in place of 4. To 3 Meinong replied that the law of non-condition does not apply to non-existents. But, Russell objected, this reply rests on a misunderstanding of the law of non-contradiction; it is not about any objects, existent or otherwise, but rather concerns what sorts of statements can be rationally conjoined.

Russell concluded that one cannot, after all, consistently reject the interdependence of being and being-thus-and-so. He then offered an "analysis" of descriptions according to which a statement applying a *simple** predicate to a non-referential description cannot be true. Indeed, Russell regarded it as a "great advantage" of his proposal that it renders every ascription of a property to a nonexistent false.** According to Russell, the undetermined statement

5. The such and such is so and so

is true just in case the conjunction of

(a) There is at least one such and such;
(b) There is at most one such and such;
(c) Whatever is such and such is so and so

---

*Complex predicates lead to some complexities in his theory that will be discussed in Chapter 10.

**B. Russell, "On Denoting", in *Readings in Philosophical Analysis*, H. Feigl and W. Sellars (ed.), (New York: Appleton-Century-Crofts, 1949), p. 106.

is true. In symbols this amounts to

> 5′. $G(Ix)Fx$

5′ is true just in case

> 6. $(Ey)(Fy \,\&\, (x)(Fx \supset x = y) \,\&\, Gy)$

is true. Now if "G" is "is gold" and "F" is "is a gold mountain", then "the gold mountain is gold" is false in Russell's theory because conjunct (a), suitably interpreted, is false.

Russell believed that difficulties of the above sort in Meinong's theory are the inevitable consequence of *any* "natural" theory that allows some descriptions to be non-referential but which regards descriptions as "*genuine constituents* of the proposition in whose verbal expressions they occur", that is, as *terms*.* The ability of his theory to avoid the pitfalls of those theories like Meinong's that take descriptions, referential and non-referential, as terms, he regarded as the major source of evidence in favor of his theory.** Russell had other inclining reasons for the view that definite descriptions are not terms. One consideration was the following: the interdependence of being and being-thus-and-so requires that every statement ascribing a property to a non-existent be false. But what then of such statements as "The gold mountain is identical with the gold mountain", which ascribes the property of being identical with itself to the gold mountain? One might feel compelled to assert the self-identity of the gold mountain in virtue of its form alone. For it appears to be an instance of $t = t$; hence it is not only true, but *logically* true. Russell's solution to this problem was to deny that expressions of the form "the so and so" are genuine constituents of the statements in which they occur, that is, to deny that they are isolable *subjects* in the statements in which they occur. To be sure, he observed, English grammar suggests otherwise; "the gold mountain" in "The gold mountain is identical with the gold mountain" is the grammatical subject of that sentence. But grammar is as misleading with respect to logical form in this case as it is in the case of "the whale" in "The whale is a mammal".

Ibid., p. 106. This was in opposition to the theory of descriptions developed by the German philosopher and mathematician Gottlob Frege. Frege's most common theory assigns some entity to all referential definite descriptions. And though Russell seems to have believed that Frege's maneuver does not lead to inconsistency, he dismissed it as "clearly artificial".

**Ibid.*, p. 106.

Since Russell set such great store in the belief that descriptions are not terms, we shall present two independent arguments that he uses to bolster his position. First, Russell considers the statement "George IV wished to know whether Scott was the author of *Waverly*, but he did not wish to know whether Scott was Scott". Then he argues

> ... as we have just seen, you may turn a true proposition into a false one by substituting "Scott" for "the author of *Waverley*". This shows that it is necessary to distinguish between a name and a description: "Scott" is a name, but "the author of *Waverley*" is a description.*

Since purely referential names are the only genuine singular terms for Russell, descriptions, he concludes, cannot be terms. His second argument against descriptions as terms is as follows:

> The central point of the theory of descriptions was that a phrase may contribute to the meaning of a sentence without having any meaning at all in isolation. Of this, in the case of descriptions, there is precise proof: If "the author of *Waverley*" meant anything other than "Scott", "Scott is the author of *Waverley*" would be false, which it is not. If "the author of *Waverley*" meant "Scott", "Scott is the author of *Waverley*" would be a tautology (i.e., logically true), which it is not. Therefore, "the author of *Waverley*" means neither "Scott" nor anything else—i.e., "the author of *Waverley*" means nothing, Q.E.D.**

Whether these arguments are valid, we shall examine presently.

To recapitulate, the two related convictions, that reason requires acceptance of the interdependence of being and being-thus-and-so and that descriptions are not terms, let alone singular terms, are the cornerstones of Russell's famous theory. In accordance with the first conviction, he regarded it as a virtue of his theory that any statements applying a *simple* predicate to a non-referential description is false; the second conviction lies behind his oft-cited claim that sentences like "the such and such is so and so" are merely *abbreviations* for sentences in which "the" does not occur.

Russell was convinced that Meinong's theory—and, indeed *any* "natural" theory that takes descriptions, referential and non-referential, as terms, that is, as "genuine constituents" of the statements in which

---

My Philosophical Development (London: George Allen & Unwin, 1959), p. 84.

**Ibid.*, p. 85.

they occur—results in "logical error".* It is ironic that his own theory apparently results in part from a logical error; for it does *not* follow that rejection of the logical truth of "the such and such is such and such" requires acceptance of the interdependence of being and being-thus-and-so. One can quite consistently reject *both* the claim that "the such and such is such and such" is logically true *and* the interdependence of being and being-thus-and-so as a principle. But apparently Russell did not see this as a possibility. What Russell's arguments against Meinong show is that the independence of being and being-thus-and-so is not *always* acceptable. In other words, if, with Meinong, we think of descriptions as terms, and hence of 1 as an accurate symbolic statement of the interdependence of being and being-thus-and-so, then rejection of 2 shows *only* that some of the evidence for the falsity of 1 rests on quicksand. Since rejection of the interdependence of being and being-thus-and-so does not lead to "logical error", Russell's basic motivation for the view that descriptions cannot be regarded as "genuine constituents" of the statements in which they occur collapses.

Nor are his pair of independent arguments (cited above) in favor of descriptions as non-terms plausible. The first argument, which purports to show a fundamental distinction between referential names and descriptions, shows no such thing. Consider the person who had the name "Cicero" and also the name "Tully". Someone who does not know this fact may well wish to know whether Tully was Cicero, but presumably not whether Cicero is Cicero. The second argument is valid but unsound because it rests on an ambiguity. For the first premise to be true "t_1 means t_2" must amount to "t_1 and t_2 have the same referent". But then the second premise is not true since if t_1 and t_2 merely *happen* to refer to the same thing, then "$t_1 = t_2$" is not logically true. To make the second premise true, "t_1 means t_2" needs to have the force of "t_1 and t_2 cannot have different referents"; but then, the first premise is not true.

SECTION 4
INTELIM RULES FOR DEFINITE DESCRIPTIONS

All of the rules of Chapter 5 carry over to analyzed singular terms. Accordingly,

1. $(Ix)Fx = (Ix)Fx$

---

*B. Russell, "On Denoting" *op. cit.,* p. 108.

is logically true, hence true. Russell's analysis of descriptions, since it renders 1 false, where F fails to be true of at least one thing or is true of more than one thing, is unacceptable. On the other hand, Russell's theory, liberalized to allow descriptions as terms, is acceptable *on the condition that the description is referential.* This implies that any statement of the form

$$2. \ (Ey)(y = (Ix)Fx) \supset [G(Ix)Fx \equiv$$
$$(Ey)(Fy \ \& \ (x)(Fx \supset x = y) \ \& \ Gy)]$$

is logically true. From this we can deduce that if the so-and-so exists, that is, if $(Ey)(y = (Ix)Fx)$, then there is exactly one thing which is so-and-so. Russell's analysis implies the converse of this; and that also seems entirely acceptable. Thus we have

$$3. \ [(Ey)(y = (Ix)Fx)] \equiv [(Ey)(Fy \ \& \ (x)(Fx \supset \ x = y))]$$

or, somewhat shorter

$$3'. \ [(Ey)(y = (Ix)Fx)] \equiv [(Ey)(x)(Fx \equiv x = y))]$$

From 2 and 3 we can deduce a restricted case of $F(Ix)Fx$:

$$4. \ (Ey)(y = (Ix)Fx) \supset F(Ix)Fx$$

(1)	$(Ey)(y = (Ix)Fx)$	
(2)	$F(Ix)Fx \equiv (Ey)(Fy \ \& \ (x)(Fx \supset x = y) \ \& \ Fy)$	(1) (2) CE
(3)	$(Ey)(Fy \ \& \ (x)(Fx \supset x = y))$	(1) (3) CE
(4)	$(Ey)(Fy \ \& \ (x)(Fx \supset x = y \ \& \ Fy)$	(3)
(5)	$F(Ix)Fx$	(2) (4) BE
(6)	$(Ey)(y = (Ix)Fx) \supset F(Ix)Fx$	(1) (5) CI

It is interesting and easy to see that 3 can be deduced from

$$5. \ (y) \ [y = (Ix)Fx \cdot \equiv \cdot (x)(Fx \equiv x = y)]$$

where x and y are distinct variables. It is even more interesting that we can also deduce 2 from 5 as follows:

(1) $(Ey)(y = (Ix)Fx)$
(2) $z \mid z = (Ix)Fx$
(3) $G(Ix)Fx$
(4) Gz (2) (3) IE
(5) $(y)(y = (Ix)Fx \equiv (x)(Fx \equiv x = y))$ (5)
(6) $z = (Ix)Fx \equiv (x)(Fx \equiv x = z)$ (5) UQE
(7) $(x)(Fx \equiv x = z)$ (2) (6) BE
(8) $(x)(Fx \equiv x = z) \,\&\, Gz$ (3) (7) KI
(9) $(Ey)((x)(Fx \equiv x = y) \,\&\, Gy)$ (8) SEQI
(10) $(Ey)((x)(Fx \equiv x = y) \,\&\, Gy)$
(11) $z \mid (x)(Fx \equiv x = z) \,\&\, Gz$
(12) $(y)(y = (Ix)Fx \equiv (x)(Fx \equiv x = y))$ (5)
(13) $z = (Ix)Fx \equiv (x)(Fx \equiv x = z)$ (12) UQE
(14) $(x)(Fx \equiv x = z)$ (11) KI
(15) $z = (Ix)Fx$ (13) (14) BE
(16) Gz (11) KE
(17) $G(Ix)Fx$ (15) (16) II
(18) $G(Ix)Fx$ (10) (11) (17) SEQE
(19) $G(Ix)Fx \equiv (Ey)((x)(Fx \equiv x = y) \,\&\, Gy)$ (3) (9) (10) (18) BI
(20) $G(Ix)Fx \equiv (Ey)((x)(Fx \equiv x = y) \,\&\, Gy)$ (1) (2) (19) SEQE

The desired conditional follows by a single application of CI from (1) and (20).

Similarly 5 can be deduced from 2, 3, and 4. The derivation sketch is as follows:

(1) $z \mid z = (Ix)Fx$
(2) $(Ey)(y = (Ix)Fx)$ (1) SEQI
(3) $F(Ix)Fx$ (2) 4, CE
(4) Fz (1)(3) IE
(5) $(Ey)((x)(Fx \equiv x = y)$ (2) 3'. BE
(6) $x' \mid (x)(Fx \equiv x = x')$ where x' is a new variable
(7) $Fz \equiv z = x'$ (6) UQE
(8) $z = x'$ (4) (7) BE
(9) $(x)(Fx \equiv x = z)$ (6) (8) IE
(10) $(x)(Fx \equiv x = z)$ (5) (6) (9) SEQE
(11) $(x)(Fx \equiv x = z)$
(12) $(Ey)((x)(Fx \equiv x = y))$ (11) SEQI
(13) $(Ey)(y = (Ix)Fx)$ (12) 3'. CE
(14) $x' \mid x' = (Ix)Fx$ where x' is a new variable
(15) $F(Ix)Fx$ (13) 4. CE
(16) Fx' (14) (15) IE
(17) $Fx' \equiv x' = z$ (11) UQE
(18) $x' = z$ (16) (17) BE
(19) $z = (Ix)Fx$ (14) (18) IE
(20) $z = (Ix)Fx$ (13) (14) (19) SEQE
(21) $z = (Ix)Fx \equiv (x)(Fx \equiv x = z)$ (1) (10) (11) (20) BI

The desired conclusion follows by one application of UQI to line (21).

Given 5 as a basis, we have therefore a pair of intelim rules for a *minimal free description theory*, which we shall call FD:

$$\text{RDE } y \ \Big| \ \dots \ \Big| \ y = (Ix)A$$

$$\cdot$$
$$\cdot$$
$$\cdot$$

$$\dots \ \Big| \ (y/x)A \ \& \ (x)(A \supset x = y)$$

$$\text{RDI } y \qquad (y/x)A$$
$$(x)(A \supset x = y)$$

where x and y are different variables

$$\cdot$$
$$\cdot$$
$$\cdot$$

$$y = (Ix)Fx$$

So FD agrees exactly with Russell's theory in the treatment of referring descriptions.

To illustrate the use of our intelim rules for descriptions we shall now prove the validity of a pair of arguments. Consider, first, the argument about the Edgar Peirce Professor of Philosophy at the beginning of this chapter. Let "*a*" be "Quine", "*W*" be "wrote *Word and Object*", and "*b*" be "The Edgar Peirce Professor of Philosophy". Then the argument may be symbolized and proved valid as follows:

(1)	$a = (Ix)(Wx)$	$\therefore Wb$
(2)	$b = a \ \& \ (Ey)(y = b)$	
(3)	$(Ey)(y = b)$	(2) KE
(4)	$z \ \big| \ z = b$	
(5)	$b = a$	(2) KE, R
(6)	$z = a$	(4) (5) IE
(7)	$z = (Ix)Wx$	(1) (6) IE
(8)	$Wz \ \& \ (x)(Wx \supset x = z)$	(7) RDE
(9)	Wz	(8) KE
(10)	Wb	(4) (9) IE
(11)	Wb	(3) (4) (9) SEQE

RDE is used in step (8).

As a second example consider the following argument:

> There is exactly one apple in the barrel and it is rotten;
> Therefore, the apple in the barrel is rotten.

Letting "F" be "is an apple in the barrel" and "G" be "is rotten", the argument may be symbolized and proved valid as follows:

(1) | $(Ey)(Fy \& (x)(Fy \supset x =y) \& Gy)$ | | $\therefore G(Ix)Fx$
(2) | $z \lfloor Fz \&(x)(Fx \supset x = z) \& Gz$
(3) | $\lceil Fz \&(x)(Fx \supset x = z)$ | (2) KE
(4) | $z = (Ix)Fx$ | (3) RDI
(5) | Gz | (2) KE
(6) | $G(Ix)Fx$ | (4) (5) IE
(7) | $G(Ix)Fx$ | (1) (2) (6), (SEQE)

Step (4) involves an application of RDI. Other examples requiring RDE and RDI are provided in the exercises below.

EXERCISES

1. Demonstrate the validity of the following arguments:
   i. There is more than one author of *Principia Mathematica*. So the author of *Principia Mathematica* does not exist.
   ii. A philosopher is an Intuitionist if and only if he is a philosopher from the University of Amsterdam. The philosopher from the University of Amsterdam exists. Therefore, the philosopher from the University of Amsterdam is the philosopher who is an Intuitionist.
   iii. Socrates is not the same as the object which is Socrates. So Socrates does not exist.
   iv. Every person is the same as the person who is himself. Hence the person who is himself is a person.
   v. The man who came to dinner does not exist. So, no one is a man who came to dinner or more than one is a man who came to dinner.

2. Produce categorical derivations or intuitive counterexamples for the following:
   i. $\neg (Ey)(y = (Ix)(x \neq x))$
   ii. $t = (Ix) Fx \supset F(Ix)Fx$
   iii. $t = (Ix)Fx \supset (Ex)(y)(Fy \supset y = x)$
   iv. $(Ey)(y = (Ix)(Fx) \supset (Iy)(Fx) = (Iy)((Ey)(y = (Ix)Fx \& Fy)))$
   v. $(x)(Fx \equiv x = t) \supset (Ix)Fx = (Ix)(x = t)$

3. Suppose x does not occur free in A. Under what conditions does $(Ix)A$ exist? Under what conditions does $(Ix)(x = x)$ exist?

4. Add the following rules to FD:

$$RD^+ \quad y|.\ldots\ |\ (y)(A \equiv B)$$

$$\vdots$$

$$(Iy)A = (Iy)B$$

$$RD^{++} \quad y|.\ldots\ |\ t \ \dot{=}\ (Ix)x = t$$

$$\vdots$$

Now produce a categorical derivation for

$$(Ix)(Fx = t) \equiv (y)(t = y \equiv\ \cdot\ Fy\ \&\ (x)(Fx \supset x = y))$$

5. Show that

 (i) $\neg (Ey)(y = t) \supset t = (Ix)(x \neq x)$

 (ii) $t = t$

are consequences of FD and RD^+ and RD^{++}.

6. Add the following rule to FD:

$$FDS \quad y|.\ldots\ |\ \neg (Ey)(y = (Ix)(Fx))$$

$$\vdots$$

$$(Ix)Fx \ \dot{=}\ (Ix)(x \neq x)$$

Now produce a categorical derivation of the following:

$$G(Ix)(Fx \equiv\ \cdot\ (Ex)(y)(Fy \equiv y = x)\ \&\ Gx) \vee\ \cdot\ \neg (Ex)(y)(Fy \equiv y = x)$$
$$\&\ G(Ix)(x \neq x)$$

PART *IV* FINITE METALOGIC

8 Metatheory of the Logic of Statements

PROBLEMS OF METALOGIC

In logic we attempt to catalogue, for example, the logical truths, and to distinguish them from other sentences. With the help of such a catalogue we can then begin the appraisal of reasoning: we can show of premises that they are inconsistent, or that they do in fact lead to a certain conclusion, or perhaps that they are not consistent with that conclusion. But suppose that someone argues

A, therefore B

and we cannot find A ⊃ B among our catalogue of logical truths. Does this show that his argument is invalid? At first sight, the answer is *no*: for who is to say whether we have managed to catalogue *all* the logical truths with our rules?

This is a question of adequacy concerning our logical system. Since it is a question *about* logic, it is called a *metalogical* question. We should like to answer it by showing that our system is indeed strong enough so that, for example, *all* logical truths have a categorical proof. The problem of showing this is called the *completeness problem*. Another metalogical problem, perhaps a more obvious one, is that of showing that our system is *sound*; that is, that any sentence which is the last line in a categorical proof is indeed logically true. Due to our informal commentary about our rules of inference, one may already be convinced that they never lead from truths to falsehoods. But, as Humpty Dumpty pointed out, it is important to see it done on paper. That is, we shall have to render our informal commentary precise.

The completeness problem is often divided into several problems. The first thing we would like to show is

    1. Every logical truth has a categorical derivation.

But in addition, we should like to show

    2. If there is a valid argument with premises $A_1, \ldots, A_n$ and conclusion B, then there is a derivation of B under $A_1, \ldots, A_n$.

In the first chapter we argued informally that an argument with premises $A_1, \ldots, A_n$ and conclusion B is valid exactly when the conditional statement with the conjunction of $A_1, \ldots, A_n$ as antecedent and B as conclusion is logically true. Assuming that this is correct, it will be sufficient to establish 1, since 2 holds if 1 holds. One of our tasks, however, will be to give precision to the arguments in the first chapter concerning logical truth and validity.

The soundness and completeness problems we have just outlined are not the only metalogical problems, although we shall concentrate on them in Part Four. Other problems studied in metalogic concern, for example, stronger versions of 2 in which arguments are allowed to have infinitely many premises ("strong completeness" or "Henkin completeness"). Still other problems concern relations among alternative logical rules and alternative logical systems. (The proofs of admissibility that we have given, especially in Chapter 3 and 5, really belong to metalogic, since they were about logical rules.) In this book we shall restrict ourselves to the most elementary metalogical problems.*

SECTION 2
STATEMENTS AND TRUTH-VALUES

The language of the logic of statements comprises a set of atomic statements, and the symbols), (, &, $\neg$, $\vee$ (logical signs). We are now leaving out the logical signs $\supset$, $\equiv$ simply because each sentence containing those signs is provably equivalent to one which does not contain them; for example $A \supset B$ is equivalent to $(\neg A \vee B)$. Therefore these other logical signs are really dispensible.

---

*See further B. C. van Fraassen, *Formal Semantics and Logic* (New York: Macmillan, 1971).

Besides atomic statements there are of course complex ones; the set of all statements can be defined as follows:

1. a. if A is an atomic statement, then A is a statement;
   b. if A is a statement then $\neg A$ is a statement;
   c. if A and B are statements, then $(A \ \& \ B)$ is a statement;
   d. if A and B are statements, then $(A \lor B)$ is a statement;
   e. nothing is a statement except in virtue of the above stipulations.

We must now consider how such statements could be true and false together. As an example, suppose that we have not introduced any logical rules yet, and we want to convince someone that $(A \ \& \ \neg A)$ cannot be true. Then we argue as follows:

> A must be either true or false. Suppose first that A is true. Then $\neg A$ is false. But clearly a conjunction is false if one of its conjuncts is false.
>
> Therefore the conjunction $(A \ \& \ \neg A)$ is false in this case.
>
> Secondly, suppose that A is false. Then $(A \ \& \ \neg A)$ is again a conjunction with a false component, and is therefore false also in this case.
>
> In other words $(A \ \& \ \neg A)$ is false in all possible cases: it is logically false.

Here the phrase "in all possible cases" could have been replaced by "in all possible worlds". And when we say: "Suppose first that A is true", we could have said "Consider first a possible world in which A is true". To abbreviate proofs of this kind, we introduce the notion of an assignment of *truth-values*.

2. An *assignment (of truth-values)* is an assignment of either T or F to each statement in such a way that in some possible world, the true statements are exactly those which have been assigned T.

We will use "v" to refer to an arbitrary such assignment, and use "$v(A) = T$" to mean that the statement A is assigned T by v, and of course "$v(A) = F$" to mean that A is assigned F by v.

On the basis of our discussion in Chapter 1, and the informal semantic commentary accompanying our rules, it should be clear that the following is a good, independent way of making the notion of assignment precise:

> 3. For all statements A,B, v is an assignment of truth-values if and only if the following conditions are satisfied:
>   (a) v assigns (in some way or other) either T or F to each atomic statement;
>   (b) $v(\neg A) = $ T if and only if $v(A) = $ F; otherwise $v(\neg A) = $ F;
>   (c) $v(A \& B) = $ T if and only if $v(A) = $ T and $v(B) = $ T; otherwise $v(A \& B) = $ F;
>   (d) $v(A \lor B) = $ T if and only if either $v(A) = $ T or $v(B) = $ T; otherwise $v(A \lor B) = $ F.

The independent characterization of assignment in 3 is important for two reasons. First, 3 contains no reference to possible worlds at all. When we consider quantificational logic, we will have to say something more about possible worlds; but for now this is not necessary. Second, 3 shows very clearly that the whole assignment is determined by the assignment to the atomic statements. More generally, if a complex sentence B has components $A_1, \ldots, A_n$, and we know what $v(A_1), \ldots, v(A_n)$ are, then we can *calculate* what $v(B)$ is.

For example, suppose that we are given

> 4. (i) $v(S) = $ T
>   (ii) $v(U) = $ F

and we are asked to show what $v(\neg(S \& \neg(U \lor S)))$ is. Then we proceed as follows:

> (iii) $v(U \lor S) = $ T   (by 3(d), i,ii)
> (iv) $v(\neg(U \lor S)) = $ F   (by 3(b), iii)
> (v) $v(S \& \neg(U \lor S)) = $ F   (by 3(c) and iv)
> (vi) $v(\neg(S \& \neg(U \lor S))) = $ T   (by 3(b) and v)

A helpful schematic way of representing the preceding calculation is the following:

S	U	$U \lor S$	$\neg(U \lor S)$	$S \& \neg(U \lor S)$	$\neg(S \& \neg(U \lor S))$
T	F	T	F	F	T

Such a diagram is a truth-table.

Turning back now to our first example, we can use a truth-table to show schematically why $(A \& \neg A)$ cannot be true.

	A	$\neg A$	$A \,\&\, \neg A$
(row 1)	T	F	F
(row 2)	F	T	F

In row 1, reconsider the possibility that $v(A) = T$; in row 2 the possibility that $v(A) = F$. Since these comprise all possible cases, the conclusion is that $(A \,\&\, \neg A)$ is logically false.

If we want to consider all possible cases, and the sentence in question has two, three, ... distinct constituents, the truth-tables get rather larger of course:

A	B	$A \,\&\, B$	$A \vee B$
T	T	T	T
F	T	F	T
T	F	F	T
F	F	F	F

A	B	C	$(A \,\&\, B)$	$(A \,\&\, B) \vee C$
T	T	T	T	T
F	T	T	F	T
T	F	T	F	T
F	F	T	F	T
T	T	F	T	T
F	T	F	F	F
T	F	F	F	F
F	F	F	F	F

The fact that we see both T's *and* F's below $A \vee B$, and below $(A \,\&\, B) \vee C$, shows that these sentences are not logically true.

SECTION 3
LOGICAL TRUTH AND VALIDITY

Truth-tables enable us to show logical truth: if a statement has only T's under it in a truth-table, then it is logically true. The precise definition of logical truth in terms of assignments (to be used in connection with the logic of statements) is as follows:

DEFINITION: A statement A is *logically true* if and only if every assignment v is such that $v(A) = T$, and *logically false* if and only if every assignment v is such that $v(A) = F$.

Similarly we can define the relation that holds between the premises and conclusion of any valid argument. We call this relation "(semantic) implication".

DEFINITION: *Statements* $A_1, \ldots, A_n$ *(semantically) imply* statement *B* if and only if for every assignment v, if $v(A_1) = $ T, $\ldots$, and $v(A_n) = $ T, then $v(B) = $ T.

We shall now prove some simple results about logical truth and implication, that will help to substantiate the informal arguments of Chapter 1, and that will be helpful later on.

I. If A implies B and $\neg A$ implies B, then B is logically true.

For suppose that A and $\neg A$ each imply B. Let v be any assignment. Then either $v(A) = $ T or $v(\neg A) = $ T. In either case $v(B) = $ T, by our supposition. Hence all assignments v assign T to B.

It is important to notice that our proof of I has the structure of a derivation in quantificational logic:

(1)	A implies B and $\neg A$ implies B	
(2)	v $v(A) = $ T or $v(\neg A) = $ T	(provable from Section 2)
(3)	$v(A) = $ T	
(4)	A implies B	(1)
(5)	$v(B) = $ T	(3) (4)
(6)	$v(\neg A) = T$	
(7)	$\neg A$ implies A	(1)
(8)	$v(B) = $ T	(6) (7)
(9)	$v(B) = $ T	(2) (3–5) (6–8)
(10)	For all v, $v(B) = $ T	(3–9)

In other words, the correctness of metalogical arguments is appropriately checked by logical methods. This means then that metalogic cannot, without circularity, be said to show the correctness of logical principles, in the sense of providing a "presuppositionless foundation". But metalogical arguments nevertheless *show* the correctness of logical rules, in the sense of making it possible to see the rationale of logic. That is, we cannot prove to an absolute skeptic that even the simple logical inferences are trustworthy. But to anyone accepting the correctness of common, simple logical steps, we can show the correctness of the complex and sophisticated systems of rules devised by logicians to catalogue logical truths.

II. If every statement implies B, then B is logically true.

Suppose that every statement implies B, and let A be any statement. Then, since every statement implies B, $\neg A$ as well as A implies B; hence, by I., B is logically true.

III. $v(A_1 \& \ldots \& A_n) = \text{T}$ if and only if
$v(A_1) = \ldots = v(A_n) = \text{T}$.

Here we are using the notation of multiple conjunction introduced in Chapter 3. The number n can be 1, or 2, or 3, or any other positive integer. Now if one wanted a simple, not too demanding, but also not too exciting, job for the rest of one's days, one could seek to prove III first for the case $n = 1$, then for the case $n = 2$, and so on.

A shorter way to prove III is as follows. We show III to hold for the case $n = 1$. Then we say: let n be any number greater than 1, and suppose that we have already proved III for all numbers less than n. Then we prove on the basis of this supposition that III holds for n also. This method of proof is called *mathematical induction*; what it proves really is that we have a recipe for a proof of III no matter how high the number n is. Written up precisely it takes the following form:

Step 1: THE BASIS STEP. III holds for a conjunction with only one conjunct. For in the case $n = 1$, III just says that $v(A_1) = \text{T}$ if and only if $v(A_1) = \text{T}$.

Step 2: THE INDUCTIVE STEP. As hypothesis of induction, suppose that III holds for any conjunction with less than n conjuncts. Then III holds for a conjunction with n conjuncts. For consider the conjunction $A_1 \& \ldots \& A_n$. If we restore some of the parentheses, it must have the form $(A_1 \& \ldots \& A_m) \& (A_{m-1} \& \ldots \& A_n)$. Now by hypothesis, $v(A_1 \& \ldots \& A_m) = \text{T}$ exactly if $v(A_1) = \ldots = v(A_m) = \text{T}$, and $v(A_{m+1} \& \ldots \& A_n) = \text{T}$ exactly if $v(A_{m-1}) = \ldots = v(A_n) = \text{T}$. But $v((A_1 \& \ldots \& A_m) \& (A_{m+1} \& \ldots \& A_n)) = \text{T}$ if and only if $v(A_1 \& \ldots \& A_m) = v(A_{m+1} \& \ldots \& A_n) = \text{T}$ (by the definition of "assignment"), and hence if and only if $v(A_1) = \ldots = v(A_n) = \text{T}$.

IV. A implies B if and only if $A \supset B$ is logically true.

Note that $A \supset B$ is short for $\neg A \lor B$. Suppose first that A implies B. Then if v is any assignment, either $v(A) = \text{T}$ or $v(\neg A) = \text{T}$. In the former case $v(B) = \text{T}$ because A implies B. So in either case $v(B) = \text{T}$ or $v(\neg A) = \text{T}$; hence in any case $v(\neg A \lor B) = \text{T}$.

Suppose on the other hand that $\neg A \lor B$ is logically true. Does A imply B? To show it does, we must show for any assignment v, that if $v(A) = \text{T}$, then $v(B) = \text{T}$. So let v be any assignment. Suppose that $v(A) = \text{T}$. Then $v(\neg A) = \text{F}$. However, since $\neg A \lor B$ is logically true, $v(\neg A \lor B) = \text{T}$, so either $v(\neg A) = \text{T}$ or $v(B) = \text{T}$. But $v(\neg A) = \text{F}$. So $v(B) = \text{T}$. (As an exercise, the reader should rewrite this paragraph in the form of a derivation, as we did for I above.)

V. $A_1, \ldots, A_n$ imply B if and only if $(A_1 \& \ldots \& A_n) \supset B$ is logically true.

This the reader can demonstrate on the basis of III and IV.

Results I–V show quite clearly that in questions concerning the adequacy of our logical system, we may concentrate either on logical truth or on validity of arguments, without loss. We shall now prove some results that have to do with negation and disjunction, and will be of use when we discuss the logical rules.

VI. If $A_1, \ldots, A_n$ imply B then $A_1, \ldots, A_n$ imply $B \lor C$.
VII. If $A_1, \ldots, A_n, B$ imply D and $A_1, \ldots, A_n, C$ imply D,
  then $A_1, \ldots, A_n, B \lor C$ imply D.

The proof of VI we leave as exercise. For the proof of VII, suppose that $A_1, \ldots, A_n, B$ and also $A_1, \ldots, A_n, C$ imply D. Now let v be any assignment that assigns T to each of $A_1, \ldots, A_n, B \lor C$. Clearly v assigns T to $B \lor C$, and hence either to B or to C. In either case, v must assign T to D, because by supposition, if v assigns T to all of $A_1, \ldots, A_n$, B and also if v assigns T to all of $A_1, \ldots, A_n$, C, then v assigns T to D.

VIII. If $A_1, \ldots, A_n, B$ imply $C \& \neg C$, then $A_1, \ldots, A_n$ imply $\neg B$.
IX. If $A_1, \ldots, A_n, \neg B$ imply $C \& \neg C$, then $A_1, \ldots, A_n$ imply B.

To prove VIII, suppose that $A_1, \ldots, A_n, B$ do imply $C \& \neg C$. This means that no assignment v can assign T to all of $A_1, \ldots, A_n$, and B; for if it did, it would assign T both to C and to $\neg C$, which is impossible. So if a given v assigns T to all of $A_1, \ldots, A_n$, it cannot assign T to B. But if it does not assign T to B, then it assigns T to $\neg B$. The proof of IX is similar and is left as an exercise. Finally, we extend result VII:

X. If $A_1, \ldots, A_n$ imply $B \lor C$; and $A_1, \ldots, A_n, B$ imply D;
  and $A_1, \ldots, A_n, C$ imply D, then $A_1, \ldots, A_n$ imply D.

The important thing to notice is that X would follow at once from VII if we had the following result (letting E be $B \lor C$):

XI. If $A_1, \ldots, A_n$ imply E, and $A_1, \ldots, A_n, E$ imply D,
  then $A_1, \ldots, A_n$ imply D.

But that is easy to establish. For suppose the antecedent of XI, and let v be an assignment. If v assigns T to all $A_1, \ldots, A_n$, then it assigns

T to E, by supposition. But if v assigns T to all of $A_1, \ldots, A_n$ and also to E, then it assigns T to D, again by supposition. Hence if v assigns T to $A_1, \ldots, A_n$ (and so *a fortiori* to $A_1, \ldots, A_n, E$), then it assigns T to D.

SECTION 4
THE SOUNDNESS OF THE LOGIC OF STATEMENTS

As we introduced rules of derivation, we argued informally that they lead from true premises only to true conclusions. We now proceed to make these arguments precise. We need to make them precise only for rules R, D, KE, KI, AE, AI, NE, NI; the other rules are shown to be admissible, given these, in Chapter 3.

Since we allow subderivations within derivations, we cannot simply consider the relations between premises and conclusions. We must consider the relations of statements written on lines in a derivation to all the suppositions under which they are derived. Since one and the same statement may occur on several lines in one derivation, as well as in other derivations, we need a precise definition. We shall say that each statement, if it occurs on a line in a derivation, has zero or more antecedents above. Then we shall show that the statement on a given line in a derivation is implied by those antecedents. (When the number of antecedents is zero, this will mean that the statement is implied by anything, that is, logically true.) It will turn out that if we have a derivation of B from $A_1, \ldots, A_n$, then in that derivation, B occurs on the last line, and there its antecedents are exactly $A_1, \ldots, A_n$. Thus if conclusion B can be derived from premises $A_1, \ldots, A_n$, then $A_1, \ldots, A_n$ imply B.

DEFINITION: Let D be a derivation, and A be the statement written on line i of D. Then:

(a) Every premise of D is an antecedent of A on i in D.

(b) If A is written on line i to the right of any scope line of any sub-derivation, which cuts line i, then the suppositions of that subderivation are antecedents of A on i in D.

(c) A has no antecedent on i in D except by virtue of clauses (a) and (b).

Note that each premise and each supposition belongs to its own antecedents. In these cases it is clear that the antecedents of A (on the line in question) imply A.

We shall now look at some of the rules in turn; but R, D, AI, KI, NI we leave as exercises.

KE: Suppose A is introduced on line i by KE from $A \& B$ (or $B \& A$) on line m. Since the two lines must have the statements written inside the same subderivation, the antecedents are the same in both cases. Hence we must show that if $A_1, \ldots, A_n$ imply $A \& B$ (or $B \& A$), then they imply A. But this follows at once from the fact that $v(A \& B) = $ T only if $v(A) = $ T.

NE: Suppose that statement A is introduced on line i by NE from lines m–n. That means that $\neg A$ is the supposition on line m of a subderivation extending from line m to line n inclusive. Within these lines we find, for some statement C, both C and $\neg C$.

The antecedents of $\neg A$ on line m are, say, $A_1, \ldots, A_n$, plus $\neg A$ itself. The antecedents of A on line i are then just $A_1, \ldots, A_n$. What we must show then is that if $A_1, \ldots, A_n$, $\neg A$ together imply both C and $\neg C$, then $A_1, \ldots, A_n$ imply A. But this follows immediately from result IX in the preceding section.

AE: Suppose that statement A is introduced on line i by AI from lines k, j–m, n–q. Then for some statements B and C, $B \vee C$ is on line k, B is on line j as a supposition, C is on line n as a supposition, and A is on lines m and q. Then $B \vee C$ on line k has the same antecedents as A on line i. And we must prove that if $A_1, \ldots, A_n$, imply $B \vee C$, and $A_1, \ldots, A_n$, B imply A, and $A_1, \ldots, A_n$, C imply A, then $A_1, \ldots, A_n$ imply A. This follows by result X.

The cases for the other rules can be proved by similar appeal to other results from the preceding section. This suffices to prove the soundness of the bank of rules for the logic of statements.

SECTION 5
THE COMPLETENESS OF THE LOGIC OF STATEMENTS

We have defined a statement A to be logically true exactly if all assignments of truth-values assign T to A. Similarly, we call A *logically false* exactly if all assignments assign F to A. Of course, we could state this equivalently as: A is logically false exactly if $\neg A$ is logically true. When we prove completeness it is convenient to concentrate on the tableau rules, and for them logical falsity is the more relevant notion.

We already know from Chapter 3 that if the tableau sequence of A terminates, then a contradiction can be derived from A by the natural deduction rules. The latter, in turn, is equivalent to: $\neg A$ has a categorical derivation. So to prove

1. If A is logically false, then $\neg A$ has a categorical derivation

it would suffice to prove

2. If A is logically false, then the tableau sequence of
A terminates.

On the other hand, to show the completeness of our logic of statements, we must prove

3. If A is logically true, then A has a categorical derivation.

But suppose we have established 2, and hence 1; and suppose in addition that A is logically true. In that case $\neg A$ is logically false, so by 1, $\neg \neg A$ has a categorical derivation. As we can easily check, however, a derivation of $\neg \neg A$ can be extended into a derivation of A:

$$
\begin{array}{lll}
 & \vdots & \\
(n) & \neg \neg A & \\
(n+1) & \quad \neg A & \\
(n+2) & \quad \neg \neg A & (n), \text{R} \\
(n+3) \quad A & & (n+1), (n+2), \text{NE}
\end{array}
$$

Therefore, to establish 3 it suffices to establish 1—and hence, 3 is demonstrated if 2 is demonstrated. This justifies our proving the completeness of our logic of statements in the following form:

If A is logically false, then the tableau sequence of A terminates.

The easiest way to prove this is by *modus tollens*: that is, we assume that the tableau sequence of A does not terminate, and proceed to prove that A is not logically false.

The important thing to notice here is that even if the tableau sequence of A does not terminate, it must still stop after finitely many steps. For an inspection of the rules shows that we only keep replacing complex statements (in the alternates) by less complex statements. For example, in the rule V, $X \& (A \lor B) \& Y$ is replaced by two alternates —namely, $X \& A \& T$ and $X \& B \& Y$—and each of these has less symbols in it than the original alternates. Since we only start with a finite number of symbols in the original formula, this process of eliminating symbols cannot go on forever.

So in the logic of statements, no tableau sequence can go on forever. This is not the case in quantificational logic, but while we have it we might as well take advantage of it.

So let A have the non-terminating tableau sequence $B_1, \ldots, B_n$, and let B_n be the disjunction $C_1 \vee \ldots \vee C_m$. Since this sequence does not terminate, at least one disjunct C_i of B is not underlined. Now what does C_i look like? It must be a conjunction $(S_1 \& \ldots \& S_k)$ where each S_j is either an atomic statement or the negation of an atomic statement. For if C_i had any more complex constituent, then one of our rules would be applicable; and if that were so, B_n would not be the last member of the tableau sequence after all.

So now let v be the assignment which assigns T to any atomic statement which is one of the conjuncts $S_1, \ldots, S_k$ and which assigns F to all other atomic statements. Then if S_i is an atomic statement U, $v(S_i) = $ T. If S_i is a negation $\neg U$ of an atomic statement, then U is not a conjunct in C_i (since otherwise C_i would be underlined, which we have assumed not to be the case), so $v(U) = $ F, and hence $v(S_i) = v(\neg U) = $ T. In other words, $v(S_i) = $ T for $i = 1, 2, \ldots, n$, and therefore $v(C_i) = $ T.

But since $v(C_i) = $ T, and B_n had C_i as an alternation, $v(B_n) = $ T. We need now to show that for any i from 1 to $n-1$, if B_{i+1} is true then so is B_i. The conclusion will then be that B_i, that is A, is also true. And this will of course establish that A is not logically false.

We must look at each of the possible ways in which B_{i+1} can come from B_i. Let the replaced alternate of B_i be E_i:

DN: E_i is $X \& \neg \, \neg A \& Y$, and is replaced by $X \& A \& Y$. If $v(X \& A \& Y) = $ T, then $v(X) = $ T, $v(A) = $ T, and $v(Y) = $ T. But if $v(A) = $ T, so is $v(\neg \, \neg A)$. Hence if $X \& A \& Y$ is true, so is E_i.

NK: E_i is $X \& \neg(A \& B) \& Y$ and is replaced by $(X \& \neg A \& Y) \vee (X \& \neg B \& Y)$. If the latter is true, one of its alternates is true. Let us assume that the first alternate is true; the contrary case is entirely similar.

If $v(X \& \neg A \& Y) = $ T then $v(X) = $ T and $v(\neg A) = $ T and $v(Y) = $ T. But then $v(A) = $ F, so $v(X) = $ T, $v(\neg A \& B) = $ F, and hence $v(\neg(A \& B)) = $ T. So in this case $v(X) = $ T, $v(\neg(A \& B)) = $ T, and $v(Y) = $ T, so that $v(E_i) = $ T.

We leave the cases V and NV as exercises for the reader; so ends the proof..

EXERCISES

1. In principle 3 in section 2, clauses (a)–(d) do not explicitly cover ⊃ and ≡. Make up cláuses for these.

2. Draw a truth-table (a *complete* one, each possible case being represented by some row) for $S \supset T$ and $S \equiv T$.

3. Given the information that (i) $v(S) = \mathrm{T}$ and (ii) $v(U) = \mathrm{F}$, calculate the truth-values that v assigns to the following sentences (in the manner of 4 (i)–(vi) in section 2):
    (a) $U \mathbin{\&} S$ (e) $S \vee \neg (U \mathbin{\&} S)$
    (b) $U \mathbin{\&} \neg S$ (f) $U \vee (S \supset U)$
    (c) $\neg (S \mathbin{\&} \neg S)$ (g) $\neg (S \supset (U \supset S))$
    (d) $S \supset U$ (h) $\neg S \supset (S \supset U)$

4. By the truth-table method, determine which of exercise 3 (a)–(h) are logically true, logically false, and neither.

5. Just as truth-tables can be used to show logical truth, they can be used to show validity of arguments (or, what amounts to the same, semantic implication). (For example, to see if A implies B, draw a truth-table for both A and B, and see if there is a T under B in *every row in which there is a T under A*.) In this way, determine which of (a)–(d) implies which of (e)–(h) in exercise 3.

6. Rewrite the proofs of IV and VII in the form of derivations, as was done for I in the text.

7. In the manner in which I was demonstrated in the text, show that
    (a) if A implies B and A implies $\neg B$, then A is logically false;
    (b) if $\neg A$ implies A, then A is logically true;
    (c) if A implies $\neg A$, then A is logically false;
    (d) if A implies B and B implies C, then A implies C.

8. Demonstrate
    (a) V by appeal to III and IV;
    (b) VI;
    (c) IX;
    (d) X by appeal to XI.

9. The rule $\mathrm{KE_1}$ leads from true antecedents to a new line which must then also be true, *just because A & B implies A*. In the same informal way, with reference to exercise 6, show that the following informally stated rules lead from truths only to truths:
    (a) ⎮ ⊢$\frac{\neg A}{A}$ (b) ⎮ ⊢$\frac{A}{\neg A}$
       ⎮ A ⎮ $\neg A$

10. Complete the demonstration of soundness in the text by examining the rules R, D, AE, KI, NI.

11. Restate in the form of a precise derivation, our argument that to prove completeness it suffices to demonstrate (2) in section 5.

12. Complete the demonstration of completeness in the text by examining tableau rules V and NV.

9 Metatheory of Free Logic

The logic of quantifiers, variables, and identity, as developed in this book with VQE and VU included, is known as "classical predicate logic with identity", or "classical quantification and identity theory". When the rules for identity are dropped, it is often referred to simply as "classical logic". This use of the term classical is somewhat ahistorical of course, since this logic was only fully developed in the present century, and postdates various disciplines referred to as "Aristotelian" or "syllogistic logic", and "modern logic". But some term was needed to distinguish the most widely studied logical system from such still later outgrowths as intuitionistic logic, modal logic, and free logic. The latter, as has already been pointed out, comprises the same logical system extended to singular terms in the way that has been done in this book, with or without the rules VQE or VU. When those rules are omitted the logic is said to be valid for all domains including the empty one, and is referred to as *universally free logic* with identity.

We shall here address ourselves primarily to the soundness and completeness of universally free logic without identity. We shall then discuss as separate topics, the elimination of the empty domain, the addition of identity rules, and the addition of the description operator.*

---

*The sources for this chapter are B. C. van Fraassen, "The Completeness of Free Logic", *Zeitschrift für mathematische Logik und Grundlagen der Mathematik,* 12 (1966), pp. 219–234 and B. C. van Fraassen and K. Lambert, "On Free Description Theory", *Zeitschrift für mathematische Logik und Grundlagen der Mathematik,* 13 (1967), pp. 225–240.

SECTION 1
SENTENCES AND MODELS

The language of free logic has as vocabulary a set of variables, a set of constants (names, or unanalyzed singular terms), a set of predicates (of various degrees), all these sets disjoint and not empty, and the logic signs $=$,), (, &, $\neg$, $\vee$. The variables and constants are jointly known as *terms*. The sentences of this language are defined as follows:

1. a. If P is a predicate of degree n, and $t_1, \ldots, t_n$ are terms, then $Pt_1 \ldots t_n$, and also $t_1 = t_2$ (when $n \geq 1$) are sentences (atomic sentences);
    b. If A and B are sentences, so are $(A \& B)$, $(A \vee B)$, and $\neg A$;
    c. If x is a variable, and A is a sentence, then $(x)A$ is a sentence;
    d. Nothing is a sentence except in virtue of the above stipulation.

A sentence with no free variables in it is called a *statement*. As before, we shall now think of $(A \supset B)$ as just an abbreviation for $(\neg A \vee B)$, and we shall also think of $(Ex)A$ as just an abbreviation for $\neg(x)\neg A$. We shall write $(t/t')A$ for the result of replacing every (free) occurrence of t' in A by an occurrence of t, but only after bound variables have been rewritten to avoid their confusion. Identity sentences will be ignored until section 6.

We shall now have to say something more about possible worlds. If $\mathcal{M}$ is a possible world, then it has a set $\mathcal{D}$ of "inhabitants"—the things which exist in $\mathcal{M}$. We call $\mathcal{D}$ the *domain* of $\mathcal{M}$, or the domain of *discourse*. This set may be empty, since it is not a logical truth that there is something rather than nothing. When the language is being used to describe what is the case in $\mathcal{M}$, its variables range over $\mathcal{D}$. That is, when we say that "Everything is black" is true in $\mathcal{M}$, we mean that "x is black" is true in $\mathcal{M}$ whatever entity in $\mathcal{D}$ x is used to designate.

It is clear that if we only know the domain of $\mathcal{M}$, we do not know yet what is true in $\mathcal{M}$. For this we need information concerning which things in $\mathcal{D}$ fall under each predicate. Suppose the predicates in our language are $P_1, P_2, P_3, \ldots$; then there must be properties (and relations) $\mathbf{R}_1, \mathbf{R}_2, \mathbf{R}_3, \ldots$ in $\mathcal{M}$ which are expressed, respectively, by $P_1, P_2, P_3, \ldots$. For example, suppose that P_1 is the predicate "is black".

Then $\mathbf{R}_1$ must be the property of being black, or, if you wish, just the set of black things. Supposing that we are using "John" to refer to some member X of $\mathcal{D}$; then the sentence "John is black" is true in $\mathcal{M}$ just if X falls under $\mathbf{R}_1$. That X falls under $\mathbf{R}_1$ we shall write as "$X \varepsilon \mathbf{R}_1$". (This is read as "$X$ is a member of $\mathbf{R}_1$", and we choose this terminology because we will just think of $\mathbf{R}_1$ as the set of black things in $\mathcal{D}$.)

In the case of relations we handle the matter as follows. Say that P_2 is the predicate "is taller than"; then $\mathbf{R}_2$ must be the relation of *being taller than*. Instead of saying "The member X of $\mathcal{D}$ bears relation $\mathbf{R}_2$ to the member Y of $\mathcal{D}$", we shall say "$< X, Y > \varepsilon \mathbf{R}_2$". This is read as "the couple $< X, Y >$ belongs to (is a member of) $\mathbf{R}_2$". Similarly, if $\mathbf{R}_3$ is an n-ary relation, we use the symbolism "$< X_1, \ldots, X_n > \varepsilon \mathbf{R}_3$".

We said above that "John is black" would be true just if $X \varepsilon \mathbf{R}_1$. This assumed that "is black" is P_1 (which applies exactly to the members of $\mathcal{D}$ that belong to $\mathbf{R}_1$) and that John designates X". Supposing that the constants of our language are $a_1, a_2, a_3, \ldots$, we must therefore also have the information which of these designate things in $\mathcal{D}$, and what those designations are. For convenience we shall assume that each thing in $\mathcal{D}$ is denoted by some constant.*

We must note here that not all the constants need have a designation in the domain; some may be non-referring terms. How can we find out whether "Pegasus flies" is true in $\mathcal{M}$ if "Pegasus" does not designate anything in $\mathcal{M}$? The answer to this question is: we can not find out. Since Pegasus does not exist, there are no facts to be discovered about him. What we can do is arbitrarily assign that sentence a value. Or we can say that due to its occurrence in some story (say, in Greek mythology), the *name* "Pegasus" has acquired a certain connotation. Due to this connotation, we may feel "Pegasus swims" is false and "Pegasus flies", true. To get all the true sentences in the language, then, we need as part of a model $\mathcal{M}$ also a *story*. This story has to be consistent with the facts in $\mathcal{M}$, of course; if $\mathcal{M}$ is the real world, the story may say that Pegasus flies, but not that Pegasus exists, nor that Pegasus is identical with some real horse.

The preceding discussion of possible worlds can now be made precise through the notion of a model.

2. A *model* $\mathcal{M}$ comprises a domain $\mathcal{D}$ (a set, empty or non-empty), an interpretation function f, and a story $\mathcal{S}$. The

---

*Our proofs would be somewhat complicated if we did not make that assumption: however, proofs of *strong* completeness are simplified by not making that assumption. The assumption is clearly a didactic convenience only.

function f assigns to each predicate P a relation $f(P)$ among the elements of $\mathcal{D}$, and each element of $\mathcal{D}$ to one or more constants. The story $\mathcal{S}$ is a set (empty or non-empty) of atomic sentences, each of which contains some constant to which f has assigned no element of $\mathcal{D}$.

When b is a constant, and element X of $\mathcal{D}$ is assigned to b by f, we write $X = f(b)$. We are clearly going to say that, for example, an atomic sentence Pab is true in $\mathcal{M}$ exactly if either Pab is in $\mathcal{S}$ or $< f(a), f(b) >$ is in $f(P)$. (And we do not at present have any atomic sentences of the form $a = b$.)

Each statement has a truth-value in a model. (Note that we say *statement*, not sentence; whether Pxb is true depends in part on what the variable x is currently being used to refer to, and not just on what the model is like.) This truth-value is either T or F; and the following spells out exactly when it is T. We shall write "$\mathcal{M} \models A$" for "the value of A in $\mathcal{M}$ is T"; let $\mathcal{M}$ comprise $\mathcal{D}$, f, and $\mathcal{S}$.

3. (a) $\mathcal{M} \models Pa_1 \ldots a_n$ if and only if either $Pa_1 \ldots a_n$ is in $\mathcal{S}$ or $< f(a_n), \ldots, f(a_n) >$ is in $f(P)$.

   (b) $\mathcal{M} \models \neg A$ if and only if not ($\mathcal{M} \models A$).

   (c) $\mathcal{M} \models (A \,\&\, B)$ if and only if $\mathcal{M} \models A$ and $\mathcal{M} \models B$.

   (d) $\mathcal{M} \models (A \lor B)$ if and only if $\mathcal{M} \models A$ or $\mathcal{M} \models B$.

   (e) $\mathcal{M} \models (x)A$ if and only if $\mathcal{M} \models (b/x)A$ for every constant b to which f has assigned an element of $\mathcal{D}$.

In more informal terms, clause (e) says that $(x)Ax$ is true in $\mathcal{M}$ exactly if Ax is true no matter what element of the domain $\mathcal{D}$ we use x to designate. Since each of these elements is assumed to be designated by some constant, that is equivalent to: Ab is true exactly wherever b is a designating constant.

SECTION 2
USES OF MODELS

Just like truth-tables, models may be used to prove logical truth and falsehood. Let us first make up a simple model and see what is true in it. Let $b_1, \ldots, b_n, \ldots$ be all the constants we have. We shall use b_2 to refer to number 1, b_4 to number 2, and so on.

Model $\mathcal{M}_1$. The domain is the set of positive integers, and the constant b_{2i} is assigned the number i by f: $f(b_{2i}) = i$. The predicate P is assigned the set of even numbers, and each of the other predicates is assigned the empty set. The story S has only one statement in it: Qb_1.

Now the following are some true statements in $\mathcal{M}_1$:

Pb_4, Pb_8, Pb_{12}, Qb_1,
$\neg Pb_2$, $\neg Pb_1$, $\neg Qb_2$, $\neg Rb_1$, $\neg Rb_4$,
Pb_4 & Pb_8, Pb_{12} & Qb_1,
$Pb_4 \lor Pb_2$, $Qb_1 \lor Qb_2$.

For example, we prove that $\neg Pb_2$ is true in $\mathcal{M}_1$ as follows:

Since $2 = 2 \cdot 1$, $f(b_2) = 1$; now 1 is not even, so $f(b_2)$ is not in $f(P)$. Therefore not ($\mathcal{M}_1 \models Pb_2$); but then $\mathcal{M}_1 \models \neg Pb_2$.

As exercises, the following may be proved:

(a) $\mathcal{M}_1 \models Pb_i$ if and only if $i = 4j$ for some $j \geq 1$
(b) $\mathcal{M}_1 \models \neg Qb_i$ if and only if $i \neq 1$
(c) $\mathcal{M}_1 \models (x)Px$
(d) $\mathcal{M}_1 \models (Ex) \neg Qx$

The construction of a suitable model can now be used to *disprove* logical truth or logical falsehood. For example, to show that

$$(x)(Ey)(Rxy) \supset (Ey)(x)(Rxy)$$

is not logically true, we only need to point to the model in which $\mathcal{D}$ is the set of humans, Rab says that b is a relative of a (living or dead). In that model

$$(x)(Ey)(y \text{ is a relative of } x)$$

is true, but

$$(Ey)(x)(y \text{ is a relative of } x)$$

is not true.

Similarly, to show that $(x)(Px \& \neg Px)$ is not logically false, we point to a model $\mathcal{M}_2$ with empty domain. This is worth describing in some detail.

> *Model $\mathcal{M}_2$.* The domain $\mathcal{D}$ has no elements. The function f does not assign anything to any constant; the set $f(P)$ is empty for every predicate P. The story $\mathcal{S}$ contains exactly the sentences Pb_1, Qb_2.

Now the following are some sentences true in $\mathcal{M}_2$.

> $Pb_1, Qb_2, \neg Pb_2, \neg Qb_1, \neg Rb_1,$
> $(x)Px, (x)Qx, (x)\neg Px,$
> $\neg(Ex)Px, \neg(Ex)\neg Px.$

Indeed, no matter what the sentence A is, we have $\mathcal{M}_2 \models (x)A$ and $\mathcal{M}_2 \models \neg(Ex)A$. The second claim follows from the first, since $\mathcal{M}_2 \models \neg(Ex)A$ exactly if $\mathcal{M}_2 \models (x)\neg A$. That $\mathcal{M}_2 \models (x)A$ for any sentence whatsoever is easily established. It amounts to the claim

(e) $\mathcal{M}_2 \models (b/x)A$ for every constant b such that b is assigned an element in $\mathcal{D}$.

And this claim is true *vacuously*, since *no* constant b is assigned anything. So specifically $\mathcal{M}_2 \models (x)(Px \& \neg Px)$; therefore the sentence is not logically false.

Logical truth can also be proved directly by considering models. For example, to prove that $A \vee \neg A$ is logically true, we argue

> Let $\mathcal{M}$ be an arbitary model. There are possibilities: $\mathcal{M} \models A$ and not $(\mathcal{M} \models A)$. If the former, then $\mathcal{M} \models (A \vee \neg A)$; and if the latter, then $\mathcal{M} \models A$, and hence $\mathcal{M} \models (A \vee \neg A)$.

This argument would be more perspicuous if we indicated, at each step, the clauses of principle 3 of Section 1. Indeed, an argument such as this can be made quite formal, along the lines of proofs by the rules of classical logic. As a final example, we derive the truth of *Henkin's formula*, $(Ex)(Fx \supset (y)Fy)$, in every model with non-empty domain:

(1)	The domain $\mathcal{D}$ of $\mathcal{M}$ is not empty	
(2)	For some constant b, $f(b)$ is in $\mathcal{D}$	(Section 1, principle 2)
(3)	b $\mid$ $f(b)$ ε $\mathcal{D}$	
(4)	$\mathcal{M} \vDash (y)Fy$ or not $\mathcal{M} \vDash (y)Fy$	
(5)	$\mathcal{M} \vDash (y)Fy$	
(6)	$\mathcal{M} \vDash (y)Fy$ or $\mathcal{M} \vDash \neg Fb$	(5) AI
(7)	$\mathcal{M} \vDash \neg Fb \lor (y)Fy$	(6) (Section1, 3b)
(8)	$\mathcal{M} \vDash Fb \supset (y)Fy$	(7) DI
(9)	For some (constant) b,$(f(b)$ ε D and $\mathcal{M} \vDash Fb \supset (y)Fy$	(8) SEQI
(10)	$\mathcal{M} \vDash (Ex)(Fx \supset (y)Fy)$	(9) (Section 1, 3b, and 3e)
(11)	not $(\mathcal{M} \vDash (y)Fy)$	
(12)	not (for all b such that $f(b)$ ε $\mathcal{D}$, $\mathcal{M} \vDash Fb$)	(11·) (Section 1, 3b)
(13)	for some b such that $f(b)$ ε $\mathcal{D}$, not $(\mathcal{M} \vDash Fb)$	(12) EQI
(14)	b $f(b)$ ε $\mathcal{D}$ and not $(\mathcal{M} \vDash Fb)$	
(15)	$\mathcal{M} \vDash \neg Fb$	(14) (Section1, 3e)
(16)	$\mathcal{M} \vDash \neg Fb$ or $\mathcal{M} \vDash (y)Fy$	(15) AI
(17)	$\mathcal{M} \vDash \neg Fb \lor (y)Fy$	(16) (Section 1, 3d)
(18)	$\mathcal{M} \vDash Fb \supset (y)Fy$	(17) DI
(19)	for some b, $f(b)$ ε $\mathcal{D}$ and $\mathcal{M} \vDash Fb \supset (y)Fy$	(18) SEQI
(20)	$\mathcal{M} \vDash (Ex)(Fx \supset (y)Fy)$	(19) (Section 1, 3b, and 3e)
(21)	$\mathcal{M} \vDash (Ex)(Fx \supset (y)Fy)$	(14–20) SEQI
(22)	$\mathcal{M} \vDash (Ex)(Fx \supset (y)Fy)$	(4–21) AE
(23)	$\mathcal{M} \vDash (Ex)(Fx \supset (y)Fy)$	(3–22) SEQE

Note that in steps (10) and (20), clauses 3b and 3e of Section 1 were used to infer the derivative principle that $(Ex)A$ is true in $\mathcal{M}$ exactly if $(b/x)A$ is true in $\mathcal{M}$ for some constant b which has a referent in $\mathcal{M}$.

SECTION 3
LOGICAL TRUTH AND VALIDITY

The exact definition of logical truth, in the present context, is that a statement is logically true exactly if it is true in every model. Similarly (semantic) implication must now be understood as follows: statements $A_1, \ldots, A_n$ imply B if and only if every model in which $A_1, \cdot \ldots, A_n$ are all true is such that B is true in it. It is easily seen that results I-XI of Chapter 8, Section 3 carry over to the present context, since models are like assignments in all respects relevant to those results. (For example, just as $v(A \& B) = T$ if and only if $v(A) = v(B) = T$, so $A \& B$ is true in $\mathcal{M}$ exactly if A and B are both true in $\mathcal{M}$.) We shall now add some further results which concern quantifiers.

XII. If A is a statement, then A implies $(x)A$.

The quantifier here is vacuous, since x has no free occurrences in a statement. So $(b/x)A$ is just A, no matter what b is. Hence if $\mathcal{M}$ is a model, and A is true in $\mathcal{M}$, then $(b/x)A$ is true in $\mathcal{M}$ for every constant b which has a referent in $\mathcal{M}$.

XIII. $(y)(x)A$ implies $(y)(y/x)A$, provided y does not occur in A.

First consider the case of a model with non-empty domain. Suppose that $(x)A$ is true in model $\mathcal{M}$. Then $(b/x)A$ is true in $\mathcal{M}$ for each constant b assigned a referent in $\mathcal{M}$. But notice that $(b/y)(y/x)A$ is just the same as $(b/x)A$ if y does not occur in A. So for every constant b with a referent in $\mathcal{M}$, $(b/y)(y/x)A$ is true in $\mathcal{M}$. So $(y)(y/x)A$ is true in $\mathcal{M}$. If the domain is empty, then also $(y)(x)A$ could not be true in the model without $(y)(y/x)A$ being true in it.

XIV. $(y)(y/x)A$ implies $(x)A$ if y does not occur in A.

The proof is similar to that of XIII. Notice that if y does not occur in A, then $S_x^y(A)$ and $(y/x)A$ are the same sentence.

XV. If b does not occur in A, and $(b/c)A$ is logically true, then A is logically true.

Let us suppose that b does not occur in A, and that A is not logically true. Then we must show that $(b/c)A$ is not logically true.

To begin, let us consider the problem informally. If A is not logically true, then there is some model $\mathcal{M}$ in which A is false. Now we can make up a model $\mathcal{M}'$ in which b plays exactly the role that c played in $\mathcal{M}'$. So we claim that $(b/c)A$ will have exactly the status in $\mathcal{M}'$ that A had in $\mathcal{M}$. And this will hold for any statement A in which b does not occur.

Before going on, let us look at a specific example, say a statement E which has been symbolized as

$$Pa \supset (Pc \supset Pa)$$

To show that this is logically true, it would not do to show that $(a/c)E$, that is

$$Pa \supset (Pa \supset Pa)$$

is logically true—because a already occurs in E. But according to XV, you could show E to be logically true by showing that $(b/c)E$, namely

$$Pa \supset (Pb \supset Pa)$$

is logically true. For suppose that E is not true in a given model $\mathcal{M}$. Then without affecting any component expression in E, we could change $\mathcal{M}$ into a model $\mathcal{M}'$ which is exactly like $\mathcal{M}$ except that b has the same status as c (so that, if we *were* using identity, $b = c$ would be true in $\mathcal{M}'$).

We return now to the general problem. Let A be an arbitrary statement in which b does not occur. Just because b does not occur in A, we can say that $(b/c)A$ is obtained by interchanging b and c; that is, by replacing occurrences of c by occurrences of b, while simultaneously replacing occurrences of b by occurrences of c. Let us, for any statement B, write B^* for the result of interchanging b and c in B. What we shall prove now (and this establishes XV) is that for any model $\mathcal{M}$ and statement B, we can construct a model $\mathcal{M}^*$ such that B is true in $\mathcal{M}$ if and only if B^* is true in $\mathcal{M}^*$.

Let $\mathcal{M}^*$ have the same domain $\mathcal{D}$ as $\mathcal{M}$. Let $\mathcal{M}^*$ have interpretation function f^* such that f^* is exactly like f for symbols other than b and c, but $f^*(c) = f(b)$ if f assigns something to b and $f^*(b) = f(c)$ if f assigns something to c. Let $\mathcal{M}^*$ have story $\mathcal{S}^*$, which is the collection of statements B^* such that B is in $\mathcal{S}$.

Now let A be any statement. We shall prove that A^* is true in $\mathcal{M}^*$ if and only if A is true in $\mathcal{M}$. We prove this by mathematical induction, ordering statements by the number of symbols that occur in them.

THE BASIS STEP. Suppose A is atomic, say A is $Pa_1 \ldots a_n$. Then A^* is $Pa_1^* \ldots a_n^*$, where b^* is c, and c^* is b, and a_i^* is a_i if a_i is neither b nor c. Then $< f(a_1), \ldots, f(a_n) >$ is in $f(P)$ exactly if $< f^*(a_1^*), \ldots, f^*(a_n^*) >$ is in $f(P) = f^*(P)$. In addition, A^* is in $\mathcal{S}^*$ if and only if A is in $\mathcal{S}$. Therefore, in all cases, A^* is true in $\mathcal{M}^*$ if and only if A is true in $\mathcal{M}$.

THE INDUCTIVE STEP. As hypothesis of induction we suppose that for any statement B that has less symbols in it than A, B^* is true in $\mathcal{M}^*$ if and only if B is true in $\mathcal{M}$. There are now various possible cases.

Case 1. A is a negation; say A is $\neg B$. By hypothesis, B^* is true in $\mathcal{M}^*$ if and only if B is true in $\mathcal{M}$. But then $\neg B^*$ is true in $\mathcal{M}^*$ if and only if $\neg B$ is true in $\mathcal{M}$. But $\neg B^*$ is just $(\neg B)^*$, that is, A^*.

Case 2. A is a conjunction; say A is $(B \ \& \ C)$. We note that $A*$ is $(B \ \& \ C)*$, which is $(B* \ \& \ C*)$. By hypothesis, $B*$ and $C*$ are true in $\mathcal{M}*$ exactly if B and C are true in $\mathcal{M}$; hence $A*$ is true in $\mathcal{M}*$ exactly if A is true in $\mathcal{M}$.

Case 3. A is an alternation, say $(B \lor C)$. We leave this case as an exercise.

Case 4. A is a universally quantified statement; say $(x)B$. Now A is false in $\mathcal{M}$ if and only if $(d/x)B$ is false in $\mathcal{M}$ for some constant d which has a referent in $\mathcal{M}$. Suppose this is so. We note that $((d/x)B)*$ is exactly $(d*/x)B*$, where $b*$ is c, $c*$ is b, and $d*$ is d if d is not either b or c. By hypothesis, if $(d/x)B$ is false in $\mathcal{M}$, then $(d/x)B*$ is false in $\mathcal{M}*$; hence $(d*/x)B*$ is false in $\mathcal{M}*$. But if d has a referent in $\mathcal{M}$, then $d*$ has a referent in $\mathcal{M}*$. So in that case $(x)B*$, that is, $A*$, will be false in $\mathcal{M}$.

Conversely, if $A*$ is false in $\mathcal{M}*$, there must be a constant e such that $(e/x)B*$ is false in $\mathcal{M}*$. Now interchanging b and c in a statement is a perfectly symmetric operation, so $(e/x)B*$ is in fact $(e*/x)B*$. Hence if $(e/x)B*$ is false in $\mathcal{M}*$, then $(e*/x)B$ is false in $\mathcal{M}$, by the hypothesis of induction. And since e has a referent in $\mathcal{M}*$ exactly if $e*$ has a referent in $\mathcal{M}$, it follows that $(x)B$, namely A, will be false in $\mathcal{M}$.

This ends the demonstration of XV. Now we shall use XV to demonstrate a principle which will have an obvious bearing on the rule U1. Essentially it says this: if you have a derivation of form

$$
\begin{array}{c|c}
 & Fb \\
 & \cdot \\
 & \cdot \\
 & Gb
\end{array}
$$

then there is also a derivation, equally correct, of the form

$$
\begin{array}{rl|l}
(m) & & (x)Fx \\
(m+1) & \quad y & (x)Fx \\
 & & Fy \\
 & & \cdot \\
 & & \cdot \\
 & & \cdot \\
(n) & & Gy \\
(n+1) & & (x)Gx \qquad (m+1)\text{-}(n),\ \text{UQI}
\end{array}
$$

We state this in a precise and general manner:

> XVI. If b does not occur in $A_1, \ldots, A_n$, B, and statements (b/y) $A_1, \ldots, (b/y)A_n$ imply statement $(b/y)B$, then $(y)A_1, \ldots,$ $(y)A_n$ imply $(y)B$.

Let us suppose that b is as stipulated, and that $(y)A_1, \ldots, (y)A_n$ does not imply $(y)B$. Then there is a model $\mathcal{M}$ with domain $\mathcal{D}$, interpretation function f, and story S such that $(y)A_1, \ldots, (y)A_n$ are true in $\mathcal{M}$ while $(y)B$ is not. So there is a constant c such that $((c/y) A_1 \& \ldots \&$ $(c/y) A_n) \supset (c/y)B$ is false in $\mathcal{M}$. So this statement is not logically true. But b does not occur in it; hence $(b/c) ((c/y) A_1 \& \ldots \& (c/y)$ $A_n) \supset (c/y) B)$ is not logically true, by result XV. Now this is just $((b/y) A_1 \& \ldots \& (b/y) A_n \supset (b/y) B$; hence $(b/y) A_1, \ldots, (b)/y A_n$ do not imply $(b/y) B$.

SECTION 4
THE SOUNDNESS OF FREE LOGIC

We would like to show that if, by our rules, B can be derived from $A_1, \ldots, A_n$, then $A_1, \ldots, A_n$ imply B. The derivation is supposed to conform to all our cautions, of course. That is, $A_1, \ldots, A_n$ and B must be statements, and if variable y occurs free on any line, that line must be crossed by a scope line flanked by y. And every new subderivation general in some variable must obey the maxim that in such a case an entirely *new* variable is to be chosen.

These general subderivations and their concomitant free variables are purely a device of convenience for us. The convenience is this: within the scope of a universal quantifier, the quasi-statements can be manipulated like statements. For example, just because Fa implies $Fa \lor Ga$, we can infer $(x)(Fx \lor Gx)$ from $(x)Fx$. And because Fa and Ga together imply $Fa \& Ga$, we can infer $(x)(Fx \& Gx)$ from $(x)Fx$ and $(x)Gx$ together.

But because these are a convenience, we can in principle do away with them: we can regard them as abbreviatory. We do away with them by converting the scope line flanked by a variable into universal quantifiers binding the free occurrences of that variable. As an example, consider

$$
\begin{array}{lll}
(1) & (x)Fx & \\
(2) & \quad y \mid (x)Fx & (1)\ \ Ry \\
(3) & \quad\ \ \mid Fy & (2)\ \ UQE \\
(4) & \quad\ \ \mid Fy \lor Gy & (3)\ \ AI \\
(5) & (x)(Fx \lor Gx) & (2\text{--}4)\ \ UQI
\end{array}
$$

We transform this into

$$
\begin{array}{lll}
(1^*) & (x)Fx & \\
(2^*) & (y)((x)Fx) & \text{from } (1^*)\ [\text{See below}] \\
(3^*) & (y)(Fy) & \text{from } (2^*) \\
(4^*) & (y)(Fy \lor Gy) & \text{from } (3^*) \\
(5^*) & (x)(Fx \lor Gx) & \text{from } (4^*)
\end{array}
$$

In this sample derivation the three rules R, UQE, and UQI appear in a typical way. And we can argue for their soundness by showing that in the transforms (1*–5*), each statement is implied by its antecedents.

That (1*) implies (2*) follows by result XII of the preceding section. That (2*) implies (3*) follows by XIII (remember that in a new general subderivation, we must choose an entirely new variable, so that y cannot occur in line 1). By XVII, and the consideration that Fb implies $(Fb \lor Gb)$, (4*) is implied by (3*). And finally, again because general subderivations are flanked by entirely new variables, result XIV shows that (4*) implies (5*).

We could expand this discussion into an inductive proof that any derivation in which quantificational rules are used corresponds to a semantic implication. (For EQE and EQI the reader is asked to supply his own arguments.) But the idea of the transformed derivations and the appeal to the results of the preceding section is no doubt clear enough so that further precision would not bring further insight.

SECTION 5
THE COMPLETENESS OF FREE LOGIC

In Chapters 3 and 5 we have established that if the tableau sequence of a statement terminates, then the negation of that statement is categorically derivable. So we can prove the completeness of our logic by establishing that

If a statement A is logically false, then its tableau sequence terminates.

(We can still call A logically false exactly if $\neg A$ is logically true; but this means now that A is false in all models.) The tableau sequence is meant to be constructed using all tableau rules of Chapter 5 except VU and I. Again we shall resort to *modus tollens*: we shall assume that A has a non-terminating tableau sequence, and then prove that A is true in some model.

Since we find ourselves now in a context in which a non-terminating tableau sequence may go on forever, a few preliminaries are necessary. First we define rigorously what is meant by a *branch* of a tableau sequence.

DEFINITION. Let $B_1, \ldots, B_m, \ldots$ be a tableau sequence. Then $C_1 \ldots, C_m, \ldots$, is a *branch* of this sequence exactly if:
(a) for $i = 1$, C_i is an alternate of B_i;
(b) if B_{i+1} is formed from B_i by a replacement of C_i, then C_{i+1} is one of the (one or two) alternates that replace C_i in B_{i+1};
(c) if B_{i+1} is formed from B_i in some other way, then $C_{i+1} = C_i$.

As an example, let us pick out the branches of the following tableau sequence:

1. $(x)Fx \,\&\, \neg(y)(Fy \,\&\, Gy)$
2. $E\{(x)Fx \,\&\, \neg(Fz \,\&\, Gz)\}$ 1, UR
3. $E\{((x)Fx \,\&\, \neg Fz)\} \vee E\{((x)Fx \,\&\, \neg Gz)\}$ 2, NK
4. $E\{Fz \,\&\, \neg Fz \,\&\, (x)Fx\} \vee E\{Fz \,\&\, \neg Gz \,\&\, (x)Fx\}$ 3, Ul

This tableau sequence has two branches:

$$B_1: \quad (x)Fx \,\&\, \neg(y)(Fy \,\&\, Gy)$$
$$E\{(x)Fx \,\&\, \neg(Fz \,\&\, Gz)\}$$
$$E\{(x)Fx \,\&\, \neg Fz\}$$
$$E\{Fz \,\&\, \neg Fz \,\&\, (x)Fx\}$$

$$B_2: \quad (x)Fx \,\&\, \neg(y)(Fy \,\&\, Gy)$$
$$E\{(x)Fx \,\&\, \neg(Fz \,\&\, Gx)\}$$
$$E\{(x)Fx \,\&\, \neg Gz\}$$
$$E\{Fz \,\&\, \neg Gz \,\&\, (x)Fx\}$$

And of these, exactly one *terminates*, namely B_1.

If the tableau sequence does not terminate, then it must have a branch that does not terminate (that is, does not have underlined formulas). When $C_1, \ldots, C_m, \ldots$, is a branch that does not terminate, let $c_1, \ldots, c_n, \ldots$ be the constants that do not occur in C_1 (and hence not in C_m, for any m), and let $y_1, \ldots, y_n, \ldots$ be all the variables we have. Then write B^* for the result of the following operation on a sentence B:

(i) drop all existential quantifiers at the beginning of B, (ii) replace any free occurrence of y_i by an occurrence of c_i. For example, $E(Fy_1 y_3) = (Fc_1c_3)$. Now we define for our non-terminating branch $C_1, \ldots, C_m, \ldots$ the following

> The branch diagram of $C_1, \ldots, C_m, \ldots$ is the set of sentences that are conjuncts of the sentences $C_1^*, \ldots, C_m^*, \ldots$.

Thus the branch diagram of B_2 in the above example is the set

$$(x)Fx, \neg(y)(Fy \& Gy), \neg(Fc_1 \& Gc_1), Fc_1 \& \neg Gc_1, Fc_1, \neg Gc_1$$

where c_1 is the first ("alphabetically the first") variable that does not occur in the branch B_2. You can see what role c_1 is supposed to play; it is the name of some existent which is such that it is a counterexample to the claim that $(y)(Fy \& Gy)$ is true. (That is, in the branch we see the assertion $\neg(y)(Fy \& Gy)$; that is, there is something that is *not* both F and G, so we say: let us call it c_1.)

Concerning the branch diagram we can now deduce the following, by considering exactly how the tableau rules operate:

(i)   if $\neg\neg A$ is in the branch diagram, then so is A;
(ii)   if $A \& B$ is in it, so are A and B;
(iii)   if $\neg(A \& B)$ is in it, so is $\neg A$ or $\neg B$;
(iv)   if $(A \lor B)$ is in it, so is A or B;
(v)   if $\neg(A \lor B)$ is in it, so are $\neg A$ and $\neg B$;
(vi)   if $(x)A$ is in it, and c_i occurs in any member of the branch diagram but not in the branch, then $(c_i/x)A$ is in it;
(vii)   if $\neg(x)A$ is in it, so is $\neg(c_j/x)A$ for one of the constants c_j which occurs in the branch diagram but not in the branch;
(viii) if A is in it, $\neg A$ is not, and conversely.

Now what we are going to do is this: we construct a model $\mathcal{M}$, such that if a formula is in the branch diagram of this non-terminating branch, then it is true in $\mathcal{M}$. The constants $c_1, c_2, \ldots$, which do not occur in the branch $C_1, C_2, \ldots$, are supposed to refer to existents. That is, C_i is true *because* C_i^* is true, for the former has the form $E\{Ry_1 \ldots y_n\}$ and the latter has the form $Rc_1 \ldots c_n$. So we interpret each such term c_i (which occurs in the branch diagram but not in the branch) in such a way that then it designates something in model $\mathcal{M}$. So we can infer that $\mathcal{M} \models C_i^*$, and then that $\mathcal{M} \models C_i$. But C_i is a alternate of B_i, so we conclude

$\mathcal{M} \models B_i$—specifically, setting $i = 1$, that $\mathcal{M} \models B_1$. But of course, B_1 is just A, so A is not logically false.

Now we construct $\mathcal{M}$ by choosing, first of all, as domain $\mathcal{D}$ the set of those constants c_i that actually occur in the branch diagram but not in the branch. Then we set $f(c_i) = c_i$ when c_i is in $\mathcal{D}$, and do not assign elements of $\mathcal{D}$ to any other constants. For a predicate P, $f(P)$ is the set of sequences $< d_1, \ldots, d_n >$ such that $Pd_1 \ldots d_n$ is a member of the branch diagram, *and* $d_1, \ldots, d_n$ belong to $\mathcal{D}$. As our story $\mathcal{S}$ we choose the set of all atomic sentences that are members of the branch diagram *and* contain some constant which is not in $\mathcal{D}$.

To prove that every sentence in the branch diagram is true in $\mathcal{M}$, we divide them into a number of classes, considering each separately. Let Q be a sentence in the branch diagram in question.

(1) Q is an atomic sentence, say $Pb_1 \ldots b_n$. Then if $b_1, \ldots, b_n$ all belong to $\mathcal{D}$, we have $< b_1, \ldots, b_n > \varepsilon f(P)$, and $f(b_i) = b_i$ in this case, so $< f(b_1), \ldots, f(b_n) > \varepsilon f(P)$. Therefore $\mathcal{M} \models Pb_1 \ldots b_n$. If some b_i does not belong to $\mathcal{D}$, then $Pb_1 \ldots b_n$ is in the story $\mathcal{S}$, and so $\mathcal{M} \models Pb_1 \ldots b_n$.

(2) Q is the negation of some atomic sentence, say $\neg Pb_1 \ldots b_n$. Then neither of the above lines of reasoning apply for $Pb_1 \ldots b_n$, and so not $(\mathcal{M} \models Pb_1 \ldots b_n)$. But then $\mathcal{M} \models \neg Pb_1 \ldots b_n$.

Now we are going to look at more complex sentences, and hypothesize that our claim holds for all sentences of length less than Q.

(3) Q is $\neg \neg Q'$. Then Q' is also in the branch diagram, so $\mathcal{M} \models Q'$ by hypothesis. But then not $\mathcal{M} \models \neg Q'$, and hence $\mathcal{M} \models \neg \neg Q'$.

(4) Q is $(Q' \& Q'')$. Then Q' and Q'' are in the diagram, so by hypothesis, $\mathcal{M} \models Q'$ and $\mathcal{M} \models Q''$. But then $\mathcal{M} \models Q' \& Q''$.

(5) Q' is $\neg (Q' \vee Q'')$. This is like case (4).

(6) Q is $\neg (Q' \& Q'')$. Then either $\neg Q'$ or $\neg Q''$ is in the diagram, so by hypothesis, not $\mathcal{M} \models Q'$ or not $\mathcal{M} \models Q''$. But then not $\mathcal{M} \models (Q' \& Q'')$.

(7) Q is $(Q' \vee Q'')$. This is like case (6).

(8) Q is $(x)Q'$. Then if c_i occurs in some member of the diagram but not in the branch, $(c_i/x)Q'$ is in the diagram. By hypothesis then, $\mathcal{M} \models (c_i/x)Q'$ if c_i occurs in some member of the diagram but not in the branch—equivalently, if $f(c_i)$ is in $\mathcal{D}$. But then $\mathcal{M} \models (x)Q'$.

(9) Q is $\neg(x)Q'$. Then $\neg(c_i/x)Q'$ is in the diagram for one of the constants c_i, and c_i is in $\mathcal{D}$, so $f(c_i) = c_i \in \mathcal{D}$. So we have $\mathcal{M} \models \neg(c_i/x)Q'$, and hence not $\mathcal{M} \models (c_i/x)Q'$. But then not $(\mathcal{M} \models (x)Q')$, and so $\mathcal{M} \models \neg(x)Q'$.

This ends the proof.

SECTION 6
REMARKS CONCERNING NON-EMPTY DOMAINS AND IDENTITY

In Part III, Chapter 5, we showed that within our proof theory, the elimination of vacuous quantifiers was equivalent to the assumption that $(Ex)(Fx \lor \neg Fx)$ is logically true. But it is easily shown that this sentence is true in one of our models *exactly if* that model has a non-empty domain. So if we use the rule VU in constructing tableau sequences, our proofs of soundness and completeness go through provided we stipulate that a model must have a non-empty domain.

The introduction of identity introduces some rather more dramatic complications. First we must say that if b designates something, then $b = c$ is true exactly if c also designates that very same thing. But if b does not designate anything, then $b = c$ is true exactly if it belongs to the story of the model.

Now to ensure that

1. $b = b$
2. $b = c \supset \cdot Fb \supset Fc$

both come out logically true we must place two restrictions on the story $\mathcal{S}$:

(a) $b = b$ is in $\mathcal{S}$ if and only if b is a constant that does not designate anything in the model;
(b) if $b = c$ is in $\mathcal{S}$ and A is in $\mathcal{S}$, then $(c/b)A$ and $(b/c)A$ are also in $\mathcal{S}$.

It can now easily be seen that 1 and 2 will hold true in any model, provided Fb is an atomic statement. But then we can also prove 2 to hold for non-atomic statements.

For let A be a sentence of any complexity, let $\mathcal{M} \models A$ and $\mathcal{M} \models b = c$ hold, and assume that for any sentence B of length less than A, $\mathcal{M} \models B'$ if and only if $\mathcal{M} \models (c/b)B$. The cases are

(i) A is $\neg B$. Then $\mathcal{M} \models B$ if and only if $\mathcal{M} \models (c/b)B$; but not $\mathcal{M} \models B$, so not $\mathcal{M} \models (c/b)B$. Then $\mathcal{M} \models \neg(c/b)B$; but that is just $\mathcal{M} \models (c/b)\neg B$.

(ii) A is $(B \,\&\, C)$. Then $\mathcal{M} \models B$ and $\mathcal{M} \models C$; by hypothesis $\mathcal{M} \models (c/b)B$ and $\mathcal{M} \models (c/b)C$. Hence $\mathcal{M} \models (c/b)B \,\&\, (c/b)C$; but that is just $\mathcal{M} \models (c/b)(B \,\&\, C)$.

(iii) A is $B \vee C$, case like (ii);

(iv) A is $(x)B$. Then $\mathcal{M} \models (a/x)B$ for any constant a which designates something in $\mathcal{M}$. By hypothesis, $\mathcal{M} \models (c/b)(a/x)B$ for any such statement $(a/x)B$. But this is just: $\mathcal{M} \models (a/x)(c/b)B$, for every designating constant a; hence $\mathcal{M} \models (x)(c/b)B$. It is easy to see that this is exactly the same as $\mathcal{M} \models (c/b)(x)B$.

We have now essentially established soundness: certainly rule I will not lead from true statements to false ones, and an underlined statement of form $E(X \,\&\, x \not\approx x \,\&\, Y)$ must be logically false.

In the completeness proof, we have this problem: if $c = b$ occurs in the branch diagram, then c and b must be treated in exactly the same way in the associated model. This means that if, for example, $c = b$ occurs in the diagram, we must set $f(b) = f(c_i) = c_i$, when c_i is one of those special constants that are used to designate elements in the domain. In addition, we must increase the story, by adding $b = b$ whenever b is not one of the designating constants. And similarly for the second restriction on the story.

SECTION 7
REMARKS ON THE SEMANTICS OF FREE DESCRIPTION THEORIES

When we introduce descriptions, we must define terms by some such clause as: constants and variables are terms, and if Fx is a sentence then $(Ix)Fx$ is a term. Note, however, that Fx may already contain a description. It is therefore impossible to define sentences and terms separately: we could not possibly define the terms first and *then* the sentences, nor define the sentences first and *then* the terms. For this reason we adopt the following complicated definitions of sentences and terms all at once:

(a)   Variables and constants are terms;

(b)   if $t_1, \ldots, t_n$ are terms, and F an n-ary predicate, then $Pt_1 \ldots t_n$ is a sentence;

(c)   If t_1 and t_2 are terms, $t_1 = t_2$ is a sentence;
(d)   If A and B are sentences, so are $\neg A$, $(A\ \&\ B)$, and $(A \lor B)$;
(e)   If A is a sentence and x a variable, then $(x)A$ is a sentence;
(f)   If A is a sentence and x a variable, then $(Ix)A$ is a term;
(g)   Nothing is a sentence or term except in virtue of the above stipulations.

It must be recalled that in $(Ix)A$, any occurrence of x free in A is bound by (Ix).

In our models, we now extend the interpretation function f to descriptions in certain cases. We go by the following principle:

> If there is exactly one member x of the domain of $\mathcal{M}$ such that $\mathcal{M} \models (b/x)A$ for any constant b such that $f(b) = \alpha$ then $f((Ix)A) = \alpha$.

In any other case, f does not assign anything to the description. (It must be added that if we were not following the fiction that everything has a name, the model theory for descriptions would be a good deal more complex.) The restrictions on the story of a model with respect to identity must be extended to descriptions, of course.

We can now prove that FD is sound and complete, if we do not modify models any further. The proofs for FD can be given fairly directly by adding a special tableau rule for descriptions. This rule is designed on the basis of the three possible cases that arise in the evaluation of $G(Ix)Fx$: that $(Ix)Fx$ exists, that nothing is F, and that more than one thing that is F exists. Note that this rule leads to the occurrence of three-way branchings in tableau sequences.

The emendations needed in the soundness and completeness proofs are relatively straightforward, but lengthy.

EXERCISES

1.   Principle 3 in section 1 does not have explicit clauses for $\supset$ and (Ex). Supply these.

2.   Show which of the following are true statements in $\mathcal{M}_1$ in Section 2:
      (a) Pb_8 (e) $(Ex)(Px\ \&\ Qx)$
      (b) Qb_1 (f) $(Ex)(Px \lor Qx)$
      (c) $\neg Qb_2$ (g) $(Ex)(Px\ \&\ \neg Qx)$
      (d) $Pb_{12}\ \&\ Qb_1$

3.   Demonstrate (a)–(e) in section 2.

4. As was done in section 2 for excluded middle and Henkin's formula, show that the following are logically true:

    (a) $A \supset (B \supset A)$
    (b) $(A \supset B) \& (\neg A \supset B) \cdot \supset B$
    (c) $(x)[(y)Fy \supset Fx]$
    (d) $(x)(Fx \supset Gx) \supset \cdot (x)Fx \supset (x)Gx$
    (e) $(x)(Fx \lor \neg Fx)$
    (f) $(Ey)(Fy) \supset (x)(Ey)(Rxy \lor Fy)$
    (g) $(Ey)(x)Rxy \supset (x)(Ey)Rxy$

5. Demonstrate XIV.

6. Supply arguments for rules EQE and EQI similar to those given in section 4 for R, UQE, and UQI.

PART *V* **PHILOSOPHICAL IMPLICATIONS
AND APPLICATIONS
OF FREE LOGIC**

10 Philosophical Implications and Applications of Free Logic

"Well, it's no use *your* talking about waking him," said Tweedledum, "when you're only one of the things in his dream. You know very well you're not real."

"I *am* real!" said Alice, and began to cry.

"You won't make yourself a bit realler by crying," Tweedledee remarked: "there's nothing to cry about."

"If I wasn't real," Alice said—half-laughing through her tears, it all seemed so ridiculous—"I shouldn't be able to cry."

"I hope you don't suppose those are real tears?" Tweedledum interrupted in a tone of great contempt.

—Lewis Carroll, *Through the Looking Glass*

SECTION 1
ARE THERE NON-EXISTENTS?

Free logic is an extension of classical quantification theory that provides principles for reasoning in situations where the objects of our discourse are either non-existent or have only putative existence. So it enables one to measure the worth of reasoning in fictional discourse as well as in discourse about, say, the hypothetical entities of science.

Consider the non-referential name "Pegasus". It is an example of an expression that is used to talk about non-existents, and in particular, about the non-existent but possible object with wings, tail, four legs, and so on, captured by Bellerophon. Now free logic validates certain reasoning containing words such as "Pegasus". But it does not follow from this fact that it is committed to a realm of entities among which

199

is included a flying horse. To be sure, one could develop a philosophical semantics for free logic that does recognize a realm of non-actual but possible beings. This, indeed, is the most natural (though not the only) way to interpret the "outer domain" semantics involved in the completeness proof for free logic presented by H. LeBlanc and R. Thomason.* But one need not develop the semantic that way—and we did not in our own presentation earlier in this book. In our development, *talk* about non-existent objects is just that—"talk" is what is stressed. "Non-existent" object, for us, is just a picturesque way of speaking devoid of any ontological commitment. In this regard our own development is motivated by what Russell called "a robust sense of reality".

SECTION 2
DO FREE DESCRIPTION THEORIES NECESSARILY SUFFER FROM SCOPE PROBLEMS?

We have had occasion in Chapters 6 and 7 to emphasize the fact that in free logic expressions such as "Pegasus" and "the winged horse captured by Bellerophon" are genuine singular *terms*, in contrast to the position of Russell. A look at our semantic development also shows that non-referential names and descriptions are not assigned anything in the domain of discourse. These features of our treatment of names and descriptions have philosophical consequences. Recall first Russell's theory of descriptions. According to Russell a statement such as "The king of France is bald" is to be analyzed as "Exactly one object is king of France and is bald". The expression "is bald" is a simple predicate. But if we replace "is bald" by the complex predicate "is not bald" in "The king of France is bald", problems arise. How shall we treat the new statement? As (a) "It is not the case that exactly one object is king of France and is bald" or as (b) "Exactly one object is king of France and is not bald"? The matter is important because, given the fact that there is no king of France, (a) is true but (b) is false. Russell responded by introducing the concept of "the scope of a description" and requiring that every descriptional statement be unambiguously rendered in the new notation with appropriate scope. We will not dwell

---

*LeBlanc, H. and R. Thomason, "Completeness Theorems for Some Presupposition-Free Logics", *Fundamenta Mathematica*, 62, (1968), pp. 123–164. See also, R. Meyer and K. Lambert, "Universally Free Logic and Standard Quantification Theory", *Journal of Symbolic Logic*, 33, (1968), pp. 93–117, for an example of an "outer domain" semantics that does not treat the entities therein as non-actual objects.

on the subtleties of Russell's treatment of the problem of scope because what is of concern to us are the circumstances that produced the problem. Notice that the ambiguity occurring in contexts containing complex predicates is harmless in cases where the definite description is referential. For example, whether "The senior author of this book is not a woman" is rendered after the fashion of (a) above or of (b) above is inconsequential; the truth-value is the same (namely, true). Accordingly, one might think that the problem of scope is produced by the semantic policy of allowing non-referential descriptions to be assigned no entity in the domain of discourse. That is, one might think that because there may be some definite descriptions assigned no entity in the domain of discourse—the natural semantic analogue of the informal concept of non-referential—that scope problems are inevitable in free logic.

It should be emphasized that in FD a statement of the form $\neg G(Ix)Fx$ is treated as unambiguous. Thus it is not equivalent either to $(Ex)((y)$ $(Fy \supset y = x) \& Fx \& \neg Gx)$ or to $\neg(Ex)((y)(Fy \supset y = x) \& Fx \& Gx)$. But is this circumstance possible only because of relatively weak character of FD? After all FD says very little about the treatment of non-referential definite descriptions. Would we run into scope problems if we tried to strengthen FD?

So the problem of scope can be put in better perspective by considering how one can strengthen the description theory developed in Part Three. That theory has been named FD, and before going on we shall now sketch the motivation and development of a stronger free description theory.*

If non-referring terms are not of great concern (as is the case for many purposes) it makes sense to treat them as uniformly as possible. In that case, we may note that the following holds for any terms t, t' which do have a referent:

1. $t = t' \equiv (y)(y = t \equiv y = t')$

So, if we wish to treat non-referring terms very uniformly, we can accept 1 as a *general* principle. Given that 1 is accepted as a general principle, for all terms t, t', we then have

2. $t = (Ix)Fx \equiv (y)(y = t \equiv y = (Ix)Fx)$

and from 2 by the principle

---

*See K. Lambert and B. van Fraassen, "On Free Description Theory", *Zeitschr. für math. Logik und Grundl. der Math.*, 13,3: 1967, pp. 225–240.

3. $(y)(y = (Ix)A \equiv (y/x)A \& (x)(A \supset x = y))$

we get

4. $t = (Ix)Fx \equiv (y)(y = t \equiv (x)(Fx \equiv x = y))$

We may note that from 1 we can also derive the following principle:

5. $(\neg E! t \& \neg E! t') \supset t = t'$

since $\neg E!t$ is logically equivalent to $(y)(y \neq t)$, where term t is not itself the variable y. Thus under the present proposal all non-existents are identified, which may be both perfectly harmless and very useful in some contexts.

The very "strong" free description theory in which (1)–(5) are theorems is called FD2. This theory results if we adopt the intelim rules

$$\text{DE} \left| \begin{array}{l} t = (Ix)A \\ \hline (y)(t = y \equiv)(y/x) A \& (x)(A \supset x = y))) \end{array} \right.$$

$$\text{DI} \left| \begin{array}{l} (y)(t = y \equiv ((y/x)A \& (x)(A \supset x = y))) \\ \hline t = (Ix)A \end{array} \right.$$

FD is part of FD2, for given DE and DI, the rules RDE and RDI can be reduced to the status of admissible rules (in fact, so can II). We leave it to the reader to establish these claims.

Returning now to the question of scope problems, we note that

$$G(Ix)Fx \equiv (Ey)((x)(Fx \equiv x = y) \& Gy) \lor$$
$$\neg (Ey)(x)(Fx \equiv x = y) \& G(Ix)(x \neq x)$$

is provable in the system FD2. But, as the reader may also verify,

$$(Ey)((x)(Fx \equiv x = y) \& \neg Gy) \lor$$
$$\neg (Ey)(x)(Fx \equiv x = y) \& \neg G(Ix)(x \neq x)$$

and

$$\neg [(Ey)((x)(Fx \equiv x = y) \& Gy) \lor$$
$$\neg (Ey)(x)(Fx \equiv x = y) \& G(Ix)(x \neq x)]$$

are logically equivalent. It follows that "The so and so is not such and such" and "It is not the case that so and so is such and such" have the same truth-values whether or not "the so and so" is assigned an entity in the domain of discourse. In short, whether a description theory encounters scope problems concerns the analysis of descriptional contexts and not just the semantic policy for treating non-referential descriptions. So it is not the case that free description theories need have scope problems.

SECTION 3
IS FREE LOGIC EXTENSIONAL?

In our semantic account, non-referential singular terms such as "Pegasus" and "the horse captured by Bellerophon" are not assigned entities in the domain of discourse. Given the further assumption that there is a predicate whose extension is the domain of discourse itself—in the present system, the predicate is "$(Ex)(x = \ldots)$", that is, "being identical with some (existent) object" will suffice—it is easy to show that free logic violates the principle that coextensive predicates can be substituted for each other in all contexts without change of truth-value (one of the set of traditional principles called principles of *extensionability*). By coextensive predicates we mean predicates true of exactly the same set of existents. For example, "being colored" and "being an existent that is colored" are coextensive, but "being colored" and "being tall" are not.

In the present development, a predicate F is coextensive with a predicate G just in case the statement "$(x)(Fx \equiv Gx)$" is true. Accordingly, we will have a breakdown in the principle of predicate substitutivity, other things being equal, if the formula "$(x)(Fx \equiv Gx) \supset (Ft \equiv Gt)$" is not a theorem. In fact this is quickly shown, simply by substituting "being self-identical" for F, "being an existent self-identical" for G, and "Pegasus" for t. For though "being self-identical" is coextensive with "being an existent self-identical", and "Pegasus is self-identical" is true, "Pegasus is an existent self-identical" is false.

As a matter of fact the argument holds even if we reject "Pegasus is self-identical" as being true. For now, interchange of the coexistensive predicate "being self-identical *if* an existent" for "being self-identical" leads from a falsehood to a truth, namely, that Pegasus is self-identical *if* he exists. So it makes no difference whether "Pegasus is self-identical" is taken to be true or false, the principle of predicate substitutivity can be shown to fail in free logic.

As indicated above, failure of predicate substitutivity is one of the ways in which a system of logic can fail to be extensional. Some philosophers regard the failure of predicate extensionality as a very serious matter. Thus Quine has suggested* that a necessary condition of "coherent" quantification is predicate extensionality; failure of predicate extensionality renders quantification "incoherent".

Quine's argument for this belief is as follows. Consider, for example, the statement that (Ex) (necessarily x is odd) in the context of a discussion about the number 9. This is a true statement. But, one may ask, what is the object x specified in the statement that makes it true? One answer is

1. the object of which the predicate "$(Ex)(y \neq x \& x = yy \& x = y + y + y)$" is true;

another presumably acceptable answer is

2. the object of which the predicate "There are x planets" is true,

a predicate that is coextensive with the first predicate because they are true of exactly the same thing. But this is paradoxical, Quine claims, because, though answer 1 supports the truth of "(Ex) (necessarily x is odd)" in virtue of the true statement "Necessarily$(x)((Ey)(y \neq x \& x = yy \& x = y + y + y) \supset x$ is odd)", answer 2 fails to support the truth of "(Ex) (necessarily is odd)" in virtue of the falsehood of "Necessarily (x) (there are x planets $\supset x$ is odd)". Note that here we have a failure of substitutivity of predicates in contexts governed by the word "necessarily"—a "modal" context. We shall discuss these contexts further in Section 7.

Now whatever may be the worth of this argument in modal contexts, it does not always go through in non-modal contexts. Imagine a language that contains as its only atomic predicate the predicate "being identical with Pegasus". Consider now the coextensive predicates "being identical with Pegasus" and "being an existent identical with Pegasus". It certainly is not the case that Pegasus is self-identical if and only if Pegasus is an existent self-identical. So here we have a failure of predicate substitutivity. Now consider the sentence "$(Ex)(x = $ Pegasus$)$"; this corresponds in our example to Quine's "(Ex) (necessarily x is odd)". Notice that Quine's argument does not get off the ground here because the sentence in question is false. So the question, "What is the object x specified that makes $(Ex)(x = $ Pegasus$)$ true?" does not arise. We conclude therefore that the admission of non-referential singular

---

*See W. V. Quine, "Replies", *Synthese*, 19, (1968), pp. 308–309.

terms, though it does bring about a failure of extensionality, does not, however, make quantification "incoherent" via Quine's argument.*

The issue is important because of the lamentable tendency to blame certain puzzling and/or questionable features of modal discourse on its non-extensional character. In view of the present argument it would be equally plausible to attribute these vagaries to the modalities themselves.

SECTION 4
APPLICATIONS OF FREE LOGIC

In free logic we admit singular terms to our language without stipulating that those terms must refer to something. There are many areas of ordinary discourse in which non-referring terms occur, and free logic is meant to be usable in the logical analysis of such discourse. Indeed, some uses of terms which do not (or perhaps may or may not) refer are of philosophical interest, and it is important not to ride roughshod over the needs served by discourse of this sort.

A novelist has complained that the grass never grows green again on the soil touched by Greek philosophy; many philosophers have voiced similar complaints about logic. There certainly is a tradition in logic that claims to know exactly the needs of science, mathematics, and linguistic analysis, and to provide philosophy with a simple, can-onical language adequate to these needs. From such a point of view, problems concerning non-referring terms and other vagaries of actual discourse are not *logical* problems. They are problems to be eliminated by paraphrase procedures leading from the tongue of the vulgar to the language of logic. Now, as we emphasized, it seems quite impossible to attain any significant level of generality unless some paraphrase procedure, some regimentation of language, is introduced. But, we be-lieve, logical analysis is nevertheless improved as fewer problems are shunted to paraphrase and more complexities dealt with on the side of logic. And we find it difficult to trust the insight into what the needs of science and philosophy are that justifies limiting attention to a single canonical language.

---

*It should be emphasized that we are not attributing to Quine the belief that failure of predicate extensionality *in free logic* leads to incoherent quantification. For he holds that this result occurs only if substitutivity of identity fails and makes quantification incoherent. But in our development substitutivity of identity holds in the form of IE.

In the sections that follow, we address ourselves to three problems that may be raised concerning our approach and its usefulness. The first concerns the use of the different free description theories: when is one appropriate rather than another? The second concerns our adoption of relatively strong rules for identity: will these prove limiting in extensions of our logic to other contexts? And the third concerns our assumption, so far, that sentences in which non-referring terms occur are all true or false, just like more ordinary sentences. We regard these as serious problems concerning the application of free logic, but shall try to show that our approach is flexible enough to handle them.

SECTION 5
USES OF DEFINITE DESCRIPTIONS

In Part Three we developed a minimal description theory, FD, whose characteristic principle is

$$1. \ (y)(y = (Ix)Fx \equiv Fy \ \& \ (x)(Fx \supset x = y))$$

Using only this principle, there is nothing special that can be said about a description, such as "the present king of France" which does not refer. The sentence

2. The present king of France is bald

is true or false, but we do not know which. (This is subject to qualifications which we shall take up in the last section.) All we can say, logically, is that *if* the king of France exists, then he is a king of France; if he does not exist, then he either is a king of France or he is not; there is no *logical* reason to choose either alternative.

Such a weak description theory seems to be needed in some contexts; or, at least, some sentences involving non-referring descriptions must be allowed to be either true or false, depending on non-logical factors. Examples seem to be

3. I am thinking of the golden mountain;
4. The rain prevented the explosion;
5. The supreme god of the Greeks is Zeus.

But perhaps we are too cautious; perhaps there are some truths to which everyone would agree. For example, Henry Leonard, who pioneered free logic,* held that

6. The so and so is to be conceived of as a so and so

must be true, no matter what "so and so" is taken to be.** If he is right, it is no doubt because of the meaning of "is to be conceived of as". Again in a context in which all meanings are abstracted from, we must hold 6 to be a non-logical principle. Another principle that has been offered as always holding is

7. $t = (Ix)(x = t)$

If that is correct, it must be because of the meaning of the description operator and identity predicate—and that is normally taken to be a matter of logic. But the theory of identity can, when extended to non-referring terms, be developed in various ways, and 7 is not always accepted.***

Most important is perhaps the consideration that there are contexts in which the theory of descriptions is useful, and where it is harmless to treat all non-referring descriptions in some uniform way. This is especially true of mathematical contexts. In such a case, we would offer the theory FD2. However, there is a similar theory, also with great convenience, which is like FD2 in accepting

8. $\neg E! (Ix)A \supset (Ix)A = (Ix)(Fx \& \neg Fx)$

but rejects 7. This theory was developed by Scott.****

The conclusion to be drawn, it seems to us, is that there are many purposes for which definite descriptions are useful, and specific descrip-

---

*See Leonard's paper "The Logic of Existence", *Philosophical Studies*, 7, 1956, pp. 49–64.

**See his Presidential Address to the Western Division of the American Philosophical Association entitled "Essences, Attributes and Predicates", Milwaukee, May, 1964.

***D. Scott, "Existence and Description in Formal Logic", in R. Schoeman (ed), *Bertrand Russell: Philosopher of the Century* (New York: Atlantic, Little Brown, 1967).

*****Ibid.*

tion theories should be tailored to fit special needs. In our opinion, the most flexible and convenient way to do this is to begin with the minimal theory FD, with 1 as basic principle, and then to add further principles as need, purpose, or convenience dictates.

Again, some philosophical puzzles and arguments may be clarified to some extent through attention to definite descriptions. Anselm's Ontological Argument may be stated as

(1) God = that than which none greater can be conceived;
(2) If God does not exist, something greater than God can be conceived;
(3) (Hence) God exists.

Of this, (1) is justified as being true simply by virtue of the meaning of the word "God". To justify (2) we can argue that we can conceive of God existing, and if one thing is exactly like another except that only the first exists, then the first is greater than the second. Finally, (3) is derived, apparently, from (1) and (2): for if something greater than God could be conceived, (1) would be false.

If we paraphrase this argument in our official idiom, and then symbolize it, we get

(1*) $g = (Ix)\neg Fx$
(2*) $\neg E!g \supset Fg$
(3*) (Hence) $E!g$

Here "Fx" symbolizes "something greater than x can be conceived" and "g" stands for "God". Now the inference from (1*) and (2*) to (3*) is not valid as it stands. It would be if augmented by the additional premise that "The being than which nothing greater can be conceived is a being than which nothing greater can be conceived". In symbols this is

$\neg F(Ix)\neg Fx$

But what are the grounds for this additional premise? Certainly not that it is logically true, as we saw in the discussion of the Russell-Meinong debate: a special case in point would be that in which $\neg Fx$ is a contradiction. This last observation is quite independent of whether we use the weak theory FD or the strong theory FD2. (Still, these brief remarks cannot, by themselves, end the debate concerning the validity of Anselm's Ontological Argument, since something essential *may* have been lost in our paraphrase and symbolization.) *

SECTION 6
SINGULAR TERMS IN MATHEMATICS

Most of classical mathematics can be developed in a framework devoid of singular terms, the logical framework developed in Parts One and Two of this book. Indeed, it is surprising how little in the way of special symbols and axioms needs to be introduced for this purpose. This recasting of mathematics in the language of quantification theory is one of the most important intellectual developments of the past century. * *

But while the language of mathematics may in principle be devoid of singular terms, it is not in practice; and convenience and elegance may be served by allowing singular terms that may or may not refer. We shall explain this briefly with reference to functions and sets.

A *function,* as is well known, has arguments and values. For example, the following is a function:

f has as arguments all real numbers, and if x is an argument of f, then the value $f(x)$ of f at x is 3-x.

Here we write $f(x) = 3$-x and usually assume that this equation by itself conveys to the readers that x ranges over the real numbers. Now there are many cases where we have to add some such clause as "provided x is not zero" or "provided x is not 2", as in the case

$g(x) = 2/(x$-$2)$

In this case we usually say that the function is *not defined* for $x = 2$. We also say that g is a *partially defined* function on the real numbers.

---

*A different approach to this argument is taken in J. Hintikka, "On The Logic of the Ontological Argument", in K. Lambert (ed.), *The Logical Way of Doing Things* (New Haven: Yale University Press, 1969), pp. 185–197. See also William Mann's paper "Definite Descriptions and the Ontological Argument", *Theoria*, 33, (1967), pp. 211–230.

* *Bertrand Russell, *Introduction to Mathematical Philosophy* (London: Allen & Unwin, reprinted 1968). This book is still one of the most readable introductions to this subject.

There are many important instances of this latter notion; for example, conditional probabilities, and partial computable functions. Now partially defined functions are not very manageable if we constantly have to add clauses concerning argumenthood. But suppose x is not an argument of f; then $f(x)$ is just a non-referring term. In fact, we can think of $f(x) = y$ as having the form $R_f(x,y)$ so that $f(x)$ is just $(Iy)(R_f(x,y))$. This reduces the theory of functions to the theory of descriptions. And for purposes of mathematics,* it is now perfectly all right to take the strongest possible description theory in which all non-existents are conveniently assumed to be identical.

Secondly, in set theory it was first assumed that any stateable condition defined a set; the well-known Russell paradox soon made it necessary to give up this principle. Using ε for the relation of set-membership, the following principle relates membership in a defined set with the defining condition

$$1. \quad (x)(x \, \varepsilon \, \{y : Fy\} \equiv Fx)$$

where $\{y : Fy\}$ is a term read as "the set of all things y such that Fy". Now the paradoxical Russell set is

$$2. \quad R = \{y : \neg \, (y \, \varepsilon \, y)\}.$$

1 and 2 entail

$$3. \quad (x)(x \, \varepsilon \, R \equiv \neg \, (x \, \varepsilon \, x))$$

which instantiated to R yields the contradiction

$$4. \quad R \, \varepsilon \, R \equiv \neg \, (R \, \varepsilon \, R).$$

There are many ways to avoid this contradiction: for example, we may revise our logic so that 4 can be true, or we may set up our language in such a way that R cannot be defined by 2, or we may give up principle 1. From the point of view of free logic, however, the above proof is most obviously seen as a proof of the non-existence of R. (It is possible to see this as an application of description theory, because the term $\{y : Fy\}$ may be thought of as shorthand for a definite description, namely

---

*When the functions are being used for other purposes this may not hold, of course.

5. $\{y : Fy\} = (Ix)(y \,\varepsilon\, x \equiv Fy)$

In this case 4 follows from 3 only on the assumption that $\{y : Fy\}$ exists.*

SECTION 7
INTENSIONAL DISCOURSE

If, in a certain formal language, replacement of one statement by another of the same truth-values always leads from true statements to true statements and from false statements to false statements, that language is called *truth functional*. Thus the language discussed in Part One is truth functional; for example,

> If A and B have the same truth-value, so do $(A \,\&\, C)$ and $(B \,\&\, C)$, so do $(\neg A \supset C)$ and $(\neg B \supset C)$, and so on.

Truth functionality is one kind of *extensionality*: extensionality with respect to statements. The language studied in Part Two has extensionality in this respect; it also has extensionality with respect to predicates. That means: if predicates P and Q have the same extension, then replacement of one by the other leads from true to true and from false to false statements.

The extension of a statement is its truth-value, the extension of a predicate is the class of things to which it truly applies, the extension of a singular term is what it refers to. The general principle of extensionality can thus be phrased as follows:

> 1. The extension of a statement is a function of the extensions of its component statements, its component predicates, and its component terms.

However, it may not be clear exactly what this means if some singular terms do not have extensions. In free logic, we may guess therefore, this principle does not hold at least under some interpretations of what it means. Certainly if the principle is meant to have as a consequence that

> 1′. $(x)(Fx \equiv Gx) \supset (Ft \equiv Gt)$

---

*There are various ways of implementing a free logic approach to this subject. See *Op. Cit.*, D. Scott, "Existence and Description in Formal Logic".

holds in general, we have already seen in Section 3 that the language of free logic is not extensional (in that sense).

There are many kinds of common discourse which appear not to be extensional in one or more senses. The blanket term *intensional* is applied to the various kinds we shall now examine. Without attempting a precise characterization, we may (roughly) classify as intensional any statement in which the truth-value does not depend on the extensions of its component parts. Examples are provided by descriptions of *acts of mind* (judgment, thought, perception, belief, knowledge) and by statements of various *modalities* (necessity, possibility, obligation, tense). Much work in philosophical logic has concerned the formal analysis of such statements, and one common scheme has been widely accepted. In this scheme, sentences are modified by expressions called "sentential operators"; in the following examples, we italicize the expressions regarded as being such operators:

> 2. *It is possible that there* are (be) griffins.
> 4. *John thinks that* there are (be) griffins.
> 5. *It is permitted that* there are (be) griffins.

In example 4, at least, it is very clear that the truth-value of the whole statement is independent of the truth-value of the component statement "there are griffins". In this section we shall discuss to some extent the role played by singular terms in intensional statements and the statements in some way related to intensional statements.*

To begin, let us point to a distinction which can apparently be made for acts of mind but not for modalities. The verb "think", for example, can be followed by one of two syncategorematic words—"of" and "that":

> 6. John thinks of Pegasus;**
> 7. John thinks that Pegasus is a flying horse.

---

*Since principle 1 appears to take for granted that every complete expression (term, predicate, statement) has an extension, it is not entirely clear whether, for example, "John thinks of Pegasus" is or is not an extensional statement in the sense of 1. But the most obvious way to read 1 is to say that this is an example of a statement which is not extensional.

**Similar to 6 would be "John perceives Pegasus", "John believes in Pegasus", and so on. "Perceive" and "know" often entail existence, but not always: consider for example, Macbeth's seeing the dagger.

It is the latter that has the form roughly of a modal statement

  8. It is possible that Pegasus is a flying horse.

In none of 6–8 is the truth-value of the total statement affected by Pegasus' non-existence. But 6 has much less internal structure than 7 or 8; it is a simple relational statement.

  This naive way of taking 6 has been challenged by many: how could a relation hold between John, a full-blooded existent, and Pegasus, a bloodless thing? Shouldn't we rather say that 6 ascribes a *property* to John, the property thinks-of-Pegasus? For how could a non-existent affect or be affected by the existent?

  In other words, many philosophers have felt that to call 6 a relational statement is to use the term *relation*, which has a proper use in ontology, in a much extended sense: that to assimilate all statements of form $F(t,t')$ to relational statements is to ignore distinctions a philosopher ought not to ignore. On the other hand, the assimilation of all relations to the kick, scratch, bite, or hammer model, in which the relata actively modify each other, has also proved no boon to philosophy.* One main point stands: that 6–8 all have the form $F(t,t')$, but that if 6 is said to have more structure than is implied by this, that must be pursuant to a specific philosophical analysis of thought. And logic wherever possible ought not to wait upon philosophy, for logic wherever possible ought to be neutral between different philosophical analyses.

  What harm would it do, however, to say that 6 merely ascribes the property thinks-of-Pegasus to John? Well, if 6 really has the form

  6′. $T^p(j)$

where T^p is the unanalyzed predicate "thinks-of-Pegasus", the following inference cannot be justified:

  9. John thinks of Pegasus, and Pegasus is the horse captured by Bellerophon; so John thinks of the horse captured by Bellerophon.

Of course, it might be argued that inference 9 ought not to be regarded as justified, because it is not valid. If that is so, we should either have

_____

  *See, e.g., B. Russell, *A Critical Exposition of the Philosophy of Leibniz*, 2nd ed. (London: George Allen & Unwin, 1937).

to symbolize 6 as 6', or reject rule IE. The latter move we shall soon have to consider again, in connection with 7 and 8. But here, we think, arguments of form 9 ought to be accepted. The obvious test case is that John might think of Pegasus without knowing that Pegasus is the horse captured by Bellerophon; in that case can John correctly be said to be thinking of the horse captured by Bellerophon? It seems to us that the answer is *yes*: If John tells us that he was thinking of Pegasus (when he said that philosophers like mythical examples, for example), and we say to Peter "He was thinking of the horse captured by Bellerophon", John might well attempt to correct us; but he would agree that we had not distorted the facts once we tell him the full *story*.

The case is very different when the verb is followed by "that", as in 7. For John might well think that Pegasus is not the horse captured by Bellerophon, but of course he would not think that the horse captured by Bellerophon is not the horse captured by Bellerophon. Indeed, this inference would not be correct even if Pegasus and that horse were not only identical but existed as well.

In other words, in *operator contexts*—statements of the form (. . . *that A*)—substitutivity of identity does not hold in general. So here we may laud the leniency of free logic with respect to non-referring terms, but it seems we must lament its acceptance of the principle of substitutivity of identity. This is not really as bad as it sounds, for several reasons. The first is that it is fairly easy to develop free logic without identity (with or without *E*! as a special predicate).* The second is that we can make a distinction (cutting across the existent/non-existent distinction) between *substances* and *accidents* (a terminology introduced by Thomason).** The defining feature of substance is precisely that if *t,t'* are substances

$$t = t' \supset \cdot A \supset (t/t')A$$

holds. Definite descriptions in general do not denote substances; however, Thomason has also shown, by precept and by example, the fruitfulness of using free description theory in this area.

More important than either of these points is the fact that our logic

---

*See K. Lambert's "Existential Import Revisited", *Notre Dame Journal of Formal Logic,* 4, (1963), pp. 288–292; and his "Free Logic and the Concept of Existence", *Notre Dame Journal of Formal Logic,* 8, (1967), pp. 133–134.

**R. H. Thomason, "Modal Logic and Metaphysics", in K. Lambert (ed.), *The Logical Way of Doing Things* (New Haven: Yale University Press, 1969).

can be reformulated, without loss, in a way that applies even to sentences with operators in them. To do this, we revise IE to

$$IE^* \quad \begin{array}{|l} t = t' \\ A \\ (t'/t)A \end{array} \qquad \text{provided } A \text{ is atomic}$$

Recall that an atomic sentence is one in which no quantifiers nor connectors (or operators) occur: for example, $x = a$ or *Paby*. Now IE* will really do, with a lot of inconvenience, what IE does, with respect to the replacement of terms that do *not* occur in an operator context. This can be proved rigorously by mathematical induction, but we shall here just illustrate the point by examples:

(1)	$a = b$		
(2)	$\neg Fa$		
(3)		Fb	
(4)		$a = b$	(1) R
(5)		Fa	(3) (4) IE*
(6)		$\neg Fa$	(2) R
(7)	$\neg Fb$		(3–6) NI

(1)	$a = b$		
(2)	$Fa \lor Fc$		
(3)		Fa	
(4)		$a = b$	(1) R
(5)		Fb	(3) (4) IE*
(6)		$Fb \lor Fc$	(5) AI
(7)		Fc	
(8)		$Fb \lor Fc$	(7) AI
(9)	$Fb \lor Fc$		(2) (3–6) (7–8) AE

(1)	$a = b$		
(2)	$(x)Rxa$		
(3)	y	Rya	
(4)		$a = b$	(1) R
(5)		Ryb	(3) (4) IE*
(6)	$(x)Rxb$		(3–5) UQI

But the rules governing operators would be such that the use of IE* would not lead to substitution of t for t' given only the information that $t = t'$ is true.

SECTION 8
QUANTIFIERS AND EXISTENCE

There exists nothing of which I think when I think of Pegasus—but surely, when I think of Pegasus, I think of something? And is it not true that some of the beings that have been believed to exist, really do not exist? And may not a person correctly be said to be seeing pink rats, or witches, or genies without specifying that he is seeing rat Bartholomew or witch Nancy or genie Hakim?

To some, the answer to these questions is negative. The phrases "there is" and "some" ought only to be used to assert existence, they argue, for what could it possibly mean to say that there *is* something which does not *exist*? And they can point to a number of conceptual muddles and puzzles, whose genesis seems intimately connected with disregard of their advice.*

We readily agree that the advice has all the justification it claims, and will cheerfully agree to use such phrases as "there is" and "some . . . are" only in the prescribed manner, in all moments of high seriousness. But there still remains the common use of these phrases illustrated rhetorically in the opening paragraph of this section. This usage ought to be explicated; it is a mode of discourse that has been exemplified amply in the mouths of babes and philosophers alike. (And, if such discourse does have a philosophically responsible explication, would it not as well be responsible thereafter to use it freely?)

Without going too deeply into the exact formal reconstructions that are open to us, we can indicate briefly how one can proceed.** Intuitively, we can divide the denizens of the world (taken in its broadest, loosest sense) into *existents*, (mere) *possibles*, and *impossibles*.

You are an existent. Hobbits do not exist, but they could have or might have, so they are possibles. Round squares do not and could not exist, so they are impossibles. (If several species of possibility, say *physical* or *logical* possibility, are admitted, this division is relative to the selected species of possibility, of course.) If you want to say that there are impossibles—if, say, you wish to disagree with the claim that nothing is impossible; or if you wish to tell Alice that you did several impossible things before breakfast—your claim may have to be con-

---

*See, for example, W. V. O. Quine, *Methods of Logic* (London: Routledge & Kegan Paul, 1952), section 33.

**For further details, see K. Lambert and B. van Fraassen, "Meaning Relations, Possible Objects, and Possible Worlds", in K. Lambert (ed.), *Philosophical Problems in Logic* (Dordrecht: Reidel, 1970), pp. 1–19, and references therein.

strued differently from the claim that there are (mere) possibles. We wll look at each in turn.

Let us take as a sample this imaginary dialogue:

1. Some things are impossible.
   Really? Name one.
   The round square. It's totally impossible!

At least one of the discussants assumes that a statement of the form "Some things are . . ." is true if some statements of form ". . . is a . . ." is true. This has sometimes been expressed as: whatever can be a subject of discourse has being. Today we refer to it as the *substitution interpretation* of quantifier phrases. For it can be summed up by

2. (Some x)A is true exactly if for some singular term b, $(b/x)A$ is true.

Under this interpretation, some things do not exist and some could not possibly exist. And this is surely one actual usage of "some".

However, something curious happens with descriptions. For any term t, the statement

3. (Some x)$(x = t)$

is logically true, given principle 2, just because

4. $t = t$

is logically true. So we have specifically

5. (Some x)$(x = (Iy)(Fy \ \& \ \neg Fy))$

but we do *not* have as even possibly true

6. (Some x)$(Fx \ \& \ \neg Fx)$.

This means that the basic law relating quantifiers and descriptions does not work here. We *cannot* accept

7. (All x)$(x = (Iy)A \cdot \equiv \cdot (All\ y)(A \equiv y = x))$

on pain of inconsistency, if "All" is here interpreted along the same lines of "Some" in 2.

So even if we accept a sense in which there are impossible things, they cannot be used as examples to substantiate impossible claims. This is confusing exactly in the case of a dispute about whether something is, in fact, possible or impossible. Impossible examples do not count; consider:

> 8. Nothing is red and green all over.
>   What about the ice-cube in my dream?
>   What about it?
>   It was red and green all over.
>   That is impossible.
>   It wasn't impossible in my dream!
>   Oh, you just *dreamt* that it was not impossible.
>   And you just aren't twink!

It is assumed by both disputants that an impossible example does not count. To refute the opening statement, you have to produce an example of a possible that is red and green all over.

This is rather an important kind of dispute in philosophy. For example, Leibniz held that if things *a* and *b* have all properties in common, then they are identical (Principle of the Identity of Indiscernibles).*
There are trivial interpretations of this, under which it is a tautology: just count *being identical with a* as a property. The opponents of the claim must therefore describe a possible world in which *a* and *b* do have all properties in common, and are not identical—but guarding themselves against the assumption that being identical or not identical with a given thing is a property. This makes their efforts *prima facie* fruitless of necessity, for if they describe such a world the Leibnizian will conclude from its description that this world contains only one thing, with two names. And if the assertion is added that there are two things in it, he will say: either you have not given me all relevant information, or your example is an impossible one—you might as well try to demonstrate that something can be both round or square by mentioning the round square!

The substitution interpretation clearly does not allow us to make a distinction between possible and impossible examples. It has the further drawback that it makes analytic the claim that there is nothing that does

---

*See also B. van Fraassen, *Introduction to the Philosophy of Time and Space* (New York: Random House, 1970), pp. 41, 63–65.

not have a name. These drawbacks can be overcome in various ways, but for further discussion we must refer the reader to the literature.*

SECTION 9
PRESUPPOSITIONS

Last of all, we shall now try to take seriously the idea that in many cases statements about non-existents are really very puzzling. It is fairly plausible that such a statement as "John thinks that the king of France is bald" or "Possibly, the king of France is bald" is true or false (depending on the empirical facts, at least in the first case). But what about the component statement "The King of France is bald"? Asked whether this is true or false, we are baffled: in the absence of the king of France, the usual tests for baldness simply cannot be applied. So we *correct* the questioner rather than answer him: we tell him that his question is mistaken, based on the mistaken *presupposition* that there is such a person as the king of France, that it just does not arise.

P. F. Strawson has made the notion of presupposition precise in the following way.** Consider the statement that the king of France is bald *presupposes* that the king of France exists. The relation of presupposition in this statement he characterizes as follows:

1. *A presupposes B* if and only if *A* is either true or false only if B is true.

So, in other words, *A* presupposes *B* if $\neg A$ does, provided we take $\neg A$ to be true if *A* is false, and conversely. Now it might be thought that to agree to this would make almost all of classical logic and certainly free logic quite useless. For after all, we have assumed throughout that every statement is true or false. So it seems that if we agree to the above we will have to say that our logic is to be applied only to the special case of statements which are true or false, and not in general, as we have apparently been at pains to mislead the reader to believe.

---

*In addition to the selections cited so far, see R. H. Thomason, "Modal Logic and Metaphysics", in K. Lambert (ed.), *The Logical Way of Doing Things* (New Haven: Yale University Press, 1969), pp. 119–146; B. van Fraassen, "Meaning Relations among Predicates", *Nous* 1 (1967), pp. 161–179; and B. van Fraassen *Formal Semantics and Logic* (New York: Macmillan, 1971), Ch. IV, section 9 "Substitution Interpretation".

**See his *Introduction to Logical Theory* (London: Methuen, 1952).

But this is not so, provided we are allowed to assume in addition the venerable doctrine that the familiar truths of logic alone have no factual content, convey zero information, and hence have no fallible presuppositions. For then we can adjust our account of any language in such a way that the applicable logic is the same before *and* after the admission of the general possibility of failing presuppositions. We do this by the method of *supervaluations*. This method has been developed for a number of purposes in a number of our publications, and we shall here present a simplified account.*

Suppose that the set of statements true in an actual situation is X; then we know various things about X. First of all, we know that

(a) X is satisfied in some model $\mathcal{M}$;

and

(b) X contains all of its own consequences by our ordinary logic.

In addition, we know that the statements in X, at least, have no untrue presuppositions. So we have also

(c) if A is in X and A presupposes B, then B is in X.

For this to provide us with real information, we must have a list of the presuppositions of each statement, insofar as these are expressed by other statements in the same language. Furthermore, if we now allow that statements that are not logically true may also have fallible presuppositions not expressed in the language in an arbitrary manner, then we arrive at the principle

2. X is the set of statements true in some possible factual situation if and only if conditions (a)–(c) hold for X.

We shall call such a set a *saturated* set. We note that what is true in the corresponding situation, that is, X can equivalently be characterized as the set of statements true in all models (our old notion) in which X is

---

*See B. van Fraassen "Presuppositions, Supervaluations, and Free Logic", in K. Lambert (ed.), *The Logical Way of Doing Things* (New Haven: Yale University Press, 1969), pp. 67–91. For an application of the method of supervaluations to the logic of microphysics see K. Lambert's paper "Logical Truth and Microphysics" in the same volume, pp. 93–119.

satisfied. Thus the possible factual situations are mathematically represented by the following functions that satisfy the following principle for some set $\mathcal{V}$ of models:

> 3. For all statements A of the language, $s(A) = \mathrm{T}$ if $\mathcal{M} \models A$ for all $\mathcal{M}$ in $\mathcal{V}$ and $s(A) = F$ if not $\mathcal{M} \models A$ for any $\mathcal{M}$ in $\mathcal{V}$ (where $\mathcal{V}$ is the set of models satisfying a given saturated set X).

Such a function s is called a *supervaluation* of the language. And now we can state the result that justifies our claim that all our previous work was not in vain, but can provide the basis for appraisal of reasoning even though we accept Strawson's theory:

> 4. If A is a consequence of X by our logic, then all supervaluations which satisfy X also satisfy A.

This means that our logic is *sound* for the reinterpreted language. In addition, to make this logic *complete* for the new case, we need only add as a rule (with reference to the list of presuppositions presumably on hand)

> 5. If A presupposes B, then the arguments from A to B and from $\neg A$ to B are correct.

But now, finally, we must urge some caution. To say that our old logic is sound means that if it justifies an argument

$$A_3, \ldots, A_n; \quad \text{hence } B$$

then this argument is indeed valid. But it does not follow that the old patterns of argument—which often involved arguments about arguments —carry over when some of the arguments in the language are valid because of the relation of presupposition. Specifically, we cannot argue:

> (i)   The king of France is bald or the king of France is not bald;
> (ii) The king of France is bald; hence he exists;
> (iii) The king of France is not bald; hence he exists;
> (iv) So, the king of France exists.

This has the form of an application of the rule AE. But this is not a correct application, since lines (ii) and (iii) are not *classically valid*, that is, not justified by the logic (as opposed to the presumed list of presuppositions). All correct applications of *logic proper* in the new context have the forms

> 6. *A* is a logically true statement; hence *A* is valid;
> 7. *A* ⊃ *B* is a logically true statement; hence the argument from *A* to *B* is valid.

EXERCISES

1. Show that the system FD is deducible from the system FD2, and that II can be reduced to the status of a derived rule.

2. In Section 3 it is claimed that a predicate *F* is coextensive with a predicate *G* just in case $(x)(Fx \equiv Gx)$ is true. Justify this claim.

3. In Section 5 it is mentioned that Dana Scott's theory is like FD2 in that it adopts (8) in Section 5 but rejects
   $$t = (Ix)(x = t)$$
   Describe some other ways in which Scott's theory differs from FD2 as a consequence of the above features.

4. Show the invalidity of the argument from 1* and 2* to 3* in Section 5; demonstrate the validity of that argument when augmented with the premise $\neg F(Ix) \neg Fx$.

5. Produce a categorical derivation for
   $$\neg (Ey)(y = t) \& Ft \cdot \supset F(Ix)Fx$$
   in FD2 (See Section 5). Would this formula be deducible in Scott's theory? Explain.

6. Present the inductive argument mentioned in the discussion of IE* near the end of Section 7.

7. In Section 8, it is pointed out that if one accepts (1) the substitution interpretation of the quantifiers and (2) II, one must give up FD. What happens in the case of FD2? In the case of Scott's theory? Why does no conflict arise between II, FD, and the more common referential interpretation of the quantifier adopted in Chapter 4?

8. In Section 9, the method of supervaluations is put forth as a device allowing one to tolerate truthvalueless statements while yet holding to the logic developed in this book. Show how that method validates the statement from $A \lor \neg A$.

9. One of the most common claims in contemporary philosophy is that existence is not a predicate. What bearing does free logic have on this claim, especially in view of the proof of Hintikka's theorem? (See exercise 4 at the end of Chapter 6.)

Index